Call to Revolution

We asked: A writer?
An artist? A politician?
A philosopher? A prophet?
Our hearts answered:
Yes, all that. But still
more than the sum
of all that. What?
came the further question.
And as answer there remained:
a great, genuine
human being.

Hans Franck

Everything that Landauer
thought and planned,
said and wrote—even when
it had Shakespeare
for subject or German
mysticism, and especially
all designs whatsoever
for the building of a
socialistic reality—
was steeped in a great belief
in revolution and the will
for it.

Martin Buber

Call to Revolution

————◆◆◆◆————

The
Mystical
Anarchism of
Gustav
Landauer

Charles B. Maurer
Denison University

WAYNE STATE UNIVERSITY PRESS
Detroit / 1971

Published simultaneously in Canada
by the Copp Clark Publishing Company
517 Wellington Street, West
Toronto 2B, Canada.

Library of Congress Catalog Card Number 75-148270

International Standard Book Number 0-8143-1441-4

To
PROFESSOR ERICH HELLER
whose counsel led me
to Gustav Landauer
and to this work

Contents

Preface

ALL cultures, even the most sophisticated, have magic formulas, words or phrases that cast an emotional spell totally unrelated to their basic meaning. No one is free from this effect of language, though the emotional response to a particular formula may be quite different in two different cultures or even for two individuals of the same culture. Witness the definition of *infidel* in Ambrose Bierce's *Devil's Dictionary:* "In New York, one who does not believe in the Christian religion; in Constantinople, one who does." A more current example, of course, is the differing reactions in the United States and the U.S.S.R. to the word *socialism.* To those who consider themselves first and foremost patriots of the United States, this word connotes a great evil, an evil of particular virulence. Their response to the word itself is so highly emotional that they become incapable, when under the influence of the word-formula's magic, of understanding the thing or things the word *denotes.* If the spell affects enough people simultaneously, it can lead even to ritualistic murder, such as the executions following the Haymarket Riot of 1886 in Chicago or the Sacco-Vanzetti trial, which ended in the death of the two defendants in 1927.

In both these cases the formula was not *socialism,* but another word that was current around the beginning of this century and then, until recently, fell into disuse. The youth rebellion of the

9

1960s has brought it to the public's attention once more, and it is obvious that the period of dormancy has in no way reduced the word's magic power. The word-formula is *anarchism*.

Ever since journalists with a historical perspective began to relate some of the attitudes held by modern, young intellectuals to the philosophies and actions of the basically nineteenth-century anarchist movement, some elements in our society have reacted in precisely the way analogous elements reacted to anarchism in the nineteenth century. For these people anarchism means violence, the hurled bomb, the hidden dagger. They see anarchists as desperate men, devoid of morality, dedicated only to destruction.

That there were once such anarchists is beyond doubt. That there are some today is equally certain. Yet the passionate reaction to the magic of the word has blinded many people to the fact that there were other anarchists as well, peaceful, contemplative men convinced that civilization had evolved a social environment hostile to the nature of man and to a valid life for the individual. These were humanitarians in the best sense of the word, men who were inspired by the belief that mankind could build a better existence for itself. These men were worth listening to. They still are. Gustav Landauer was one of them.

Landauer called himself an anarcho-socialist, a term making him doubly liable to rejection by many victims of word magic. He was an anarchist in that he considered the state to be the enemy of its people and wished to see it destroyed, as the German critic Julius Bab said, not by bombs and daggers, but by increased recognition of the state's artificiality. He was a socialist because he understood socialism to be the process of cooperation among individuals; he saw in such cooperation the basis for a better life for mankind. He believed that the personal freedom necessary for real cooperation among men would evolve when the power of the state had been overcome and that a new and better society would be the inevitable result. He once wrote to Bab: ". . . anarchism is the negative side of that which, positively, is called socialism." [1] His message to mankind was that these two concepts formed a unity that pointed the way to a glorious future.

For most of his life Landauer lived and worked in isolation from the main political currents of his time; but his efforts were, nonetheless, rooted in a tradition of social philosophy established and perpetuated by some of the most original personalities of the eighteenth and nineteenth centuries. The English clergyman William Godwin (1756–1836) and the French aristocrat Claude de Saint-Simon (1760–1825) were early figures in this tradition, as was the British industrialist Robert Owen (1771–1858), who helped to introduce it in the United States. Pierre Joseph Proudhon (1809–65) rose from humble origins to become, with his concept of property as theft, one of the leading theoreticians of anarchism. He was joined in his rejection of Marxism by Mikhail Bakunin (1814–76) and Pëtr Kropotkin (1842–1921), both from aristocratic Russian backgrounds, each in his own way convinced that the state is the root of human misery. Like Bakunin and Kropotkin, the Italian Errico Malatesta (1853–1932), son of a wealthy family, took part in the First International but soon broke with it, feeling it to be as much a danger to personal freedom as the state. From his remote outpost in Russia, Leo Tolstoi (1828–1910) dedicated his later years to the propagation of a rejuvenated Christianity that was basically anarchist. In the United States the idea of a stateless society was supported in the writings of men such as the inventor Josiah Warren (c. 1798–1874), Henry David Thoreau (1817–62), and Benjamin R. Tucker (1854–1939), editor of the journal *Liberty* (1881–1908) and publisher of many works on anarchism. The theories and methods of these individuals varied greatly, but all of them, and many others like them, dedicated much of their lives to the development of what they held to be a human society worthy of human life. Landauer's place in this tradition is discussed in Chapter 8.

The intellectual world of early twentieth-century Germany was well aware of Landauer and his message, but little of his work has become known outside the German-speaking areas, and none of it has been translated into English. This is also true for the most part of comments made by other Germans about him and his writings. With the exception of extracts from a few pertinent books available in English (noted in the selected bibliography), the translations in the present volume are my own.

I am much indebted for bibliographic assistance to the late Mr. Jackie Renka, book dealer in Munich, whose success in find-

Call to Revolution
The Mystical Anarchism of Gustav Landauer

ing necessary materials for this work seems almost to have had a touch of the supernatural, and to the staff of the Labadie Collection in The University of Michigan General Library. I offer my gratitude, too, to Professor James H. Meisel, who gave generously of his time to read the manuscript and to make numerous highly valuable suggestions enabling me to correct sins both of omission and commission. And very special thanks are due to my wife for the patient and effective way she carried out the various editorial tasks that are the inevitable lot of the academician's spouse.

The primary purpose of this book is to make available to English-speaking scholars an accurate and fairly detailed discussion of Landauer and his works. Though he was well known throughout the German intellectual world during the first two decades of this century, it is only his connection with Kurt Eisner and the Bavarian Revolution of 1918/19 that people now remember. His name appears frequently in accounts of modern German cultural history, but details of his writings and personality have been all but totally obscured, even in Germany, during the past fifty years. It is true that his impact was small, but the nobility of his intentions and the philosophic grandeur of his dreams for a better world deserve to be remembered.

I hope, too, that this volume will serve as a contribution to the knowledge of anarchism as a philosophy, to help remove the magic from the word, so that those whose rejection of anarchism has been an emotional reflex may come to a more realistic judgment of it, and so that those who have subscribed to it as a way of life may better understand its pitfalls.

C. B. M.
Ann Arbor, Michigan
1970

1

The Bismarckian Reich

In the last third of the nineteenth century Germany hovered between the political past and the economic future. The European revolutionary wave of 1848 had made little immediate impression on the political structure of the German states, but it left a legacy of nationalism that the princes and politicians of the nearly forty independent states in the German-speaking region of Europe could not ignore. It became ever more obvious that the principle of particularism—so long a dominant feature of German political organization—would have to give way; the form a unified Germany would take, however, was by no means so clear. Demands for democratic processes and economic liberalism were accompanied by the desire for national unification, all three opposed by the established nobility and its governments. A governmental structure uniting all the German states on a liberal, democratic basis would have aligned Germany with Western Europe as a nation politically consistent with its era. But the unification that came had a very different face: one state, Prussia, reached out to comprehend all the others, and it was the traditional Prussian authoritarianism that characterized the German Reich.

This nation, founded on 18 January 1871 at the seat of government of a just conquered foreign state, is often called the "Bismarckian Reich." It was Bismarck's creation. Otto von Bismarck-

Call to Revolution
The Mystical Anarchism of Gustav Landauer

Schönhausen (1815–98) descended from an old line of East Prussian nobility, and throughout his career, no matter what power alliances and maneuvers political exigencies dictated to him, he was above all a Prussian monarchist. The Junker tradition from which he came strongly rejected nationalism and liberalism, and his own attitudes reflected this tradition. When his experience in Prussian government service convinced him that the force of nationalism was irresistible, he concluded that it must be directed toward the preservation of Prussian power. Becoming prime minister of Prussia in 1862, he worked tirelessly toward the foundation of a German Reich, one that Prussia could shape and control. His efforts were startlingly successful; his methods foreshadowed the kind of absolutist state he would create.

The political strategy Bismarck followed was to make use of established government forms when they suited his purposes and to defy them when they did not. For four years he pursued a policy contrary to the Prussian constitution, ignoring the complaints of the Prussian parliament. He brought about the downfall of the Austrian-controlled German Confederation, since 1815 the guardian of German affairs, and replaced it with the North German Federation, in which all the German states north of the river Main submitted to Prussian leadership. Even before the founding of this political organization in 1867, Bismarck had concluded a secret defense treaty, directed against France, with the southern German states. The revival of an old customs union enhanced relations between the Federation and the southern states and further strengthened Prussia's position. In five years he had gone a long way toward his goal of a German Reich, without Austria, under Prussian control. After 1867 he had only to wait.

In 1870 a dynastic quarrel arose between France and Prussia. King Wilhelm I of Prussia was conciliatory, but French belligerence inflamed the situation; and Bismarck, by deliberate public misrepresentation of a French letter to the Prussian king, enraged both France and all Germany. France declared war (July 1870), and the combined armies of the North German Federation and the southern German states marched. France was routed in six months. In the context of this military success, the spirit of nationalism ran high throughout Germany. Even before the war was

14

over, the southern states formally united with the Federation; the Bismarckian Reich was founded in France's Palace of Versailles.

In an era when the ideals of liberalism, democracy, and nationalism were influencing the thinking and actions of so many political figures in Western Europe, Bismarck based his German Reich on nothing but power and the conviction that that power must be kept in the hands of the Prussian monarchy. He allowed no ideals, laws, or loyalties to interfere with this policy. It is obvious enough that a state founded on such a principle will operate on the same principle, and so it was with the Reich. The parliament of the Reich, following the pattern set earlier in the constitution of the North German Federation, had a lower house (the Reichstag) elected by universal male suffrage, but this was only the slightest veneer of democracy. The electorate was never redistricted, despite great changes in population distribution; and the power of the Reichstag was so limited as to place it at the mercy of the chancellor and upper house (the Bundesrat), which continued to represent the dynastic interests of the various states in the Reich. In addition, the Reich's parliamentary policies and actions were much influenced by the Prussian state parliament, whose structure and attitudes were even less democratic. The position of the rich was repeatedly reinforced by the Prussian parliament. Prussia's laws of the press were extremely confining: press offenses could not be tried before a jury. Police powers were nearly all-inclusive and police spying was rampant. Many new laws for all of Germany were based on Prussian repressive prototypes. This was the heritage with which Bismarck's Prussianized German Reich began its existence.

The autocratic government of the Reich was backward looking and remained so. The political history of Germany from 1871 to Bismarck's resignation in 1890 is largely the story of his efforts, in internal and foreign policy, to preserve the state he had brought into being. In 1871 the German economy was backward looking as well; but its modernization was already in progress, and the changes of the following two decades were to put Germany in the forefront of European and world history.

The real significance of the industrial revolution is sometimes lost on the modern man, who lives amid its fruits—sweet and bitter. In most of Western Europe the process of industrialization took more than a hundred years to become the all-pervading way of life, a time span that can obscure the truly revolutionary nature of the event. The real magnitude of the transformation was more conspicuous in Germany, however, for the upheaval and adjustment attendant upon the triumph of technology were compressed there into little more than forty years. In contrast to Britain, where the first steps in industrialization were taken around 1770, it was not until the late 1840s that the typical combination of iron, coal, machinery, and transportation began to develop in Germany, and at first this represented little more than the old manufacturing facilities using new methods. There were some industrial strikes in the 1860s, but at that time there were still only 750,000 industrial workers in a population of about 40,000,000. In 1871, 63 percent of the German population was still rural. The Bismarckian Reich was established in a country beginning its way from an agricultural to an industrial economy.

The great impetus toward industrialization in Germany came with unification. The spirit of nationalism sweeping the country in the wake of victory over France—the feeling that Germany was invincible—contributed to this development. So did the generally held belief that the money exacted from France as part of the peace treaty, five billion gold francs paid in the remarkably short period of two years, provided a completely new basis for the German economy. Actually, the German government held this money as a gold reserve until 1914, but the belief in its presence in the economy was sufficiently encouraging.

The years 1871 to 1873 have been nicknamed *"Gründerjahre"* ("founders' years"), an expression reflecting the great commercial activity of that time. Numerous industrial ventures were begun; the trend toward industrial centralization became apparent, to the detriment of small producers; modern financial methods—stock companies, large banks—began to take a firm hold on the economy. And with this came financial risk-taking and unscrupulous speculation. This sudden burst of activity slowed toward the end of 1873, when there was a depression of international dimensions. Yet even this crisis could not halt the momentum of German industrialization; and, except for agricultural interests, the German economy held better than that of the other industrialized or industrializing nations. By 1890, Germany was challenging Britain's output in coal and iron and had surpassed it in steel. German railroad mileage increased twelvefold from 1840 to 1870, eightyfold from 1840 to 1890. Partly because application of important scientific discoveries was immediate, especially in the chemical and electrical fields, German technology captured a leading place in world economy. The products of that technology were distributed by a splendidly organized commercial network supported by a government solicitous of industrial growth and protective of those whom industrial growth benefited financially. By 1895 only 36 percent of the population was involved in farming.

When one compares this with the 63 percent rural population in 1871, the truly revolutionary character of industrialization becomes clear. It is an occurrence of major proportion when in twenty-five years nearly one-third of the inhabitants of a large country basically alter both their way of making a living and their way of life. Under such circumstances the entire social fabric of the nation must experience drastic strains, strains sometimes intense enough to produce serious rents. This was certainly the case in Germany between 1871 and 1890. The traditional place of the nobility as the dominating force in German society was still protected legally by the government of the Reich, but the source of their power—wealth based on agriculture—was failing. A new group, the commercially successful, was becoming socially ascendant; sheer wealth, without title and without the traditions pertaining to title, became ever more powerful. Despite the reactionary policies of the government, Germany was developing into a bourgeois nation.

This is not to say, however, that one established class was replacing another in social prominence. The old middle class—artisans, self-employed shopkeepers, and professional people—experienced the same shattering effects of industrialization as the aristocracy to which it had traditionally looked for leadership. Some members of this group, like some aristocrats, successfully took part in the rush of economic expansion and secured for themselves a position in the new bourgeoisie. Others, the majority, were unable to change quickly enough with the times. As large industry and corporate finance made older methods obsolete, these people found the basis for their previous economic independence diminished, and they were forced into the salaried class, a class that had much in common with the ever-growing industrial proletariat, yet that for the most part disdained it.

The working class was also victimized. What the worker of the preindustrial era lacked in material goods and economic opportunities was usually made up for by the paternalism of the employer. The baron or master, in return for work and loyalty exacted, had a responsibility for his workers' well-being; and since it was in his own interest to have strong and loyal workers, he usually took the responsibility seriously. Furthermore, until the founding of the Reich, by far the majority of workers were rural. The society they lived in was close-knit, bound together by ties of neighborhood, religion, traditions, and personal relationships. In return for a relatively uneventful life of hard work in the fields, they generally enjoyed good health and an adequate diet. Industrialization broke this pattern too.

The tremendous migration to the city between 1871 and 1895 had two interrelated causes. Growing industry needed workers, and the lure of a supposedly exciting new life drew many to factories—either in large cities, where the principal industries were concentrating, or in developing rural areas rapidly being urbanized by industrialization. At the same time, declining agricultural prices and some effort to mechanize agriculture forced many workers from the land to the factories. Whether they went by choice or necessity, to the big city or the urbanizing industrial village, they found the same conditions and experienced the same fate. They became members of the industrial proletariat.

No nation could provide a smooth transition for such a large body of people moving from one way of life to another in so short a time. Adequate living conditions were simply not available. The industrial worker lived inadequately, therefore, and little effort was made to improve his condition. His wages were low and his hours long, as they had been in agricultural life, but the paternalism he had earlier relied upon to offset this was lacking. As the labor force increased and industry became mechanized, the employer was able to replace a sick worker either with a healthy one or with a machine. The worker looked after himself as best he could. If he could not, he was abandoned by the industrial system. If he managed to survive, he had little to look forward to but year after year at his machine. The glamour and excitement of life in the industrial city applied only to the owners. There was little chance that the worker would ever advance to a place in the bourgeoisie. In this regard the industrial white collar workers—the remnants of the old middle class—were scarcely better off.

Yet in this society the worker, white collar or blue, initially had no model for life to emulate except that of the owner class, the new bourgeoisie. The hold of religion on the population had weakened immeasurably during the nineteenth century. In the Reich nationalism replaced religion as a unifying force among the people, and the saints of this nationalism were the commercially successful. They were very materialistic saints, and their materialism replaced traditional cultural values throughout the society. The worker—isolated from genuine human contact by the anonymity of factory and city, believing in the materialism of the bourgeoisie but unable to achieve its material benefits, condemned to a way of life without promise of a better future—finally turned away from the wealthy as his model and looked upon them as his enemy.

Fortunately for the German worker, he was not entirely on his own. He had the experience of decades of labor struggle in Britain to learn from and the sympathy of a few individuals in the upper classes who were willing to interpret this experience for him. As early as 1850, worker cooperatives, proposed in England at the beginning of the century by Robert Owen, were founded on a modest scale in some German states. German unionism made a brief appearance in 1848, but was suppressed after the revolution. Its real inception came in 1863 with the founding of Ferdinand Lassalle's Universal German Workingmen's Association. This was meant to be a political party whose function would be to gain the vote for the workers so they would have some control over their own destinies. Though the vote was obtained when the North German Federation was established four years later, the effect was not as Lassalle, who died in 1864, had envisioned it, since the political organization of the Federation effectively separated power from the vote. In 1868 three lasting trade union organizations came into being, two of them based on Lassalle's approach to labor questions. The churches, too, both Catholic and Protestant, supported labor organizations that had paraunion characteristics. The principle of collective bargaining was accepted by the Prussian state in 1869, though the right to strike was not recognized. Yet unionism exerted relatively little influence upon economic affairs until the 1890s (there were only 50,000 union members in 1877), and by that time it was largely combined with another movement of far greater significance for Germany: socialism.

The utopian socialism of early nineteenth-century France, best represented by the work of Claude de Saint-Simon (1760–1825) and Pierre Joseph Proudhon (1809–65), had very little effect in Germany. It was not until the influence of Karl Marx (1818–83), with the *Communist Manifesto* (1848) and the International Workingman's Association (First International, 1864–73), that socialist ideas gained a foothold. Largely through the efforts of August Bebel (1840–1913) and Wilhelm Liebknecht (1826–1900), the basis for the German Social Democratic Party (SPD) was laid. These two men persuaded a congress of south German workingmen's education associations, meeting at Eisenach in 1869, to combine its participating organizations into a political party for labor. The Marxist orientation of the party founded there led to conflict with the Lassalle party, but in 1875 at a joint meeting in Gotha the two groups united in a single party dedicated to Marxist principles. Though the name German Social Democratic Party was not finally set until 1890, the 1875 coalition was essentially the SPD.

It had great appeal to the workers, not only because of its economic goals but because, unlike Marxist parties in Western Europe, where democracy was already established, the SPD combined its economic program with a struggle for truly representative democracy in Germany. Basically a workers' party, it promised constant opposition to the autocracy of the Reich, an autocracy that even the industrial white collar workers, themselves dangerously close financially to the proletariat, seldom opposed. Its strength at the polls showed its appeal: in 1871, before unification of the Bebel and Lassalle groups, both together received only 125,000 votes in the elections for the Reichstag. In 1877, after unification, the SPD won twelve seats in the Reichstag, receiving a popular vote of about 500,000, ten times the number of trade union members. The union movement, previously unable to establish itself as an independent force, now profited from the success of the SPD; as the party grew, so did the unions, most of them affiliates of the party.

Though the party and the unions had been significant steps toward improvement of the workers' condition, they did not culminate in the promised triumphal march into the workers' paradise of the new century. Bismarck prevented it. The hopes, vain or otherwise, of the proletariat were threatening to the autocratic structure of Bismarck's Reich, and in 1878 he moved to meet that threat. He obtained from the parliament a series of laws against the socialist organization. The SPD was not abolished; its deputies continued to sit in the Reichstag and, protected by parliamentary immunity, to criticize the government. But everything possible was done to undermine the power of the party. All socialist societies were banned; publication and distribution of socialist literature was forbidden. All labor organizations came under government control; ninety-five socialistically oriented unions were ordered disbanded. Police power was expanded to give officials all but absolute domination over anything that seemed tinged with Marxism. Nearly all the socialist leaders were arrested at one time or another, some of them repeatedly. The police had the power to expel even Germans from the Reich without trial. These laws were rigorously enforced.

At the same time, however, Bismarck realized that the problems of labor had to be solved before the strength of labor's party could be significantly assailed. Already in the 1870s two laws had been passed obligating employers to contribute to accident and relief funds for workers. Beginning in 1883 the Reich passed a series of social insurance acts covering sickness, accidents, and retirement, and initiated government controls on working conditions and hours. The only lack in this series of industrially related legislation was a provision for unemployment insurance. These laws, the first of their kind, became a model for social legislation in all industrialized countries. In 1881, after three years of the antisocialist laws,

SPD strength at the polls fell to about 300,000; but thereafter it grew steadily until it reached 1,427,000 in 1890, when the repressive measures were allowed to lapse. There were evidently many who surmised that socialist agitation was the motivating force behind official recognition of the workers' plight; and socialist ideas, even when promulgated by Bismarck's regime, were well received by the workers.

But there was another reason for the continued growth of the SPD despite Bismarck's campaign against it, a reason that goes beyond the borders of Bismarck's Reich and is connected with what is perhaps the major development in the intellectual history of late nineteenth-century Europe. For it was not only social reformers and socialist politicians who concerned themselves with the conditions of society in the industrial age. Some artists, writers, and philosophers saw what was happening and set out to express it in their own way. About the time the Reich was founded, the brooding psychology of Dostoevski, the penetrating grandeur of Tolstoi's work, the obsessive concentration upon the details of life reflected in the work of the French brothers Edmond and Jules de Goncourt, Zola's campaign to depict precisely the entire spectrum of contemporary society, all began to impinge upon the consciousness of German intellectuals. From Switzerland, Nietzsche was soon thundering out his condemnation of the cultural values upon which post-1870 Germany was being built. In the late seventies and early eighties, Ibsen's social dramas were appalling the establishment but winning praise from German writers and were soon being emulated by them, especially by the younger German writers. There were those, to be sure, who carried on the traditions of preindustrialization and pre-Reich literature to the end of the century, but during the eighties this old guard met increasingly derisive opposition from a rising generation whose attention was fixed rigidly upon the conditions surrounding them. In 1889 this attitude reached a climax with the appearance of *Papa Hamlet* by the early naturalists Arno Holz (1863–1929) and Johannes Schlaf (1862–1941), a collection of three short sketches that combined the technique of microscopic observation of life with a strongly critical vision of the prevailing society. In the same year Gerhart Hauptmann (1862–1946) achieved sudden fame when his first drama,

Vor Sonnenaufgang, brought to the stage the specter of social problems as they really existed. With these two works was born a German literature responsive to the temper of German intellectuals who were growing ever more antagonistic toward the bourgeois German Reich.

Though most intellectuals came from the middle class, they found, during the first twenty years of the Bismarckian state, that their problems and desires were in many ways parallel to those of the workers. Opposition to the government was characteristic of both workers and intellectuals. Both were victims of government repression: antisocialist laws stifled workers' complaints, and censorship watched over newspapers and the book trade. Though a relative relaxation of control came with the newspaper act of 1874, there were still many arrests and convictions during the eighties on charges stemming from governmental objection to critical articles. Lese majesty was an oft-committed offense. So was lese Bismarck. Opposition to the government was considered unpatriotic. In economic matters, too, the intellectual was frequently as much at the mercy of the bourgeoisie as were the workers; some writers, indeed, became true members of the proletariat in a financial sense. If the workers were eager to achieve democracy as a means of improving their condition, the intellectuals strove ardently toward the same goal from philosophic conviction. Both these in many ways so disparate castes stood alone against the rest of society and the government in their alienation from the establishment. They soon came to stand together. When Bismarck moved against the SPD with the antisocialist laws, he forced the intellectuals toward the SPD, and the support they provided contributed significantly to its survival and growth during the years of repression.

The focus of the struggle against the autocracy of the official Reich, as of so much else that took place in Germany between 1871 and 1890, was Berlin. Capital city of Prussia and of the Prussianized Reich, symbol of the young nation as Vienna and Paris were the symbols of their centuries-old states, largest and most vital of the German cities, nucleus of German industrialization, Berlin attracted people of all classes from all over the country and from abroad. Financial opportunities, real or only imagined, together with the lure of life in a modern city, a city of a new kind, where all the cultural streams of the time were throbbing with ever-increasing energy, created a magnetism irresistible to many. For the young writers and artists Berlin seemed to be the environment where talent could thrive, be acknowledged, and exert a lasting influence; and in ever-increasing numbers they were drawn to it. One of these young men was Gustav Landauer.

Gustav Landauer was born, almost simultaneously with the Reich, on 7 April 1870, in Karlsruhe. He was the son of a fairly well-to-do merchant family. The family was Jewish in background but was not religious, and Landauer's contact with the faith and the synagogue was slight. It was evidently intended that he should follow some commercial career, for he was sent for most of his preuniversity schooling to the Realgymnasium in Karlsruhe. This must have been an alien environment to a young man who very early in life began to exhibit an unusual sensitivity to music and literature; and, as his involvement with the arts grew, it became apparent that he was more suited for a university education and some profession than for a career in business. In preparation for this he attended a humanistic Gymnasium for two years, but like so many of his contemporaries who later became recognized figures in the literary world of the early twentieth century, Landauer found the formal classical instruction offered there boring and stultifying. His real education was obtained, not from the Gymnasialprofessor, but from the theater, books, and music, which provided the vital experiences of his early life. Though he learned his Latin and developed a deep respect for the classical authors, the focus of his interest lay elsewhere. He showed this plainly enough as a seventeen-year-old, when, taking part in one of the numerous patriotic festivities that punctuated the school year of the German Reich, he delivered to schoolmates and faculty a mildly revolutionary speech that drew much of its inspiration from the then academically unacceptable German poet Heinrich Heine (1797–1856). The school director publicly reprimanded him.

Neither the director nor Landauer himself was aware of how often in the future this young man would draw the wrath of authorities for statements far more radical than any he made as a student in the Gymnasium. Indeed, his first experiences with art tended to lead him away from problems of a social nature into the world of pure aesthetic effect. At fifteen he fell victim to the magic of Wagner and for awhile spent as much time as he could wandering in the cataclysmic universe of the music-drama. It was Ibsen's works that brought him back to earth and began to inspire him to accomplish something here, something that would be consistent with the dream of beauty Wagner's work had given him. Spinoza, Schopenhauer, and especially Nietzsche further influenced his sensitive nature and brought him more and more to face the problem of reconciling the world around him with the intimations of the perfect that art communicated to him. It was from this beginning, not from dedication to an egalitarian social justice, that his anarchism and socialism grew. All his efforts in the social sphere were dominated by the belief that such a reconciliation between art and social reality was possible.

From 1888 to 1891, Landauer studied at the universities of Heidelberg, Berlin, and Strassburg, concentrating on Germanics, philosophy, and history. He became proficient enough in French and English to translate literary works from these languages into German. He was especially drawn to the writers of the German romantic period; just how deeply he delved into the works of Tieck, Novalis, Brentano, and their contemporaries is clear from a review he wrote in 1900 discussing a collection of romantic lyrics entitled *Die blaue Blume* (*The Blue Flower*).[1] Reverence for the material in the anthology, as well as the self-assurance only vast knowledge provides, speak from every line of this essay as it points out omissions, provides corrections, and offers perspectives on the poems and the poets. Landauer's years of study had been profitable.

In 1891 he went to Berlin a second time, intending to continue his studies. But his institutional education was over. There were new stirrings in Berlin, and Landauer was prepared to be caught up completely in their currents. In 1888 the proud and erratic Wilhelm II had become emperor of the Reich, and after two years of conflict with him, Bismarck, now 75 years old, was forced to resign. Before his resignation he saw his antisocialist laws discredited and allowed to lapse (1890); the SPD had won. Once Bismarck was out of office, it became apparent that the web of political and social constructions Bismarck had created to support his Reich required a man of his determined genius for its continued functioning. The international horizon was becoming clouded with threats from various sources, and there seemed to be no one in power in the Reich with the capacity to fend them off short of war. Furthermore, the idea that a war would be desirable was taking hold. Was not Germany's army the greatest in the world? Was not German steel production now greater than England's? And was not that the prime requisite for building a modern battle fleet that could challenge Britannia's rule of the waves? German nationalism had not flagged since the war against France, and such thoughts were the logical consequence of unlimited nationalism. Most dangerous of all, the emperor was the Reich's greatest patriot.

There was, to be sure, a peace movement in Germany, as there was in the other countries of Europe; in its foremost ranks stood the labor organizations, united to some extent by the Second International, founded in 1889. This was a more impressive aggregate than the First International, which, discredited by the Franco-Prussian war and the Paris Commune uprising following that war, had ceased to exist in 1873. The First International had been little more than an assemblage of individual revolutionaries. The Second International was a *Bund* of well-established political parties and as such promised for awhile to be an effective instrument for social change. It was the Second International that set the First of May as an annual celebration of universal worker solidarity.

In Germany, however, the solidarity was beginning to crumble. At a party meeting in Erfurt in 1891, the SPD adopted a new, more strictly Marxist program, an act that drove many people, especially intellectuals, away from it. Some rejected politics altogether as a social instrument and, under the growing influence of Nietzsche and the egoistic philosopher Max Stirner, turned to various types of anarchism. When Landauer arrived in Berlin to stay, the young literary group in the capital of the Reich was in a revolutionary mood. Discussion concerning the proper approach to social and literary problems was building to a climax of fury against tradition and the status quo. Amid this ferment the direction and tone of Landauer's life was permanently set.

2

The
Sozialist
Years
1891–1900

THE personal circumstances surrounding Landauer's coming to Berlin, without reputation and with few resources other than three years of university training, made him just one more young intellectual seeking a life for himself in the big city. Yet within two years he was associated with some of the leading Berlin literati and was accepted and taken seriously by them. Though his own personality and acumen obviously contributed to this, much of the credit for his entrance into literary society is unquestionably due to his acquaintance, evidently initiated during his first stay in Berlin, with the drama critic and novelist Fritz Mauthner. Mauthner was a forceful interpreter of the new spirit awakening in German literature in the 1880s and 1890s; he was one of the first to recognize and report on the significance of Ibsen's work when it began to appear on the Berlin stage.[1] In all likelihood it was he who introduced Landauer into a group, consisting of nearly all the progressive literary figures in Berlin, working toward the implementation of a plan to expand massively the effect of the theater upon society.

During the nineteenth century Berlin gradually became the center of theatrical activity in Germany, by 1900 surpassing even Vienna in importance and vigor. As early as 1831, Goethe had remarked on the growing preeminence of the Prussian capital in theater. The literary developments of the 1880s brought the theater into conflict with the government, and steps were taken to counter official interference and to keep alive the new social force in literature. One answer to the problem was the Freie Bühne (Free Theater), founded in 1889 under the stimulus of Otto Brahm, a leading theater director. This organization, because it was instituted as a private club, was beyond the sphere of the censors and was therefore able to mount works that would have been banned from any other stage. Its first two presentations were Ibsen's *Ghosts* and Hauptmann's *Vor Sonnenaufgang*. The venture was artistically a success; but because of the high membership dues by which the organization was financed, working people were for the most part excluded from it. Some of them, however, wished to share in the experience the new trends in literature offered. The urging of three young workers prompted Bruno Wille, a writer and poet who had come to socialism by way of Lassalle's philosophy, to propose a subscription drive among the Berlin workers so a theater could be established to serve the workers' needs. The response exceeded all expectations, and in 1890 the Freie Volksbühne (Free People's Theater) was started, a theatrical experiment in which not the company but the audience was organized. Wille conceived of it as an educational institution for the proletariat, a private club to make available to the working class the social insights of the drama the Freie Bühne provided for the bourgeoisie. Membership fees were very low; actors donated their time to give Sunday afternoon performances in rented theaters, and the seats, distributed to the members by lot before each performance, were always filled. The success came not only from the workers' interest in the works performed; the list of intellectuals who contributed in some way is almost a directory of Berlin literary life at that time. Otto Brahm, Ludwig Fulda, Otto Erich Hartleben, Richard Dehmel, Maximilian Harden, Julius and Heinrich Hart, and Wilhelm Bölsche, among many others, all had a part in the realization of the original concept. When difficulties arose in 1892, it was certainly not from doubts about the efficacy of the project.

The directors of the Freie Volksbühne were all socialists of one shade or another, and disagreement arose among them after the Erfurt party meeting of the SPD in 1891 as to how the more

Marxist program issued there should influence the work of their theater. There were differences over matters of administrative control and artistic integrity as well. Increasing conflict finally led a number of the principal figures, including Wille, to resign. Landauer and Mauthner joined those who left and helped establish a rival theater to operate on the same basis as the Freie Volksbühne. Their efforts led to the institution of the Neue Freie Volksbühne (New Free People's Theater) in November 1892; the soundness of the original concept is demonstrated by the fact that both people's theaters flourished side by side until 1913, when they united in a cartel and began construction of their own theater building, the Theater am Bülowplatz in Berlin.

The Neue Freie Volksbühne movement continued to prosper despite occasional governmental interference until 1933, when the Nazi regime imposed controls that at first crippled the spirit of the Theater and finally forced it to close in 1939. During most of the period from 1892 until his death, Landauer remained connected with the Neue Freie Volksbühne, serving for many years on its artistic committee. Combining dedication to art and to social reform, the program of this institution commanded and received his unwavering allegiance.

About the time when the Neue Freie Volksbühne was founded, Landauer's allegiance was also enlisted by another project, one he felt was in no way inconsistent with his work at the Volksbühne. This was a newspaper called *Der Sozialist*, a name that unintentionally disguised the purpose of the journal. Like the Neue Freie Volksbühne, this paper owed its existence to the events that had taken place in 1891 at the Erfurt party meeting of the SPD. The program adopted there suggested to many that the older leaders of the party who had guided its fortunes through the period of the antisocialist laws had become so enmeshed in the political structure of the Reich that they threatened to strangle the party's revolutionary fervor in the coils of parliamentarianism. The rebels held that nothing could be accomplished by work within the established governmental forms. The party expelled those who represented this viewpoint, and the exiles formed a new party, the Independent Socialists, which never gained much influence and soon splintered into various groups. *Der Sozialist* was founded in

1891 as a voice of the apostates, and an important aspect of the ideological development some of these dissenters underwent is mirrored in the subtitle the paper eventually assumed: "Organ of Anarchism-Socialism." It became the first and best of the journals to propagate the ideas of anarchism then beginning to enjoy some acceptance in Germany.

Landauer once wrote in *Der Sozialist* that in February 1892 he was still outside political life.[2] He did not maintain this independence much longer. His intellectual background made him very susceptible to the revolutionary currents of the time, and the influences he was exposed to encouraged active involvement in them. He associated with a radical group led by Benedikt Friedländer, an anti-Marxist socialist, author of a brochure entitled *Der freiheitliche Sozialismus im Gegensatz zum Staatsknechtsthum der Marxisten* (*Free Socialism in Contrast to the State Slavery of the Marxists*). He read *Freiheit*, the anarchist journal published in New York by the German-expatriate revolutionary Johann Most. Landauer was writing, too, and the tone of his articles—interestingly enough some were published in *Die neue Zeit*, an organ of the SPD—show that his thinking was, if not politically oriented, then certainly concerned with social questions. In January 1892 appeared an essay with the title "Die Zukunft und die Kunst" ("The Future and Art"), in which Landauer claimed that the times were not ripe for real art in Germany, because the production of art is based on passive observation, and the modern world demanded action. He suggested that the great literature of the past seemed out of place now—Shakespeare frequently seemed bombastic and Goethe boring—because people—the young and the workers, in any event—were living for the present. The worker who had found his way to socialism was the person living at the pinnacle of his time, as Landauer put it; the classics had nothing to say to him. The modern German writers were drawing their materials not from tradition but from the real world around them. Although this did not result in great literature, Landauer argued, it did honestly reflect the conditions of the moment and held promise for their betterment. Yet even this was not enough. Action was necessary so that contemporary mankind could serve as a model for a new florescence of art in a better future. The young men who in the past would have become the Goethes of their day would now be more useful as statesmen or socialist agitators.

Landauer was twenty-one years old when he wrote this. He had his convictions, and if his inexperience and youth did not keep him from challenging the great literary giants of the past, it would certainly not cause him to be timorous when discussing the leading German writers of his day. In February 1892, *Die neue Zeit* printed a second article in which Landauer took up the question of Gerhart Hauptmann. He saw the author of *Vor Sonnenaufgang* as a promising revolutionary writer who had been spoiled, at least temporarily, by the literary theories of Arno Holz and Johannes Schlaf. The youth of Germany were not interested in matters of form and style but in reality, and Hauptmann had failed to depict it except in his first drama. His psychological treatment of his characters was accurate and penetrating, Landauer maintained, but this approach resulted in the creation of weak personalities. What was needed was strong men who could overcome their environment and show the way to a better world. In *Kollege Krampton* (*Colleague Krampton*), Hauptmann had to some extent created such a character; Landauer expressed his hope that this was a sign of future masterworks from Hauptmann's pen.

The editors of *Die neue Zeit* found it wise to state in a footnote to this article that the views expressed there as well as in the earlier article by the same author were not necessarily those of the editorial board. It was a year later before the next, and last, Landauer essay to appear in this journal was printed. It is doubtful, however, that Landauer offered *Die neue Zeit* many articles from 1892 to 1893, because it was soon after the appearance of the Hauptmann piece that he joined the staff of the *Sozialist* and became an editor in his own right. The decision to associate himself with this paper may be taken as Landauer's act of commitment to anarchism. Throughout most of the nineties, his life was largely determined by the fate of this publication.

Working with Landauer were Albert Weidner, later the editor of *Welt am Montag*, and Wilhelm Spohr, a writer and translator. The paper was well received in anarchist circles: the German-American anarchist Johann Most, the Italian revolutionary Errico Malatesta, and the prince of anarchists, Pëtr Kropotkin, all considered it the best of several European German-language journals supporting the antistate philosophy. Weidner maintained that its success was largely owing to Landauer, who became chief editor in 1893.[3] There was much to write about. Opposition to the SPD continued to grow within the Independent Socialist groups. The unions, on the other hand, became more and more deserving of support as their strength increased and their potential power was felt. The First National Trade Unions Congress was held in Germany in 1891, and strikes were occurring with greater frequency and intensity. And there was the task, always a dominating aspect of Landauer's efforts, of educating the proletariat to the possibility of a better life.

This purpose is apparent, too, in Landauer's first book, *Der Todesprediger* (*The Preacher of Death*), published in 1893. In the afterword to the second edition issued ten years later, Landauer wrote that the book was the product of a twenty-year-old. Interpreted loosely, this statement may be taken to mean that the book was written between 1890 and 1892. The political philosophy presented there suggests that it was not before 1892, however, because firm dedication to the cause of anarchism is a salient feature of its plot.

It is a strange work. The title page of the third edition (1923) bears the designation "Novel by Gustav Landauer." Landauer's friends, as well as literary reference books, also call it a novel, but Landauer himself never used that term, preferring to call it "my book" or "my story." *Der Todesprediger* is certainly not typical of the novel genre. Thirty-six of its one hundred and twenty-five pages are devoted to three philosophical essays written by the leading character. Moreover, it is precisely the central portion and the end of the book that are reserved for these essays; everything else is made to revolve around or lead up to them. And this "everything else" is by no means all plot. Twelve pages are filled with speeches on socialism, anarchism, or bourgeois politics presented by minor characters or, in one case, by the protagonist himself. Add to this more than twelve pages of rather extensive background material describing the youth and early manhood of the hero, and there remains only about half the book for the events and descriptions normally constituting a novel. Over half of this space contains philosophical speculations of the hero and the author's comments on the hero's state of mind. There is almost no action.

In a book with such a structure, the story is necessarily simple. The hero, Karl Starkblom, is a withdrawn, reflective widower who becomes financially independent at the age of forty-two and retires from his judgeship to dedicate himself to the study of philosophy. He intends to direct his speculations, with an uncompromising rationalism, toward the betterment of mankind. He finds, however, that reason cannot lead him to a justification for life; and, unable to justify it, he becomes convinced of its futility. He tries to escape this, first by concerning himself with art and then by taking a leading role in the revolutionary socialist movement. Suddenly overcome by the apparent meaninglessness of life, he withdraws once more from society and writes two essays extolling death as the only value in life. These essays fall into the hands of a woman who is prompted by them to save him. She does so by awakening in him an appreciation for natural drives, thereby showing him that reason is not the only aspect of existence, that sensual experience and the emotions are values in life. Having come to a love of life because of his love for the woman and having learned through the agency of a long lost brother, the woman's former paramour, that there are other people in the world for whom he can feel love, Starkblom decides to return to the socialist movement and work for a society in which everyone will be able to love life. As the first step toward this society, Starkblom writes an essay describing it. With this essay the book closes.

This plot, in which an intellectual man is freed from an emotional impasse by a "liberated" woman, has the flavor of Hauptmann's play *Einsame Menschen* (*Lonely Lives*), and one wonders whether that drama was not the inspiration for Landauer's book. *Einsame Menschen* had its premiere in Berlin just two years before *Der Todesprediger* appeared; in his essay on Hauptmann, mentioned above, Landauer wrote that its playwright had portrayed a common enough event—the fatal enmeshment of an intellectually superior man in the banalities of social convention—but had been remiss in not showing how such an individual might rise above conventionality and attain fulfillment. Landauer never mentioned a relationship between the two works, but there is no doubt that he tried to achieve in *Der Todesprediger* what he accused Haupt-mann of failing to do in his play.

If *Der Todesprediger* is meant to be an answer to the problems posed in *Einsame Menschen,* it is an insufficient one. The overall structure of the book, with its essays and speeches, is objectionably clumsy. The characters are ideals, not people. Landauer's attempt to symbolize his insights into reality does not succeed: wishful thinking, not the postive force of the creative imagination, make up the warp of the book's artistic fabric; the woof is political philosophy.

Yet the book cannot be simply dismissed as the naïve work of a literary apprentice. Landauer had it republished in 1903, although he expressed sorrow that he was unable to revise it at that time, and reaffirmed his satisfaction with the material. If this is difficult to understand from a literary point of view, it becomes clear enough in light of his later work; for *Der Todesprediger* has nearly all the elements that constitute Landauer's vision of a better life for man-kind. If he failed to articulate here the reality he understood, he made up for it by spending the rest of his life at the task. His be-lief in the validity of that reality never wavered.

It is noteworthy that the hero's last essay in this book is ad-dressed to artists and writers who live isolated from society, not to the proletariat. The hero recognizes that the workers are not in a position to digest the philosophical fare he offers. This too is true to Landauer's personality. He wanted to reach everyone with his vision of a better life; yet, whereas his call was understandable to the intellectual, the worker could make little of it in this form. It was Landauer's hope that intellectuals would join to raise the level of the proletariat's understanding so that it could grasp the concrete reality behind the poetic images.

If Landauer's writings were often beyond those whom he wished to lead, his activities were not. It was most probably through his support of the union movement that he met his first wife, a seamstress named Grete Leuschner. They were married late in 1891 or early in 1892, and if Landauer did indeed write *Der Todesprediger* during the latter year, it must reflect some of his emotional fulfillment as a new husband and, soon after, as a father. His work on the *Sozialist* made him a leader among the anarchists in Germany and prompted his selection as an anarchist delegate to the International Workers' Congress held at Zurich in August 1893. A pamphlet he wrote for consideration at this meeting is no longer available; but his actions there show very plainly that in dealing with the hard facts of the moment, he could use language understandable to everyone.

The relationship of anarchists to the international labor movement had been problematic even in the First International. That organization had been weakened by the disagreement between Marx and the notorious anarchist revolutionary Mikhail Bakunin (1814–76) over methods for achieving the dictatorship of the proletariat. The Second International, therefore, was wary of the anarchists. At its congress at Brussels in 1891, steps were taken to exclude them, a move that laid the groundwork for serious conflict at the meeting of 1893. The conflict came. After much angry debate the congress finally passed a motion by August Bebel excluding all those who—as he put it—refused the workers the right of parliamentary action. Bebel was fighting the battle of the 1891 SPD meeting at Erfurt all over again—and again he won. This so-called "Zurich Resolution" unseated the anarchists, who maintained that parliamentarianism served the purposes of the bourgeois state alone. The deliberations proceeded from verbal bouts to physical violence, and the German anarchists, including Landauer, were finally ejected bodily from the congress. The anarchists then held a meeting of their own at which Landauer spoke "about the general strike and the economic struggle. The May Day celebration should be combined with the general strike, and the latter should be the introduction of the revolution." [4] This was a very different tone from the one used by the SPD, which depended upon political strength in the Reichstag to achieve its goals and did not accept the general strike as a political weapon until 1905. From this fiery statement can be measured the ideological gap between Landauer's colleagues and the official socialism of the SPD. These ringing words also make it easy to understand why the first political recognition Landauer received was imprisonment.

The immediate cause of the legal action against him was material in the *Sozialist*. As chief editor Landauer was held responsible for content that the government decided advocated civil disobedi-

ence (*"Aufforderung zum Ungehorsam gegen die Staatsgewalt"*).
He was sentenced to two months in prison on 1 November 1893
and then, in December, given an additional sentence of nine
months because of "incitement" (*"Aufreizung"*). Political persecu-
tion of left-wing journalists by means of prison sentences was, even
after the antisocialist laws had lapsed, common in the Reich, the
expected price of dissent. Although, as Weidner noted,[5] Landauer,
in contrast to the treatment normally afforded political prisoners,
was forced to perform convict labor, his active spirit was not
shackled by the experience. In addition to carrying on various
studies during his period behind bars, he again turned to writing
fiction, this time the *Novelle* "Arnold Himmelheber." His real
difficulties began after his release from prison, for by then the
government had also put Spohr in prison and suppressed the
Sozialist (1894); without his earlier activities Landauer found himself cut adrift and in serious financial straits.

Money problems were to plague him throughout most of his
life. This time he was given financial assistance by relatives, particularly his sympathetic cousin Hugo Landauer, a man who
shared some of Landauer's socialist ideas. The forced break with his
earlier work made Landauer consider an entirely new course for the
future: he tried to enroll at the University of Freiburg to study
medicine. This plan collapsed in March 1895 when the university
refused to admit him because of his prison record. He then decided that journalism was, after all, the career most consistent
with his real desire, to write, so he accepted the editorship of a
newspaper in Bregenz, Austria, and entered upon his duties there
sometime after April 1895. He was back in Berlin by the end of the
year. Before its close he helped reestablish the *Sozialist* (Spohr was
out of prison again) and became engaged anew in anarchist activities. A remark in a letter written 2 March 1911 to the effect that
he was still forbidden to enter Austria suggests that Landauer's
Bregenz paper, like the *Sozialist* before it, was too revolutionary to
please the authorities, and that he was evicted from Austria as a
result.

It is clear that Landauer's prison term did not cure him of the
social disease for which the government had prescribed that treatment. His commitment to anarchism was as firm as ever, but he be-

gan to make statements indicating that the revolution he promoted
had nothing to do with the violence normally associated with anarchism. He proposed the eradication of force, not the use of it.
Toward the end of 1894 he wrote an article which appeared in
January 1895 in *Zukunft*, defining for the mostly bourgeois, but
educated, audience of that journal the positive factors of anarchism.[6] In this piece Landauer maintained that everyone, rich and
poor alike, is a victim of the historical accidents by which modern
society has developed. The intellectual limitations of the masses
and the struggle of man against man—especially of the privileged
against the nonprivileged—have until now hindered mankind's attempts to better its fate. Anarchism wishes to end the struggle
so that every individual can achieve for himself the place his nature
entitles him to. In place of social institutions that demand blind
allegiance—state, church, sanctity of property—the anarchists
wish to establish natural groupings of individuals, groupings to help
all of their members achieve some specific social goal without sub-
merging anyone in organizational structure. Collective ownership
of natural goods is not the goal, but rather social organization that
obviates ownership so that resources necessary for life are available
to everyone. Anarchism is by no means directed toward the establishment of a proletarian dictatorship; but anarchists tend to associate with the proletariat, because that caste, since the class
struggle has been forced upon it, is the most active in its efforts to
restructure society. And action now is important, because the condition of the masses may lead to a deterioration of the proletariat's
potential for intellectual growth; if the time comes when the
masses will no longer have the capability to improve themselves,
then the other classes will indeed be to blame. It is not love for the
masses, Landauer concluded, but disgust with present conditions
that leads the anarchist to his point of view. The revolution he
seeks is one of spiritual rejuvenation. Force and repression are not
the path of the anarchist.

   This was written during a period when some anarchists were
advocating violence, the so-called "propaganda of the deed." It is
obvious from this essay that Landauer, when he called for action,
meant action of a different kind. He was more specific about it in
a pamphlet entitled *Ein Weg zur Befreiung der Arbeiterklasse*

37

(*A Way to Freedom for the Working Class*) issued at the end of 1895. In this is found the first concrete formulation of an idea that occupied Landauer for the rest of his life: the anarchist settlement, where individuals would join together, within but separate from the bourgeois society, to build a life free from the pressures of modern civilization and consistent with the dignity of the human being. This proposal was based on the concept of mutual aid, which the workers had seen in action in their unions and cooperatives; and because they had seen it, Landauer was able to express to them his seemingly fanciful vision for the future in terms that had a certain relevance and validity, even for the uneducated.

His efforts to address the workers directly now became more intense than ever before, both through articles and speaking engagements. He had reason for haste. Within the anarchist camp there was an ever-growing tendency toward the violence that Landauer abhorred. This provoked vigorous repression by the authorities; Landauer was arrested again in March 1896, in the middle of a speech to a workers' group. His release the next day shows that there was nothing alarming in what he was saying, but still the meeting was disrupted by official action. Police harassment at the headquarters of the newspaper was common. On one such occasion officers arrived with a confiscation order for an issue of the literary supplement that regularly appeared with the *Sozialist*; the sensibilities of some dignitary had evidently been offended by the serialization of a story containing some rather frank sexual details. The next issue of the *Sozialist* (18 April 1896) reported that five policemen spent two hours searching the premises, even to Landauer's pockets, for the manuscript of this pornographic piece. As the search progressed, the guilty journalists found it difficult to conduct themselves with the seriousness the occasion called for. The offending work was indeed on the premises, but not in manuscript form: these dangerous anarchists had been printing excerpts from J. J. W. Heinse's *Ardinghello und die glückseligen Inseln*, a minor classic of German literature that had been available to the literary public since 1787. The book lay open on the windowsill while the official defenders of decency and virtue diligently searched. Decency and virtue, however, won out in the end. Gustav Diesner, who was serving as editor at the time,* was later sentenced to a short prison term on the grounds that only those parts of Heinse's book pertaining to sexual matters had been published and that the material was therefore dangerous to women and children.[7]

Another issue was confiscated early in October of the same year, when the paper printed an article concerning police spying into anarchist affairs, detailing the specific case of a young anarchist, named Theodor Machner, who was bribed by a police official to spy on the activities of the *Sozialist* and its staff. Machner, who was in prison at the time, readily accepted the offer so as to gain his freedom. He went to Berlin where he immediately reported the intrigue to Spohr, Landauer, and Weidner. They decided to take advantage of the situation; together the four men composed a report to the police, which was later published in the *Sozialist*; and when Machner went to an arranged meeting with the official, Commissar Bösel, the others, disguised, stood nearby. As Machner handed over the report, Spohr, Landauer, and Weidner came forward and identified themselves. The several policemen present, caught in their attempt to incriminate these three men, fled in embarrassment, pursued by four-part anarchist laughter. Machner then left the country.

Proceedings were brought against Landauer as the presumed author of the article on the adventure, and harassment, including house searches, increased over the next months. But it was impossible for the officials to keep the story quiet. Though the *Sozialist* had to be careful about printing the details, the other Berlin newspapers of all political leanings continued to report on the case as it developed. After being interrogated a number of times, Landauer was arrested on 24 December 1896 and held without bail until 6 February 1897, when his trial for insulting an official took place. Asked about his political position, Landauer made a statement repeating much of what he had written in his *Zukunft* article of January 1895 about anarchism. There was nothing in-

---

* It was not uncommon in the Bismarckian Reich for secondary figures on the staff of opposition journals to assume the title of editor to help protect the real guiding spirits from the authorities. Such a person was called a *"Sitzredakteur."* There was a rather frequent change of "editor" on the *Sozialist*.

flammatory in that statement, and the prosecutor could present no firm evidence that Landauer was the author of the offending *Sozialist* article, so he was set free. The ostensible editor of the paper at the time the article appeared, a carpenter journeyman named Gustav Friedrich, was given a two-month sentence on the same charge, however, and Commissar Bösel was found to have acted indiscreetly but in no way improperly.

Though copies of the 3 October 1896 edition of the *Sozialist* are all but impossible to find, a reproduction of the upper part of the front page can be seen in Wilhelm Spohr's little book *O ihr Tage von Friedrichshagen!* Immediately below the masthead is a photograph of Spohr, Landauer, and Weidner in the costumes they wore on the night of their intrigue, complete with beards (in this case false) such as all dangerous anarchists wear. Landauer sent a copy of the photograph to Commissar Bösel with an appropriate inscription, reminding him of their pleasant evening together. The photograph is a singular document of German cultural history.

Apprehension about the possibility of growing violence and worry that official action might finally destroy all opportunity to reach the people were not the only reasons why intensive propagandist activity was in order early in 1896. The Fourth International Workers' Congress was scheduled to be held during August of that year in London, and the anarchists were eager to have as much support as possible from the people for their renewed attempt to be accepted by the Second International. As early as 18 April of that year, the *Sozialist* carried an article by Landauer on this subject, giving a historical sketch of the struggle between the German anarchists and the official socialist party and suggesting that if Bebel's Zurich Resolution were upheld at the 1896 meeting, all of the anarchists, not only the German ones, would be forced out, and the strength of the International would be seriously weakened. He had shown with an article in the 4 April edition that his own position in regard to the SPD had not changed since 1893; he stated there that the May Day celebration should be abandoned because it had lost its revolutionary meaning. He proposed a general strike in its place.

It was obvious, however, that the old struggle between anarchists and the official International organization would be continued, and Landauer prepared for it with a long lead article entitled "Von Zürich bis London" ("From Zurich to London") in the 18 July issue of the *Sozialist*. This was reprinted as a brochure in October of the same year and also appeared in English, published in London during the same year, under the title "Social Democracy in Germany." The first paragraph of this article proclaims it a kind of minority report: "This report is meant to give a picture of the German workers' movement as it appears to us anarchists who are within the workers' movement but outside the Social Democratic Party." [8] Landauer asserted that the SPD represented not the proletariat but the bourgeois society. The socialist members in the Reichstag were interested only in votes, allowing parliamentary procedures of the state to stifle the desires and efforts of the working class. The party's failure to work within the governmental structure for a socialist revision of society and to support direct action by the masses proved the SPD's remoteness from true socialist ideals. Ignaz Auer, member of the party directorate, showed the true nature of the party when he said in a speech, "It must be strange workers indeed who object to the structure of a national state." [9]

It is little wonder, then, that when delegate tickets for the congress were sent for distribution in Germany to the SPD newspaper *Vorwärts*, the editor, Wilhelm Liebknecht, refused to provide any for the anarchist delegates, headed by Ladislaus Gumplowicz and Gustav Landauer. The German anarchists went anyway and prior to the congress attended a special international meeting of anarchists, where they were cordially greeted by their English hosts, among them Keir Hardie and Tom Mann, both leaders of the British labor movement. Among the matters discussed was the agrarian question. Landauer's statement in this discussion, as reported in the *Sozialist* of 10 October 1896, was as follows:

The anarchists no longer believe in the fatalistic and Jesuitic teaching of Marx, which declares the concentration of capital and the eradication of small farmers as a necessary condition for the realization of socialism.

In the agrarian question they are of the following opinion:

(1) We reject all state assistance—not because, for revolutionary reasons, the small farmers should not be helped, nor because it would be impossible to help them, but solely because every act of state interference leads to perpetuation of the state and of suppression.
(2) We wish to propagate understanding of free socialism among the workers and also among the farmers.
(3) We want the farmers to prevent their proletarianization by joining with farm workers in agrarian cooperatives, thereby heading off further expansion of large landholdings and creating organizations suitable to serve as nuclei for the socialist society.
(4) In recognition of the fact that the above will in many cases remain nothing but a pious wish, we urge workers as well as tenant farmers and farmers to unite in energetic economic struggle against their exploiters.

Much that was said here would recur later in Landauer's social writings.

Events at the congress itself transpired much as had been expected. Although many people, some of them very influential in international socialist circles, spoke in favor of admitting the anarchists, the meeting was stacked against them, and after much bitter argument they were excluded. The bitterness continued after the German delegates returned to their homeland. The SPD called a large meeting to report on the congress. Landauer attended with his wife and Weidner, hoping to be able to speak for the anarchist cause. One of the SPD leaders, Richard Fischer, who was in charge of the meeting, attempted to incite the crowd against Landauer even before he spoke. Fischer read aloud a quotation from one of Landauer's articles in which Wilhelm Liebknecht, a party saint, was called a scoundrel (*Lump*). The crowd responded angrily, and threatening moves were made toward Landauer and his two companions. Landauer calmly demanded the floor and spoke over the noise of the crowd for ten minutes, explaining why he had written what he had and saying that he saw no reason at that time to retract it. The crowd was subdued, but the breach between him and the party leadership was wider than ever.

Between his return from England and the Bösel trial, Landauer's life continued very much in the pattern it had followed since he had returned to Berlin from Bregenz. He wrote articles for the

Sozialist, took part in public meetings, gave speeches to workers' groups. Late in October he went on a speaking tour in southeast Germany, reporting to anarchist meetings on the London Congress and propagandizing for the establishment of cooperatives and the use of the general strike as a weapon in the struggle to better society.

After the Bösel trial, however, he set out on a course he hoped would draw him less to the attention of the authorities and at the same time be more in keeping with his real desires. On 7 February 1897, the day after the Bösel case was settled, he wrote to his cousin Hugo that he intended now to be extremely careful, and later in the same letter said that his principal concern was not with the details of immediate political struggle. He felt himself to be primarily a writer and wanted above all to have the opportunity to write. Fritz Mauthner was trying to find some means of financial support so that his younger friend might have that opportunity. It looked for awhile as if Landauer was about to embark upon a new life. In any event, some aspects of the old one were over.

One such aspect was his association with the *Sozialist.* Though it was by no means broken off, it was altered, removing from him the burden—and the danger—of editorial responsibility. This must have taken place about the same time that Landauer and his wife separated. Bab wrote of her that "she was for a long time a clever, brave, self-sacrificing companion to him"; [10] but their marriage had certainly not been an easy one, and it is little wonder that it was not of longer duration. Aside from the unrest caused by Landauer's activities, they had been constantly plagued by money problems combined with a long period of ill health Landauer suffered; and there seemed little hope that the financial situation would soon improve. It is quite possible too that differences in background and intellectual experience played a role. The wife and daughter, Charlotte (a second daughter died when two years old), set up separate quarters, and Landauer went to live in Friedrichshagen, headquarters of the famous literary colony where German literary naturalism and the Volksbühne movement had been born. He was among friends there: Spohr, Weidner, and many of the people with whom he associated at the Neue Freie Volksbühne were either residents of the area or frequent guests.

Call to Revolution
The Mystical Anarchism of Gustav Landauer

It was not until 1898 that Landauer again became active publicly, this time in an undertaking that attracted much attention and involved many prominent figures, including his old bête noire Wilhelm Liebknecht, all under the leadership of the remarkable Moritz von Egidy. At the height of a brilliant military career in which he had risen quickly to the rank of lieutenant colonel, Egidy was forced to leave the army when, in 1890, he published a brochure entitled *Ernste Gedanken (Serious Thoughts)*, expressing his rejection of the traditional structure of organized religion and calling for a revitalization of Christianity. Though officialdom was horrified by this pronouncement, Egidy became a hero to many and a leader in numerous social causes. The people at the *Sozialist* knew him by 1894—he once visited Spohr in prison—and he was treated with great respect by the paper, though his views were not always consistent with its policies.

In December 1897, Egidy called a public meeting in Berlin at which he spoke about the case of a man named Ziethen, who had been in prison since 1883 serving a life sentence for the murder of his wife. Egidy had reason to believe that the man was innocent, the victim of police chicanery, and called for the establishment of a committee to secure Ziethen's freedom. The committee was formed with Landauer as a member. The anarchists had a particular interest in the matter, because the same police official suspected of misrepresentation in this case had also been involved in the condemnation of three anarchists for a supposed bomb plot; and here too the actions of police had not been beyond question. Landauer accepted Egidy's suggestion that he write an article for the *Sozialist* attacking the manner in which the police had handled Ziethen so as to provoke a charge of libel. Should Landauer be tried on this charge, the Ziethen case would have to be reexamined, and Egidy felt he could then prove Ziethen's innocence. The attack appeared originally in the *Sozialist* of 5 February 1898, but the police took no action until it was repeated in a pamphlet six months later. Thereafter things went according to plan, except that just before the trial date Egidy suddenly died and with him Landauer's chances for acquittal. He was sentenced to six months in prison on 22 March 1899.

The Ziethen affair was, of course, not the only thing to concern Landauer during 1898. He continued to write for the *Sozialist* and, beginning in March of that year, gave a lecture series, this time not on social problems, but on literature. Yet this was no indication that he was abandoning social concerns; for it was at this same time that he began to take part in a project proposed by two of his colleagues at Friedrichshagen, a plan that for a time seemed to hold promise of thorough rejuvenation of society. It was an organization appropriately called "Neue Gemeinschaft" ("New Community").

The brothers Heinrich and Julius Hart are best known for their literary criticism and their support of new directions in German literature, especially in their series of essays *Kritische Waffengänge* (*Critical Jousts*), published in 1882. They formed the nucleus of a bohemian literary group in the eighties and were members of the Friedrichshagen colony during the nineties. Though they associated with bohemian artists and writers, they did not have the antisocial attitudes that motivated many of their friends; and they developed an interest in revitalizing society as they had wanted to do with literature. The Neue Gemeinschaft was to be their vehicle. Its basis was mystical metaphysics explained by Julius Hart in books with titles such as *Der neue Gott* (*The New God*, 1899) and *Die neue Welterkenntnis* (*The New World-Understanding*, 1902). A religious aura surrounded the undertaking, and many members were attracted by that. Not so Landauer. As Bab put it, he participated ". . . not because of the very problematical philosophical theorems of the brothers, but because he believed he had found in their *practical* program the basis for a highly fruitful, exemplary social structure." [11] For awhile Landauer was satisfied with the program. He gave lectures for the members. His essay "Durch Absonderung zur Gemeinschaft" ("Through Separation to Community"), expanded as the first part of the book *Skepsis und Mystik*, appeared in one of the organization's pamphlets. The close relationship with the Harts, however, could not last long. By August 1900, Landauer was writing of them critically in his letters, and his association with the Neue Gemeinschaft was terminated about one year later. Martin Buber, who knew Landauer well, later wrote that Landauer learned from this experience how community does *not* come about.[12] * When he discovered that there was little substance beneath the mystical mood, Landauer had no further interest in the organization. Others must have been equally disenchanted, for the association soon dissolved. It failed so completely in its attempts to influence society that scarcely a trace of its memory remains today.

More significant for Landauer than the effect of the Neue Gemeinschaft upon him were the personal relationships he established while working for it. Two of the most important were with Julius Bab and the young poet Erich Mühsam. Mühsam's introduction to Landauer was as the author of "Durch Absonderung zur Gemeinschaft," which impressed him deeply. A close friendship developed quickly between them. This was in 1901, however, after Landauer's prison term. Still a third acquaintance, made at a meeting of the Neue Gemeinschaft in March 1899, was of far greater importance for Landauer's life and work. There he met the poetess Hedwig Lachmann, whom Bab called "one of the most individual and strongest women that this entire German generation produced," [13] and who would some years later become Landauer's wife.

Hedwig was born in Swabia in 1865, the daughter of a Jewish cantor in the village of Krumbach. She had gained some reputation as poetess and translator by the middle 1890s, but her life was not happy. Her poetic sensitivity made her withdraw from life, and family troubles constantly tormented her. In the last decade of the nineteenth century, these factors were aggravated by a deep, difficult emotional relationship with the poet Richard Dehmel. The intensity with which Dehmel reacted to her demonstrates the effect Hedwig could have on a kindred artistic nature. Dehmel had met her through his wife Paula in 1892 and had immediately fallen in love with her. There is no doubt that she loved him too, but her shyness and her loyalty to Paula prevented her from giving in completely to her feelings; and the relationship went on for several years, unfulfilled and unfulfillable, a torment to them both. For

* All references to materials in *Gustav Landauer: sein Lebensgang in Briefen,* edited by Martin Buber, will not be documented further if the specific date of the letter is given in the text.

Dehmel, at least, it was a productive torment. Bab maintained that it was Hedwig's influence that brought Dehmel's poetry to fruition.[14] Dehmel himself once wrote her, "Don't you feel how everything in me began to bloom anew since I saw you? I found a new art in you, a new sensuality, new thoughts! not just for me." [15]

The writer Hans Blüher called Landauer's letters to Hedwig the finest love letters of the twentieth century.[16] If ardor is the standard for judgment, Blüher was probably right. Landauer seems to have recognized the possibility of a new life for himself the moment he set eyes on the shy poetess, and he wasted no time in informing her of his feelings. Her reaction to his approaches was calm but not cold, and he felt much encouraged by her attitude. On 24 March 1899 he wrote to Hugo that he was in love and had regained his self-assurance. This was two days after he was sentenced in the Ziethen case. Landauer was allowed to postpone the beginning of his imprisonment until late summer. During these months Landauer and Hedwig saw each other only infrequently but corresponded constantly, and in this way he drew her more and more into his life. When he entered prison on 18 August 1899, it was with particular regret but also with a special new hope for the future.

3

Mauthner
and
Mysticism
1900–1906

No century in the history of the Western world was looked forward to with such hopeful expectations as the twentieth. Technology had advanced to a stage where its beneficial effects would begin to be felt by everyone, while more and more attention was paid to the social evils the industrial revolution had caused. Some steps had already been taken to alleviate them, and progress in all fields of human life was in the air. Politicians of all parties made glowing promises to their followers; the party faithful—partly because of these promises, partly because of the mood of the times—believed the ultimate in human achievement was just around the corner. Gustav Landauer began this century in prison.

Years later, when he was editing the material for his *Briefe aus der französischen Revolution* (*Letters from the French Revolution*, 1919), Landauer included a letter by Madame Roland (1754–93) saying that she was quite comfortable in prison. To it he appended the wry footnote: "The editor has, perhaps, more experience in prison letters than most readers have, so for the benefit of increased understanding he may be allowed the comment that it is not always quite so comfortable inside as one describes to loved ones outside." [1] Yet he had learned earlier that a jail sentence was not without its positive side, and this one in particular had certain attractive features. He had been able to spend the summer months actively and happily; he now had the prospect of a winter with no financial worries and with a prescribed period of uninterrupted time to dedicate to literary activities of a compelling nature. This included editorial work for Fritz Mauthner, who was at the time preparing a major work for publication.

The friendship between Landauer and Mauthner had grown constantly during the 1890s. Though he held himself aloof from Landauer's political activities, Mauthner followed his personal fortunes closely and sympathetically. Mauthner's intercession and the work he provided allowed Landauer to be exempted from convict labor during this prison term. Landauer expressed some of his admiration and appreciation in an essay about Mauthner's literary work, offered as a birthday greeting to Mauthner, in the 18 November 1899 issue of Zukunft. The article was signed: "Gustav Landauer, Strafgefängnis Tegeler Landstrasse" ("Tegel Road Prison"). In a footnote to this article, Maximilian Harden, the editor of the journal, added his best wishes for Mauthner's fiftieth birthday, a greeting also written from prison. The life of an opposition journalist remained difficult in Germany.

As work progressed on Mauthner's manuscript, Landauer found time also for some writing of his own. For two months he translated into modern German some sermons and other writings by the medieval German mystic Meister Eckhart (?1260–?1327). As will be seen later, this work arose directly from the materials in Mauthner's book. After the translation was finished, Landauer turned to fiction, as he had in his first prison term, and wrote a Novelle entitled "Lebendig tot" ("Dead Alive"). As the date of his release—26 February 1900—approached, Landauer grew impatient for freedom, but this restlessness was tempered by the knowledge that his months in confinement had been extremely fruitful.

His release brought with it the same problems he had faced six years earlier. The Sozialist, after a moribund last year, had once again ceased publication (1899), this time not because of government action but because its readership had fallen off. Landauer had much to occupy him—his connection with the Neue Gemeinschaft was still strong—but nothing that provided a steady income. His best personal asset was that his work was recognized by some important journals, so he had no choice but to return to the life of a free-lance journalist with all the uncertainties inherent in that life. He had things of interest to write about, but for nearly two years he felt that his life was drifting aimlessly. This no doubt explains in part the great sympathy he felt for a writer who had experienced uncertainty for most of his life.

That writer was Eduard Douwes Dekker (1820–87), a Dutch citizen who wrote under the name Multatuli. Thanks to translations by Landauer's friend Wilhelm Spohr, Dekker's work began to become available in Germany in 1899. He had spent nearly twenty years as a colonial official in the Far East, but came into conflict with his superiors over the manner in which the natives of Java were exploited by the Dutch government. Forced out of the colonial service in 1856, he returned to Holland and began writing —first the startling novel *Max Havelaar*, in which, on the basis of his own experiences in Java, he indicted the Dutch government and bourgeoisie for the situation in Holland's colonial empire, then a series of other works, ever more bitter ones, as Dekker saw that his words were accepted as literature, but had no social impact. He left Holland and went into exile, wandering for years, mostly in western Germany, almost always in penury, forever renewing his attack upon his homeland. His last few years were spent in relative security owing to his publisher and his second wife, but he died thoroughly embittered about European society and having concluded that violence was the only means by which social injustice could be eradicated.

In 1899, Landauer's first review of Spohr's translation helped introduce *Max Havelaar* to the German public.[2] The second review, written in 1900 after Landauer's release from prison, shows why Landauer found this work so important. Landauer stressed that Multatuli was a man of action who had turned writer, not to create literature, but to change the social order. The intention was not to improve the conditions of the Javanese, but to show European society at its worst. His great success at this task was the sign of greatness in the man and his literature, even though he did not achieve the social improvements he hoped to.[3]

In contrast to the feeling of comradeship Landauer felt for Multatuli was his growing disaffection from the philosophic visions of the brothers Hart and their Neue Gemeinschaft. In 1900,

Landauer reviewed a collection of essays by both Heinrich and Julius Hart.[4] This was *Das Reich der Erfüllung* (*The Kingdom of Fulfillment*), but Landauer saw little fulfillment in it. As in a review he had written a year earlier of Julius Hart's *Der neue Gott*,[5] Landauer took his friends and fellow Friedrichshagener to task for making ecstatic promises of a new world but ignoring the practical sobriety and skepticism Landauer felt would be necessary for life in the twentieth century. Landauer was becoming ever more certain that a better future would be possible only if old social structures that stood in its way could be eliminated. The Harts seemed to be attempting a rejuvenation of old social structures by glossing them with consecration and jubilation.

The year from February 1900 to February 1901 brought Landauer little satisfaction except for the continuing work with Mauthner. By early 1901, however, he was at last able to settle one of his central concerns. For most of the period since Landauer's release, Hedwig had been living at her family's home in Krumbach, Swabia. They had remained in contact by letter, and the depth of their relationship had grown, but for a long time she had felt unable to commit herself to a life with the thoroughly unorthodox Landauer. In February 1901 he began to press her with greater urgency and finally forced her to a decision. She chose in his favor. Landauer spent the summer living with a cousin in Ulm so as to be near her while she tried to persuade her family to accept him. This attempt was unsuccessful; but despite her family's objections, she joined him in September and went with him to England where they hoped to be somewhat free from the censorious attitudes they would have had to face in Germany. The journey was made possible by a long-term loan from the popular novelist Auguste Hauschner, Mauthner's cousin, who at Mauthner's request first helped Landauer financially as early as 1896 and again in 1900. Auguste and Landauer developed a friendly acquaintance in 1900 and remained on very good terms for the rest of his life. Her support had always been generous; she now made possible for him the one thing he felt to be most important: a life with Hedwig.

Landauer and Hedwig remained in England, first in London, then in Bromley, until June 1902. In Bromley they were close neighbors of Kropotkin and through him associated with a number of English and other European anarchists. One may surmise, however, that these contacts were not without some friction, for Landauer's concept of anarchism was still very much at odds with the philosophy of violence espoused by many anarchists. He made this clear in an article written immediately upon arrival in England and published in late October in the *Zukunft* under the title "Anarchische Gedanken über Anarchismus" ("Anarchic Thoughts on Anarchism").[6] It was a denunciation of the anarchist murders that had punctuated European history in the previous decade. He admitted that he had once subscribed to the concept of achieving a nonviolent society by violent means, but he now believed that such an approach was nothing more than an emulation of methods used by political parties, while true anarchism demanded new methods consistent with what the new society was to be. For this the individual must first find within himself the principles by which a truly free, anarchist life can be led, and then begin living it within the existing society. For revolutionaries schooled in the writings of Bakunin and Malatesta, such a statement must have been difficult to reconcile with what they held to be their mission.

Whether because of doctrinal differences with other anarchists or as a matter of choice, the two expatriates remained relatively isolated. They were very happy with each other and were satisfied with their situation for the time, but it became evident that they could not live permanently in England. All attempts by Landauer to find a regular source of income ended in failure, and he and Hedwig soon learned that life in England was more expensive than they had anticipated. When she became pregnant, they decided to return home. Though their sojourn in England had not provided the personal independence they had hoped for, it had given them the confidence and assurance needed to carry on their life together in Germany.

Back in Germany they settled in Hermsdorf near Berlin, their home until 1917. The stability implied by such a permanent residence actually existed for awhile. Their first daughter, Gudula, was born late in 1902. In March 1903, Landauer was able to obtain a divorce from his first wife, and his formal marriage to Hedwig followed soon after. About the same time he finally found a position somewhat commensurate with his own interests: he began working for Axel Junker Nachfolger (Karl Schnabel), booksellers and publishers. The firm published his Meister Eckhart volume (1903) as well as a translation (with Hedwig) of Oscar Wilde's essay "The Soul of Man under Socialism" (1904). Other translations of Wilde's works, including *The Picture of Dorian Gray* (1907), were to follow. This represented the first real commercial success of an activity that Landauer had been engaged in since the *Sozialist* days. Translations of his from English and French had appeared there, and the Neue Freie Volksbühne had presented Octave Mirbeau's drama *Les Mauvais bergers* in Landauer's German version during the 1901/02 season. After 1903 he received many translation assignments and for a number of years devoted much of his energy to this work.

Along with the feeling of having achieved financial security, Landauer had the satisfaction of seeing his own fiction receive wider recognition. The second edition of *Der Todesprediger* appeared early in 1903, and though it was scarcely hailed as a literary tour de force, it was not without its admirers. Richard Dehmel wrote to Landauer expressing great appreciation of the book, adding, "I do not understand how such a book could remain unnoticed for so long; perhaps it appeared a few years too early for its time and for the people who should take it to heart." [7]

About the same time a book containing Landauer's two *Novellen* was published under the title *Macht und Mächte* (*Might and Destinies*). The two stories in it, though written six years apart, belong together, for both concern human love and its effect upon the individual and upon society. The first *Novelle*, "Arnold Himmelheber," had been written secretly during Landauer's prison term in 1894 and was, therefore, from the same period as *Der Todesprediger*. A first version of the story had appeared in the literary supplement to the *Sozialist* during 1896, then with the title "Lebenskunst" ("Art of Life"). Like the title, the story was altered significantly before publication in its final form. It insists that love with its inevitably attendant sensuality is necessary for the happy human being, so necessary, in fact, that conventional moral considerations must not be allowed to stand in its way. The characters all act under the influence of Himmelheber, a sixty-two-year-old giant with magnificent intellectual and physical vitality, whose life and actions symbolize the story's message. A physician, he allows a patient to die under his hand because the injured man is a barrier to a love that, in the context of the story, has the ultimate sanction of nature. Incest and murder are more acceptable in the world created here than is acquiescence before impediments to love. Himmelheber is a superman, beyond good and evil. His will to power is the will to love, expressed in his relationship with his daughter, Lysa, who became her father's beloved after her mother died. The characters in this work feel themselves to be parts of the great continuum of nature and in this feeling recognize a new reality for which a new morality is necessary, a feminine morality, meant to replace the Christian ethic, which has not succeeded in bringing love to the world. Lysa proclaims this in one short statement that symbolizes both the philosophical content of the story and the new morality Landauer felt to be necessary for mankind: "I and my mother are one. . . ." [8] This story presages the development of a super race, totally dedicated to love and therefore worthy of the new reality that fosters love.

The stress in this story on the positive aspects of sensuality relates it closely in theme to *Der Todesprediger*. In contrast, the second *Novelle* in *Macht und Mächte*, "Lebendig tot" ("Dead Alive"), written during Landauer's second prison term in 1900, is concerned with the fact that sensuality, though it is an essential feature of love, can also exist without love. When it does it is destructive, not only to individuals victimized by it, but to love itself. This is the least complex—and least successful—piece of fiction Landauer wrote. It is the story of a man whose life is ruined by his purely sensual relationship with a sexually precocious girl. The spell she casts upon him in his youth remains with him even after he frees himself from her physically; the possibility of love has been destroyed within him. Though he finds another woman with whom love seems attainable, fate reveals that his hope for this attainment is vain. The woman dies bearing his stillborn child. All that is left to him is a life devoid of love, devoid of the fundamental essence of life. Without love he is forced to exist as a totally isolated intellect. He is dead as a human being.

This story is not convincing. In "Arnold Himmelheber," despite its fantastic morality and idealistic vision of a new race, Landauer manages to convey the impression that a weird universal necessity underlies the events. "Lebendig tot" lacks this necessity at the climactic point: the second woman's death is coincidence, not fate. Still, Landauer's intent is clear. Love concerns the whole being; without love the rages of passion are destructive. This contrasts with part of the message in "Arnold Himmelheber": without passion there can be no life; love is a metaphysical imperative. Of all Landauer's characters only the hero of "Der gelbe Stein" ("The Yellow Stone") finds by himself a way to blend the sexual and the spiritual in a manner within the reach of everyday humanity.

"Der gelbe Stein," written in 1910, was included in the second edition of *Macht und Mächte* (1923). The inclusion is appropriate, for this somewhat obscure story serves as a synthesis of the two earlier ones. To achieve this synthesis Landauer used a fairy tale. The story is based on a tale from Celtic literature, "Pwyll, the Prince of Dyfed," found in the first of the *Four Branches of the Mabinogi*. This tale relates how Pwyll changed places with Arawan, the king of fairyland, in order to overcome the king's enemy, Hafgan. Pwyll spends a year disguised as the king but in all that time never touches the queen. Scholars of Welsh literature see significant elements of ancient Welsh culture reflected in the tale:

We see, for instance, an extreme punctiliousness in the matter of
personal honor, a rigid adherence to the sanctity of the spoken word,
and an exalted view of chastity, especially male chastity. We find in
"Pwyll" . . . that feeling in regard to sex honor which Renan speaks
of as the electrifying influence on the manners of the Middle Ages,
which was the contribution of Welsh literature to the times. . . .[9]

Landauer's approach to the material is, of course, quite different. The hero in his version is the "König von Tagland" ("King of the Day"). It is the "König von Traumland" ("King of Dreamland") with whom Tagland changes place, and the exchange is forced upon Tagland by the other. Tagland lives most intimately with Traumland's red-haired queen; and, upon his return to his own palace, is troubled by a longing for her, though he holds his own blond wife in as much respect as ever. He finally returns to Traumland and attempts to bring the red-haired queen back with him. She is willing, but they become separated in the darkness between the two palaces. He returns to his blond queen, who assures him that she is the red-haired one. Believing her, he then searches his palace for the blond queen, though the one he is with tells him that she is the blond queen as well. He asks her to go to Traumland with him, and when they reach the yellow stone marking the boundary between the two kingdoms, he recognizes both of his queens in her.

As is often the case with fairy tales, many elements of this story elude interpretation, and one cannot hope to understand the tale rationally. It moves simultaneously in the spheres of waking and dreaming, and the experiences within one sphere are as real and as valid as those within the other. The passage of time is different in the two kingdoms, but still forms a unity in which all the events take place. There are mysterious dark forests and areas of blinding light. The fairy dogs of the original tale, great white beasts with luminous red ears, are retained in Landauer's version, but they serve no particular purpose. Most puzzling of all is the yellow stone, which is not mentioned in the *Mabinogion.* That a stone is used as a marker between the two kingdoms is understandable enough, but there seems to be no special reason why it is yellow. Neither Welsh nor German mythology offers a precedent or an explanation. The stone is phosphorescent and associated with sunlight, but it does not represent the sun itself. The reader is forced to take Landauer's word that the stone is yellow, and that is the end of it.

No one experts to find his way through a fairy tale by the rules of logic, however, and fascination with these obscurities should not obliterate the story's total impact. Close acquaintance brings a general feeling for the thought behind it, and this general feeling is undoubtedly what Landauer, who trusted words only as metaphorical symbols, was trying to evoke. What Landauer did was to take a legend praising chastity and turn it into a symbol of man's search for the answer to the totality of his needs, for a reality that suited the duality of his being. Tagland's relationship with the blond queen is primarily a spiritual one. Both suffer because of this, and his sensual needs torture his dreams. In the end, Tagland comes to understand that his wife, the blond queen, should be his partner in all his being, that the sensual is as valid a part of their lives as the spiritual. The blond queen, being a woman, knows this and offers her support as he struggles to understand it. In his revision of the tale, Landauer challenged the stress on chastity that informs the Welsh legend and that still degrades the sensual in our own society. In place of the individual bound by accepted and unexamined custom, Landauer offered the complete, free personality.

This is poetically the most successful of Landauer's works; it reflects a maturity of personality that had come only after he had spent years grappling with the philosophical questions touched upon in *Der Todesprediger* and these three stories. The first concrete result of his philosophic speculations was published in the same year that *Macht und Mächte* appeared, *Der Todesprediger* was reissued, and the Eckhart work was printed. In 1903 the little volume *Skepsis und Mystik* (*Skepticism and Mysticism*), which bears the subtitle "Essays in Connection with Mauthner's Critique of Language," was published. Years later Landauer wrote in various essays and letters that acquaintance with his earlier works was important for understanding the later ones as he meant them, and *Skepsis und Mystik* was the one he always listed as the starting point. But underlying everything he wrote, as he himself freely admitted,[10] was Mauthner's great *Beiträge zu einer Kritik der Sprache* (*Contributions to a Critique of Language*).[11] *

Mauthner was born in Bohemia in 1849. After schooling there and a few years of journalistic apprenticeship in Prague and Vienna, he went to Berlin in 1876 and began building the powerful reputation he was to achieve as journalist, writer, and theater critic. For a short period he edited his own journal, *Deutschland*, in which Landauer's first serious literary efforts were published. Neither man left a record of when or how they first met, but it must have been early in Landauer's adult life, for Mauthner was familiar enough with the younger man's first writings to know that some of Landauer's articles from this period were written under the influence of the egoist philosopher Max Stirner and published

* Hereafter cited as *Sprachkritik*. All page references within the text below through p. 65 are to the *Sprachkritik*.

under Stirner's real name, Caspar Schmidt.[12] Well-known in Berlin for his fiction and literary criticism, Mauthner had a second intellectual bent. Since his youth he had been deeply interested in the effect of language upon human life, and during the nearly twenty-five years he spent as a public literary figure, he quietly gathered materials for a gigantic work on this subject, a work that was to be one of the cornerstones of Landauer's philosophy.

It was this work, the *Sprachkritik*, that Landauer had edited while in prison. When the first volume was finally published in 1901, Landauer helped introduce it by an article in *Zukunft*.[13] He had "lived" the *Sprachkritik* for years, Landauer wrote there, and so was able to judge its importance. He maintained that this work made Mauthner one of the most significant figures in contemporary European culture. More important for Landauer than the *Sprachkritik*'s compelling discussions about the effects of language upon human life were the possibilities Mauthner's skepticism offered for a completely new view of life, for a mysticism that would unite mankind in a society not previously possible in this world. Landauer's intimate knowledge of this book was unquestionably the most decisive intellectual factor of his life and determined much of what he did in his life. It is essential, therefore, that some consideration of the materials presented in the *Sprachkritik* be given here.

One must note at the outset that Mauthner was not a linguistic scientist; he was a philosopher concerned with the theory of knowledge. Early in the first volume of the *Sprachkritik* he provided a concise statement of purpose: "The inquiry in this book is dedicated exclusively to the question of whether human language is a useful tool for understanding the world . . ." (I, 70). A lifetime of research had convinced him that it was not. He came to reject the idea that human thought corresponds to reality; reality, he concluded, cannot be known. Years later he told how he felt his work fitted into the historical development of philosophy:

Locke, the first to criticize the senses, proclaimed the hominism of secondary characteristics like colors and musical tones; Kant, who believed he was criticizing pure reason, asserted boldly and grandly the hominism of some primary characteristics, of space, of time, of causality; the critique of language demands complete resignation: human language, dependent upon chance senses, can never achieve a view of nature, which it pretends to investigate, other than the limited hoministic one.[14]

The idea of *"Zufallssinne"* ("chance senses") is formally the point from which Mauthner set out to demonstrate the reasons for his epistemological skepticism. For millions of years, he said, our five senses have developed because we needed them to get along in the world. There is, however, no reason to believe that these five are the only possible senses. We might, for instance, have become equipped with a sense for electricity. Since we have no such sense, our experience of electricity must come to us through the senses we do possess. But our senses, as Kant had shown, do not place us in direct contact with reality; we know only sense data, not what the senses themselves experience; and, Mauthner went on, we know *nothing* that we have not learned from sense data. Thus, our isolation from reality is total.

Perhaps it was the Darwinian influence on the thinking of the late nineteenth century that caused Mauthner to put so much stress upon the idea of development. In any event, this emphasis was basically what set him apart from and carried him beyond Kant. Mauthner accepted nothing a priori concerning human thought. For him space, time, and all other concepts are created by the senses, but not by the senses alone. Concepts are linguistic devices, repositories of sense data in the form of language. In Mauthner's words: "From whatever side one observes the development of concepts, they always reveal themselves to be pure conveniences of language usage . . ." (III, 278).

The evolutionary process that led to the formation of concepts involved a number of steps, according to Mauthner. The requirements for survival of the individual caused the particular senses we possess to develop. The needs of the individual also determined the use of these senses, caused them to be concentrated repeatedly upon certain things in his environment (e.g., specific sources of food, shelter, danger) until these things became familiar and were retained in the mind as concepts. Concepts are the counters or tokens the mind uses to keep track of sense impressions, and the structured collection of these concepts is called memory. Mauthner equated language with memory, because he saw no difference between words and concepts. Both terms denote the same thing. Language is the storing of sense impressions in the mind. Words or concepts are the convenient categories into which language sorts the experience of the individual. The structure of memory is what we call grammar.

This storing process frequently leads to a misapprehension of reality, for words or concepts take on an existence of their own when they become established in the mind; they affect and influence each other and in this way lead to the formation of ideas (*Vorstellungen*), which the individual often fails to recognize as being based on sense data. He assumes that these ideas represent something in reality, something he "knows," and he projects this assumption into the world outside himself. This confusion of ideas with reality is in some ways advantageous to the individual, for the ideas become additional categories into which new sense data may be placed—new experience is "understood" when, by treating it metaphorically, it can be associated with some already existing concept, a process that usually brings about some change in that concept itself—but it causes the individual to force reality into the molds of his own mental abstractions. Mauthner considered the interaction of concepts the province of "reason" (*Vernunft*) while "understanding" (*Verstand*) is concerned directly with sense data as they are being experienced. "Thought" (*Denken*), supposedly the product of reason and understanding, must be understood neither as the precursor nor the result of language but, like memory, as language itself, ". . . the same thing looked at from two not quite identical standpoints . . ." (II, 661). Or, as he had written earlier, ". . . there is no thinking without speaking, that is, without words. Or more correctly: there is no such thing as thinking, there is only speaking. Thinking is speaking judged according to its retail value" (I, 176). This is the basic tenet of Mauthner's philosophy of language.

This philosophy seriously questions the validity of all abstractions and the justification for their tremendous influence upon human life. Mauthner called abstractions "word superstitions" (*Wortaberglauben*), pointing out that they exist only in the minds of individuals, that they have no reality outside the mind. Recognition of this fact, however, does not free individuals from the tyranny of language. Mauthner showed clearly how subservient we are to language, to our own individual language. In each individual the form and content of language is the form and content of memory: "We can only think what language allows, what language and its individual usage permit us to think" (II, 533). Language, therefore, ties us irrevocably to the past, because it stems from our attention to those things that fulfilled our needs in the past: "We can only think what we *have* wanted to and what our ancestors *have* wanted to. Former desire created former interest and thereby our language" (II, 533).

This necessary orientation toward the past makes the validity of science suspect. Mauthner asserted that scientific knowledge is only a "richer" everyday knowledge, not different in kind from that of the most simple-minded individual, and thus equally circumscribed by the limitations of language. The scientist's observations would surely be more complete than those of a country bumpkin, but scientist and dunce alike observe only what senses and language allow. The scientist's observations are valid only as observations—that is, as sense data—they are not a true representation of reality. The scientist can describe what he has seen, but he cannot explain it in terms of reality. Scientific laws are abstractions, often useful for predicting future occurrences but never able to provide a reason for them. To explain the presence of an ineffable necessity in nature, the scientist must resort to the law of cause and effect and thereby confess his ignorance:

The idea of cause and of an order in nature, added by our normal thinking processes from our own being to our inductive observations, this idea alone transforms for us a concept into a law (III, 470).

What we think we know becomes a concept for us; what we definitely do not know, but would very much like to know, that is a law (III, 472).

The past thrusts itself upon the individual in terms of cultural traditions as well; and language is, of course, the bearer of these traditions. But Mauthner went even further, saying, ". . . tradition is not only preserved in language, but is, moreover, language itself" (I, 31). Just as memory underlies the individual life—memory that is indistinguishable from language—so language serves the members of any culture as the collective memory of that culture. Looked at in any other way the term *culture* is another meaningless abstraction. Looked at in any other way the term *language* (as opposed to the specific language of an individual, his idiolect) is also a meaningless abstraction. "Only as a social factor does language become real. It is a social reality; aside from that, it is only an abstraction for certain movements [of the speech organs]" (I, 17–18). Thus, language restricts the individual not only in his thinking, but also in his relationship to society. One might almost go so far as to say that language *is* the individual *and* his place in society. The interaction of individuals depends upon communication, and the members of any culture can communicate with each other because their language contains all the values and orientations that have become inherent in their culture. A culture develops when a group of people is exposed to the same series of sense data and when all come to react to this data in a fairly uniform way. A constant exchange of concepts—the memory-tokens of the individuals—is the foundation of a common language. Ideas, abstractions, can be exchanged, too, so that the unreal abstractions of individuals can be applied as values for the entire culture. "Ethics results from the fact that there have arisen among men concepts of value which impose themselves as value judgments whenever human activities are examined" (I, 30). Following from this, what we call the human spirit (*Geist*) is the sum of those things *all* languages have in common, those reactions *all* human beings have stored as memory-tokens. Differences in reactions, and in the memory of reactions, to sense data account for the differences among cultures.

Differences among individuals within a culture can be explained the same way. Since one's memory is based not upon reality but upon sense data, and no two individuals experience precisely the same sense impressions, the image of the world that develops in each individual is necessarily different from that of any other individual:

The language of an individual is not a false picture of his thinking,
but a false picture of his exterior world; he can say everything
that he thinks as an individual, but his thinking about the real world
is individual and therefore false (I, 193).

While language as culture is a strong bond among individuals, language as the memory of particular individuals is an obstacle to their complete knowledge and understanding of each other. It sometimes even causes an individual to misunderstand himself, for the content of concepts is never precise and is always changing.

Since the individual cannot experience reality through sense data and language, his only direct contact with it is his own being, his own memory. Yet even this is of no value for an understanding of reality. "*Cogito, ergo sum,*" to be sure, but does one know the true nature of the being one is? Consciousness gives assurance of being, but aside from this certainty one's experience of oneself is based entirely on sense data, and there is no reason to suppose that sense experience of oneself is any more true to reality than other sense data. Thus, Mauthner's resignation becomes complete:

. . . so we must reckon with the possibility that the feeling of individuality is also only an illusion, generated in us as the reflection of
some totally unknown life form, just as our senses of sight and hearing,
all our sense impressions, are in the last analysis only normal illusions
of the senses, reflections of some facts or other that we now explain
[scientifically] as movements (I, 661).

Interesting implications about the nature of life arise from this view of individuality. Death becomes a relative concept, life an enduring unity. The individual is one manifestation of that unity. What we call heredity is the memory—that is, the being—of each individual, passed on in altered form from generation to generation in a chain of individuals. Heredity may even be a trait of inorganic matter if heredity-memory can be thought of as a specific structural principle, such as that of crystals, which determines the identity of a particular kind of matter. The organic individual would then have two kinds of memory: a personal one, which develops as language in each individual, and a hereditary one, which is his own physical structure, as we call it, and which is fundamental to the develop-ment of the personal memory. It must be noted that Mauthner stressed the organization of matter and the propensity to that organization, not matter itself, as the essence of memory:

Our entire investigation is removed from the empirical or materialistic
word-superstition by the fact that we assume as a basis for every ex-

perience an inherited memory or the disposition of the memory to work in a certain way (II, 714).

Mauthner would have been the last person to suggest that his theoretical structure was an unquestionably true representation of reality. All of his metaphysical conclusions, however, are consistent with his views of language and its failure as a tool for grasping reality and are, therefore, no less valid than the abstractions normally accepted as truths. Perhaps they are more valid, for we know that our customary abstractions, based as they are on sense data and language, are certainly not correct. Others before him had recognized this. In the *Sprachkritik* Mauthner discussed several poets who had understood the inherent failure of language, among them Goethe and Maeterlinck. Mauthner felt that Maeterlinck had shown an unusual sensitivity to the problem, especially in his essay glorifying silence (I, 118–19).

Mauthner, however, was no Buddhist ascetic. He did not advocate the abandonment of language because it fails us in our attempts to grasp reality. On the contrary, language, understanding, memory, reason are all necessary mechanisms for the preservation of life. Mauthner insisted that utility is a characteristic of language (I, 78–79). Language is the means for orientation in the world; our practical life would be impossible without it. Mauthner admitted that he himself forgot his philosophic skepticism in the conduct of daily affairs and pointed out that some individuals rise above daily affairs and the pains of life by objectivizing them through the use of language. It is the possibility of objectivizing afforded by language that allows philosophers, who all to a greater or lesser extent recognize the curtain language hangs between the individual and reality, to maintain an optimistic outlook (I, 88–90).

There is a further service, too, which language can perform for those who are able to take advantage of it: the very uncertainty that makes language an inadequate tool for the kind of knowledge toward which science strives makes it an excellent vehicle for artistic expression:

The difference between language as a medium of art and language as a means of understanding is to be sought in the fact that the poet needs and possesses indications of mood, symbols of the spirit, while the thinker has to have tokens of value, standards, and does not find them in words (I, 95–96).

The poet's task is to create metaphors for reality; and language, which is itself a metaphor for reality, is well, if not ideally, suited to his needs. Through language he can reveal his experience of the world to the sensitive reader or listener far more completely than a scientific disquisition could. Are the poet's images closer to reality than the scientist's observations? Mauthner felt that they are. He could not totally reject the hope that we do have some valid contact with reality (III, 615), and if this contact does exist, the poetic, not the scientific, personality is the one with the possibility of discovering it: "Language is metaphor; but the metaphor somehow coincides with the world" (II, 453).

The nonpoet has one chance for true experience of reality, a chance that bypasses, even scorns, language. Bismarck was a successful statesman despite language. He experienced reality because he took an active part in it. That is Mauthner's answer to the problem of tearing through the language curtain around us:

Only through action do we understand the world of reality, only when we stand actively amid reality, never when we want to assume a reflective posture in regard to it. However the human being may presume, with superhuman energy, to discover the truth, he always finds only himself, a human truth, an anthropomorphic vision of the world (II, 479).

The first two volumes of Mauthner's *Sprachkritik* appeared in 1901 and received immediate, though not always favorable, critical attention. Many people were misled by the title into thinking the book was about linguistics. But the linguistic scientists of the time were not overly impressed with it, and one suspects, as Mauthner suggested in the foreword to the second edition, that many of them did not know what to make of it. In the nonacademic public the book found some enthusiastic supporters, and even in the scholarly world it was granted an occasional word of acknowledgment. The noted Germanist Wolfgang Golther, writing in the section "Geschichte der neuhochdeutschen Sprache" in the *Jahresbericht für neuere deutsche Literaturgeschichte* for the year 1901, expressed the opinion that the book would have to be considered seriously by academic linguists. In the 1903 edition of the same publication, in the same section, Ludwig Sütterlin, professor of philology at the University of Heidelberg, commented upon the critical acclaim the *Sprachkritik* had been accorded in 1902, the year in which the third volume appeared. Sütterlin went on to say that the most enthusiastic supporter was Gustav Landauer, who not only wrote an essay about Mauthner's work for the *Zukunft*, but also a book, *Skepsis und Mystik*, which, Sütterlin said, was "basically nothing but an urgent, sometimes even importunate, recommendation of Mauthner's *Sprachkritik*." This statement as well as the brief, derogatory review of *Skepsis und Mystik* with which he closed his article on Mauthner show plainly that Sütterlin failed to grasp what Landauer intended his little book to be.

Skepsis und Mystik is not easy to understand, a fact for which its structure is largely responsible. It consists of a number of basically independent essays, several of which were published separately before the book appeared. The essence of the first chapter, "Das Individuum als Welt" ("The Individual as the World"), was initially the essay "Durch Absonderung zur Gemeinschaft," written by Landauer for the Neue Gemeinschaft in 1901. The most important material in the second chapter, "Die Welt als Zeit" ("The World as Time"), was printed with that title in *Zukunft* on 23 November 1901. Also included as part of the second chapter was a critique of Julius Hart's book *Die neue Welterkenntnis*, a review Landauer had written for the journal *Kultur* in 1902. The rest of the second chapter and all of the third, "Die Sprache als Instrument" ("Language as Instrument"), was appearing in print for the first time. Much of this new material was formulated for a series of lectures Landauer had given in 1902/03 on the *Sprachkritik*. It is not clear whether he had originally intended all of this material to appear together eventually in book form; but the inclusion of several self-contained essays, together with additional writings, in a format rigidly prescribed by external considerations (Landauer wanted three chapters, each one coordinated with a volume of the *Sprachkritik*) led to an awkward organization and some puzzling repetition, which hide the book's underlying concept. In a letter written 3 January 1910, Landauer admitted the structural failings and said he would recast it if he were to publish a second edition.

The difficulties are not insurmountable, however; and once the basic idea of the work has been grasped, Sütterlin's notion that it is a critique of, or commentary on, the *Sprachkritik* is no longer supportable. *Skepsis und Mystik* might be called Landauer's philosophic manifesto. It attempts to go beyond what Mauthner had done in the *Sprachkritik* and, as one commentator pointed out, succeeds in a way that was quite surprising to Mauthner.[15] Landauer felt that the skepticism Mauthner had applied to language destroyed forever the accepted human illusions about reality and thus created a desire for a new, better understanding of the world. In *Skepsis und Mystik*[16] he tried to provide that understanding: "It is necessary to reorganize the entire stock of our intellect, not because of new certainties, but because of new doubts" (p. 64).* Mauthner had hinted at the way, the only way, this understanding might be achieved when he quoted an aphorism of Nietzsche: "When skepticism mates with yearning, the progeny is mysticism."[17] *Skepsis* describes the reality mysticism can create.

His first attempt in this direction had been the Eckhart translation. He explained in his introduction to this book that he considered Eckhart a superb epistemologist who had used the traditional language of Christian dogma to express a unity of God and the universe transcending that dogma—pantheism, but in quite a different sense than Spinoza's pantheism. Eckhart had assumed a nonmaterial basis for all being, a basis he sometimes called "*Gottheit*" ("Godhead"), but which he understood to be something far different and more pervasive than the term signifies in Christian orthodoxy. Landauer insisted that this metaphysical approach was vitally meaningful for twentieth-century Western man; those writings that had only historical or scholarly interest Landauer had omitted. What he wished to convey with this book was the practical value of the mystical personality.

In *Skepsis und Mystik*, Landauer characterized the mystic as a person who constantly searches for metaphysical peace but who can find it only in a union of personality and world. Few have reported the attainment of this state, he said, and even for them the harmony is tenuous and temporary; yet the desire for it continues.

---

* All references in the text here and below through p. 74, except where otherwise noted, are to *Skepsis und Mystik*.

Landauer mentioned the poets Alfred Mombert and Johannes Wedde as modern exponents of this desire—individuals who sought freedom from the senses, language, space, and time so that they might become one with the world (pp. 46–47). Mauthner made the achievement of this freedom possible, according to Landauer, by demonstrating that our knowledge of the world consists of mere metaphors based on sense data. Since we know that we cannot place any absolute trust in sense data, why should we accept the particular metaphors we have? It should be possible to express the world in new ones. Our metaphors have always been determined by our will, by directing our attention toward those things that help preserve our existence. This will can now be redirected toward the creation of a better world for mankind.

The starting point for such an undertaking is obvious enough. It is the one thing each individual can be sure of in the world: the self. Mauthner had stressed that our most immediate experience of reality is awareness of self. Landauer pointed out that this awareness could easily lead every individual to a feeling of isolation from the world. But Landauer argued that this isolation may not be real because, as Mauthner had demonstrated, the true nature of the self cannot be known. And Landauer *willed* that any such feeling of isolation is wrong: " . . . because I will not be satisfied with the terrible isolation. . . . In order not to be an individual, alone in the universe and God-forsaken, I recognize the universe and thereby give up my individuality; but only so as to feel myself as the universe into which I am absorbed" (pp. 7–8).

We must finally realize once again that we do not just perceive parts of the world but that we are ourselves parts of the world. He who could completely understand the flower would understand the universe [Meister Eckhart]. All right: let us return completely into ourselves, then we shall have found universe incarnate (p. 10).

We have been satisfied until now to transform the universe into the human spirit, or better, into the human intellect; let us now transform ourselves into the universal spirit (p. 9).

It is unimportant that Landauer could furnish no proof for the validity of his standpoint; no proof could be brought against it either. What for Mauthner had been a possible inference from his theory of language became for Landauer a metaphysical imperative, "that the psyche [*das Seelenhafte*] in the human being is a function or manifestation of the infinite universe" (p. 7).

As arbitrary as Landauer's basic philosophic axiom might seem, it was related to a tradition with which Landauer was to some extent familiar and which was attractive to many individuals unable to accept the philosophic materialism prevailing at the turn of the century. The work of Gustav Theodor Fechner (1801–87), whom Mauthner much admired, anticipated the concept of the universal psyche, as did the book *Das Liebesleben in der Natur* (*Love in Nature*) by Landauer's Friedrichshagen comrade Wilhelm Bölsche. Landauer had reviewed the first volume of this work when it appeared in 1898.[18] A second assumption of *Skepsis und Mystik*—namely, that the psyche is not merely a human abstraction but really exists—is also consistent with this tradition. Landauer could not accept the materialistic view, which is forced to interpret personal feelings in terms of nerves and gray matter. If new metaphors for reality are to be constructed, Landauer held, they must rest on the conviction that matter itself is a metaphor for reality, for psyche, as differentiated and interpreted by the senses. Psyche is the real "stuff" of all existence, the *"Ding an sich."*

This view brought Landauer into conflict with Mauthner over the relationship of time and space. Mauthner considered space to be a metaphor of the senses, a creation of the sense of sight working in conjunction with the sense of touch. In the *Sprachkritik* (II, 659) he discussed Lazarus Geiger's theory that human language is based primarily upon sight, and later (III, 118 ff.) he added his own idea that space might have been the first sense impression retained by the brain, the initial step in the development of individual memory, and that all other concepts arose on the basis of that one. The true nature of space, like the true nature of anything we know from sense data, is, of course, hidden from us; the fact that we possess senses by which we can account for our interpretation of space, however, convinced Mauthner that time, for which we have no sense, is actually memory's way of dealing with one characteristic of space (the fourth dimension). Landauer felt that time is something inherent in the psyche, that a being is aware of the passage of time without reference to sense data, and that the concept of space is dependent upon time. What seems to us from our interpretation of sense data to be either constant or changing spatial relationships are actually manifestations of the passage of time. Then, Landauer concluded, space is an illusion created by the sense of sight. If one ignores this sense momentarily and concentrates on the impressions the other senses give, one finds that all these impressions can be regarded as changes in the self through time. Without reference to sight, one can as well think, "My fingertips become hard," as, "My fingertips touch something hard." "While it is impossible for me to ignore time and my feeling of self, from the sense of touch I can very well form the judgment necessary for the explanation of physical appearance as psychic phenomena: there is no space" (p. 54). Accordingly, "world" is represented as the changes that take place in the individual as time goes by. If the effects of vision are interpreted in the same way, then everything the individual "sees" is actually part of himself. Then *all* sense perception records only changes in the self, not data external to the self. "I" and "world" become one.

Most of the preceding considerations are based upon the second chapter of *Skepsis und Mystik*. The first chapter is concerned with a question that, in a systematic presentation, could be asked only after the conversion of world and self into a continuum of psyche —namely, the question of death. Landauer considered the flow of psyche to be eternal; but all men, all individuals, are mortal. The individual consciousness can perhaps convince itself that it is a manifestation of world, but the changes the individual experiences within himself as time passes lead eventually to a moment when the individual, the consciousness, ceases to exist, at least in any form we can recognize. The individual and the eternal world psyche seem, therefore, to be somewhat different.

Landauer's answer to this problem was implicit in Mauthner's discussion of the individual. Mauthner had maintained that the individual is the only sure reality, the concept of species an unreal abstraction. However, he was willing to entertain the possibility that since beings of a given "species" propagate only their own species, there might be some reality to which the concept "species" corresponds.[19] If this is the case, he conjectured, then the individual is only one manifestation of an unknown organism that goes on for an untold period, present in each generation as the structural memory of the species (*Artgedächtnis*), which we call heredity. The death of the individual is then only a phase in the life of the organism.

Landauer offered further justification for this idea. Interpreted materialistically the term *heredity* is a metaphor for both a series of sense data and for a force we postulate as having caused the things observed. This force, it must be assumed, is exerted upon living individuals by their forebears, many of whom have been dead for hundreds of years. Such a separation in time between a cause and its effect is absurd from the materialistic point of view, but is entirely consistent with the hypothesis that the world is differentiated, undying psyche. Therefore, what the materialist must describe vaguely as a force and what Mauthner attempted to explain as memory Landauer was able to define as the presence of the everlasting psyche:

Heredity is a very real and always present energy working for the continuing life of the ancestral world in new shapes and forms. The individual is a flash within the stream of psyche, which one calls according to the context "human race," "species," or "universe" (p. 13).

This position allowed Landauer to develop another of Mauthner's speculations in a surprising way. In the third volume of the *Sprachkritik* (p. 293) Mauthner had spoken of heredity as "the newest formulation of [the concept of] the eternal form" and had suggested its similarity to the Platonic idea. Consistent with this he had speculated (p. 498) that the realism of medieval philosophy might sometime return as the accepted method for describing reality. In *Skepsis und Mystik* Landauer proposed that the time for this return had already come:

. . . it is time for the insight that there is no individual, but only unities and communities. It is not true that collective names designate only a sum of individuals: on the contrary, individuals are only manifestations and points of reference, electric sparks of something grand and whole (p. 13).

This idea restores to such terms as *human race, species,* and *universe* a reality they had lost when Mauthner's skepticism had proclaimed them all abstractions and metaphors. Landauer felt that Schopenhauer's statement ". . . all reality has an effect" (quoted on p. 15) must be reversed: everything that has an effect is real. Since heredity affects the individual, and since the notion of heredity makes sense only when understood as a continuum of psyche, a continuum reflected in such terms as *human race, species, universe,* these terms must represent a reality that transcends the individual. Landauer wrote, "We are moments of the undying ancestral community" and "The great hereditary communities are real; because the ancestors still have an effect today and must therefore still be alive" (p. 15).

The conviction that reality exists as a supraindividual organism leads to some new observations about the individual. Whether we call this organism human race, species, or universe, it remains the essential part of the individual, the thing determining the nature of the individual:

What the human being basically is, what his innermost, most secret, most inviolable possession is, that is the great community of living beings in him, that is his lineage, the commonality of his blood with that of his ancestors (p. 17).

In contrast to this, that part of the individual that is memory based on sense data is superficial; sense data of the present world have little effect on the essence of the individual compared with the influence exerted by all previous generations. This is true also of customs and traditions that, unless they have become part of the hereditary memory, are foreign to the nature of the individual. To be true to his real nature, the individual must search within himself, as Landauer did in *Skepsis und Mystik,* to discover a mode of life in which his essence, the eternal organism, can best express itself. This search demands an isolation of the self from other individuals, but it leads to a new union of all individuals within the eternal psyche:

For this individuality, rooted in the depths of the past, is community, humanity, the divine. And after single individuals have recreated themselves as community, they are ready for the new community of associating individuals, for the community of those who have found the courage and the need to disassociate themselves from common superficiality (p. 18).

The search for the new life is still dependent upon sense data and language, however; and since Mauthner had destroyed the validity of science and religion as vehicles for the explanation of being, another means must be found for understanding the universal organism, which in Landauer's *Weltanschauung* is recognized as reality. The means, suggested in the second chapter of *Skepsis und Mystik,* is art. Landauer's definition of art is consistent with Mauthner's discussion of the subject: "By art I mean here the symbolic or metaphoric interpretation of the metaphors of the senses and the metaphors of our inner consciousness. It must replace that which until now science thought it was providing" (p. 49). Because we can no longer believe in words as concrete reflections of reality, Landauer continued, we must regard them as symbols, symbols that we can believe in, symbols that represent the real world for us. "That is art in this highest sense: a compelling symbol of the universe" (p. 49). In the new approach to being for which Landauer was striving, the function of science is to provide the sense data, the raw material for understanding. Instead of accepting the findings of science as fact, as we have in the past, we must henceforth look to the artist to interpret them symbolically before we may add them to our concept of reality.

A still richer source of symbols for reality than science, however, is music. Like the psyche itself, music consists of time and intensities and is unhampered by the materialism that clings to word-concepts because they are derived from sense data. As Schopenhauer had suggested, music is the most appropriate method of communication between the individual and the world. In the last three paragraphs of the second chapter (written after the first edition of *Skepsis und Mystik* for inclusion in later editions), Landauer carried this idea further by offering a metaphoric description of being in terms of music.

Although music is the best source of symbols, the individual is, as the short third chapter of *Skepsis und Mystik* shows, still fettered to language as the most common means of understanding the world. Because of this, the poet must be heavily relied upon to be intermediary between man and the world; Landauer believed that a number of poets writing in his time were providing the symbolic interpretation necessary for a valid grasp of reality. As early as

September 1900, Landauer had remarked to Hedwig that much of the newest art was in the same vein as Mauthner's extreme skepticism.[20] Now, in *Skepsis und Mystik*, he specifically pointed to Stefan George, Richard Dehmel, Alfred Mombert, and Hugo von Hofmannsthal as poets whose work paralleled Mauthner's thought. Landauer was convinced that Hofmannsthal, when he wrote the essay "Brief des Lord Chandos" (1901), was directly influenced by the *Sprachkritik*. There is certainly a similarity of ideas in these two works, although Hofmannsthal did not mention Mauthner's book. In contrast to the "new" poetry, which began with Goethe and led through Novalis and Brentano to those men named above, Landauer placed Schiller's poetic work. He felt that Schiller had been a rhetorician in contradistinction to the others, the difference being that Schiller, although he understood that "the world of the senses is not utterable" (p. 73), had been unable to apply this insight to his poetry, while the others had based their work upon the recognition that only symbols provide true understanding. These poets had grasped this fact for themselves. Mauthner had made it clear for the rest of us:

Mauthner has shown us that conceptual science can never satisfy our yearning to understand the universe and ourselves in other than anthropomorphic terms; art can do it, however, in those moments when we live in it. We win and create worlds and lose ourselves (p. 73).

Thus, Mauthner's *Sprachkritik*, as interpreted by Landauer, not only destroyed the illusions of which mankind has always been the victim, but in addition provided a hope for a new, truer view of reality.

The publication of three books and the republication of a fourth in 1903 made that year in one sense the close of an era in Landauer's life. In reviewing the works from the ten-year period between the first publication of *Der Todesprediger* and 1903, a number of observations can be made. The first concerns Mauthner's influence; there is strong evidence that it was present even at the time Landauer wrote *Der Todesprediger*. The socialism that the hero of this book finally espouses is not based on the supposedly scientific Marxist approach. On the contrary, one finds here the view that pure rationalism can lead only to despair. It is of course possible that Landauer adopted this position on his own, but the idea is so consistent with some of Mauthner's epistemological conclusions that the reader must suspect a direct relationship. The suspicion becomes even stronger when the hero overcomes his problem by involving himself actively in life, especially the life of the senses, instead of thinking about life. This is just what Mauthner had suggested as the path of escape from linguistically confined rationalism. The idea of the continuum of nature, discussed above as it is revealed in *Skepsis und Mystik*, also appears much earlier. In *Der Todesprediger* it is hinted at very slightly, and man stands outside it. The hint is somewhat stronger in the first version of "Arnold Himmelheber"; in the second version, written between 1896 and 1903—in the period when Mauthner's influence was becoming ever more important—this idea is the dominant aspect of the story, and the characters recognize that they as human beings are very much a part of the continuum. The step from here to the metaphysics of *Skepsis und Mystik* is an easy one.

Another thread running through all the works of this period and reaching far beyond them is the relationship of life, love, sensuality, and society. In *Der Todesprediger* the hero is freed from his intellectual paralysis by a very sensual love and finally wishes to work for a better world because through love he has found a reason to live in the world. In "Arnold Himmelheber" sensuality is seen as a demand the psyche places upon the individual for the expression of love; the story promises that a new race, which recognizes love as a fundamental part of the natural continuum, will make a better society. The hero of "Lebendig tot" must withdraw from society when there is no longer any possibility of love for him. And in *Skepsis und Mystik*, Landauer proposed that the individual, by recognizing his place in the eternal continuum and thus his intimate relationship with all other individuals, can prepare himself for a communal life in which the psyche can manifest itself in its most glorious form.

It is typical of Landauer that he thought of these stories and the philosophical speculations in *Skepsis und Mystik* as practical tools for influencing human life, tools with social implications. He expressed this to Julius Bab in a letter written 16 June 1903, saying, "I want to understand for the purpose of creating," and two paragraphs later, "We know *nothing* about the purpose of our life, therefore we must set ourselves a purpose!" His work from 1893 to 1903 had been an attempt to define the purpose—not only for himself, but for everyone.

To the extent that his attempt was intended to influence society, it must be judged a failure. Especially after 1900, Landauer was working in isolation; a book such as *Skepsis und Mystik* was scarcely a tool with which the masses could rebuild their lives. But recognition was not totally lacking. Intellectuals did respond favorably to Landauer's work. During the years between 1900 and 1906 his relations with Bab grew closer; and he met Constantin Brunner, a young philosopher who became a good friend and intellectual companion in the philosophical studies Landauer was pursuing. Contacts showing mutual respect also arose with Hugo von Hofmannsthal, the critic Hermann Bahr, the poet Alfred Mombert, and various other literary figures. Late in 1906 a rapprochement with Richard Dehmel and his second wife began, initiated by a favorable article about Dehmel that Landauer wrote for the magazine *Blaubuch*.[21] Dehmel felt that no one else had written so perceptively of his poetry.[22]

Recognition from the literary world had, however, never been Landauer's goal, and this superficially peaceful and successful period—a second daughter, Brigitte, was born in 1905, adding to the domestic happiness of the family—had an undertone of restlessness that Landauer could not ignore. His life as publisher and critic did not provide him an opportunity to produce the social effect he sought to achieve. In October 1906 the frustrations of this uninvolved existence brought him to leave the publishing firm and strike out once again on his own. The outlook for the future was uncertain, but it held the possibility of being a future Landauer could shape to his own desires.

4

The
Search for
Society
1906–1908

In 1904, Auguste Hauschner wrote a brief essay on Landauer's work and personality, stressing that for him the motivating force was always ideas, not events, and that his desire, like that of the romantic tradition in which he stood, was to renew the spiritual life of his times.[1] Between 1906 and 1911 this purpose was served by three works that grew directly from the discussions in *Skepsis und Mystik*. They represent in part an attempt by Landauer to work out a philosophical terminology by which he could present his understanding of the past and his hopes for the future. Beginning with "Volk und Land: Dreissig sozialistische Thesen" ("*Volk* and Land: Thirty Socialist Theses"),* published in January 1907, continuing through *Die Revolution*, also 1907, and culminating in the *Aufruf zum Sozialismus (Call to Socialism)*, published in 1911 but presented earlier as a lecture in May 1908, certain terms were defined and redefined as Landauer struggled to reach a small but increasingly receptive audience with his message of a new society, a society dominated by *Geist*.

Geist is a word that resists translation. It is rendered into English in various ways depending on the context: spirit, intellect, genius, soul, all are attempts at possible English equivalents. But for Landauer's use of the word the problem of finding a single,

* Hereafter cited as "Thirty Socialist Theses."

concrete English term becomes insurmountable, for in his texts its employment is essentially poetic. Landauer was trying to deal with reality, and he was convinced that only poetic symbols are adequate for that. *Geist* is such a symbol. Martin Buber in his *Daniel* (1913) attempted to define *Geist* in terms of human potential:

'The human being must apply himself completely to create something that then becomes valuable because of him. That is, what is needed is not the reproducing but the producing, the creating individual. This leads to a completely new, unsuspected permeation of the universe with the human element, and this spontaneous, characteristic human element—that is Geist'. [2]

The implication that *Geist* is inherent in humanity is fully in accordance with Landauer's view. At one point he called it "a natural, not an imposed compulsion." [3]

Far more important than a precise definition of *Geist*, however, is a description of its effect upon mankind. In *Die Revolution*, Landauer called it a bridge of love between individuals, but this does not really further the understanding of *Geist*—it merely exchanges one metaphor for another: love for *Geist*. In *Skepsis und Mystik*, Landauer had defined love as the relationship of an individual to his own forebears and progeny (and thus himself): one might then describe *Geist* as that which unites contemporaries with an intensity of feeling and closeness similar to that of parents and children. This is still far too abstract, however, to satisfy the student of a writer who had forsworn abstractions; and a better picture of the workings of *Geist* within and upon the individual can be found in Landauer's writings, though the search necessarily leads rather far afield.

In 1912, Landauer wrote, "*Nation* is the best example of what I call *Geist*, because it is the only real example of it in social relationships." [4] A description of *Geist* in terms of *Nation* is not a substitution of one undefined metaphor for another, for Landauer was very specific in his use of the word "*Nation*" and went to great pains to define what he meant by it. Probably the most concise definition appeared in the essay "Zum Problem der Nation" ("On the Meaning of *Nation*," 1915): "*Nation* is the particular way in which human nature in general and the unique traits of the individual express themselves within a community whose element of cohesion is a common historical background." [5] As early as 1906, in the "Thirty Socialist Theses," the concept of *Nation* was presented and contrasted with the concept of the state, the latter being an artificial, fortuitous, political structure based on accidents of history rather than on a mutual experience of history. At this point Landauer suggested that a common language is a symptom, though not a requirement, of a *Nation*; the Christians of the Middle Ages and the Jews, for example, were *Nationen* * not identifiable on the basis of language. More significant than language as a characteristic of *Nation* was race: Landauer categorized the two terms together in the "Thirty Socialist Theses," and in 1912 he equated them:

What is called *Nationen* or races is only incidentally the result of differences in blood mixture, physical structure, and physiological functions. Much more important is the common communal history of language, customs, and intellectual experience. The mixing of peoples and heredity contribute; but just as one cannot say with certainty whether peoples borrow from each other because they are related, or whether they become related because they have borrowed from each other over a long period, by the same token it can no longer be decided whether national correlation comes from physical and intellectual similarities or causes them.[6]

Landauer left no doubt about his dedication to the concept of *Nation*. His letters contain numerous references to it. In one he wrote that he, as a German, a south German, and a Jew, belonged to three *Nationen* at the same time.[7] In another, written in March 1915, he stressed his belief in the value to humanity of different *Nationen* or races and showed clearly how his concept of *Nation* was an outgrowth of the metaphysical position he had assumed in *Skepsis und Mystik*. Discussing a Chinese girl who had been raised in Germany, he asserted:

Everything that has become physical appearance is a sign of a characteristic residing deep in the soul: I grant that the Chinese child is German in all superficial respects; but the unnameable Chineseness is still spiritually in her and in her progeny as long as it is physically visible.[8]

* For consistency the German plural of *Nation—Nationen*—will be retained.

79

In essence this is a restatement of the idea that the individual is a combination of two memories, a superficial one based on his own sense experience and a hereditary one linking him to the past and future of his own family and thus to the great universal psyche. *Nation* is a community of families just as family is a community of individuals. The common experiences of families who represent a *Nation* become part of the memory of these families and are passed on by heredity to their progeny, thus forming a unique body of experience for all members of the *Nation*. One's nationality is an essential part of one's being. From this concept one can understand why Landauer, though he rejected the Jewish religion, always put great emphasis on the fact that he was a Jew.

Without this understanding of his approach to the question of race or *Nation*, the stress he laid upon his own Jewishness seems to be inconsistent with his concern for the fate of humanity as a whole. This stress is succinctly revealed in a letter to his philosopher friend Constantin Brunner, June 1909, which praises some of Eugen Dühring's work despite certain anti-Semitic strains in it, but which also states: "Rest assured, I have not the slightest inclination to forget my joy in my Jewishness, even for a day." [9] He expected other Jews to have this same "joy in their Jewishness," and became embroiled in a friendly dispute with Mauthner when the latter denied possessing any traits he felt to be essentially Jewish. Mauthner felt only German, and his wife wrote, ". . . I do not even know what it means to be a 'German'. I only know what I call being human." [10] Landauer was not satisfied with this and reiterated in a letter to Mauthner (20 November 1913) the importance he placed on a traditional bond he experienced with other Jews.

This dispute offers a hint concerning Landauer's means of reconciling his self-affirmed Jewishness with his concern for humanity. In answer to Mauthner's wife's statement, Landauer wrote, ". . . since humanity is not a porridge nor even tutti frutti, but a garden, it is certainly allowable that all the trees do not have the same bark." [11] This garden analogy fits Landauer's position very well. All of the individual plants go together to make the garden, and the garden might be better for the fact that there are different varieties of growth within it. A more direct expression of Landauer's stand on the matter came in some letters to Bab from the year

1913. Bab had published two articles about the place of Jews in modern German life. Landauer disagreed with these essays and expressed his disagreement in a published article as well as in these letters. Once again Landauer stressed his awareness of being Jewish and ended with the statement: "We strive toward humanity as an external goal: the way leads not only through our humanness, but primarily through our differentiated nationality, which is a part of the differentiation of the individual." [12]

This is the same argument Landauer presented in the article "Sind das Ketzergedanken?" ("Heretical Thoughts?"), also from the year 1913; but in this essay, written at the request of a Zionist organization, the stress was shifted from the idea of Judaism to that of humanity. This essay first appeared in a collection titled *Vom Judentum* (*On Judaism*). The editor made it clear in his foreword that the publishers of this book were Zionists and that the contributors were of Zionist persuasion as well:

. . . we want to hear people who, from urgency and desperate indignation, seek a path, a path to the realities of *new* Jewish *life*. A path that denies the present, because it is slavish and unbearable, and that leads through communality to the creation of the future.[13]

This statement does indeed sound like a description of Landauer's lifetime endeavors; but the Zionist context in which it was made was alien to Landauer, and "Sind das Ketzergedanken?" was probably among those contributions the editor went on to say could not be considered programmatic for Zionism. Landauer, although he staunchly proclaimed his own Jewishness, used this essay to castigate the overweening zeal of Zionists. Jews, he said, can be assured of living the full benefits of their Jewishness only when they no longer find it necessary to hold fast to it consciously. "Strong emphasis on one's own nationality, even when it does not lead to chauvinism, is weakness." [14] Though Landauer recognized the Jewishness in everything he was and did, he also had an awareness, equally strong, that he was German, and he could not become involved in a movement inimical to an essential part of his being. He was more concerned with another movement he saw developing, a movement in which Jews had a leading role, and in which the best of many *Nationen* was being united for the cause of humanity. He recommended this as the true Zionism:

Call to Revolution
The Mystical Anarchism of Gustav Landauer

Like a wild cry over the earth and like a soft whisper in our innermost heart, a voice tells us urgently that Jews can find salvation only in common with all humanity, and that it is the same thing to await the Messiah in banishment and Diaspora and to be the Messiah for all peoples.[15]

It must be noted here that Landauer did not reserve this view for the strictly Jewish audience of the book *Vom Judentum*. He reiterated it the same year for the general public with the article "Zum Beilis-Prozess" ("On the Beilis Trial"). Mendel Beilis was a Jewish resident of Kiev, accused in 1911 by the Russian government of ritualistic murder. He was finally exonerated in October 1913, after two years in prison and despite the anti-Semitic attitudes of the official investigators. Landauer's essay is not a discussion of the trial, but a call to non-Jewish populations to put aside their prejudices and understand the Jew for what he really is. In this context the author's concept of Zionism is an answer to the charge of separatism so often leveled against the Jews:

The movement going through the world of Jewry, generally under the name Zionism, should have, whatever its external forms and fluctuations, the following purpose: that Jews, under the leadership of spiritual and strong individuals, mold purely and creatively that particular nature which they, like every *Nation*, have developed over thousands of years; that in the battle for that which is holy they save their souls from the chaos of misunderstanding and superficially mechanical custom; that they fill their souls with urgent life and present themselves and their nature to developing mankind, which can as little stand to do without the Jews as it can any other level or gradation of humanity. Humanity does not mean identity; humanity is the union of the manifold.[16]

Since the middle of the nineteenth century, racial philosophy, under the spell of evolutionary theories but totally without the methodological rigor and observational basis that gave those theories scientific validity, had exercised an increasing influence upon social philosophy. A significant number of Germans subscribed to the elitist Aryanism of Houston Stewart Chamberlain (*Foundations of the 19th Century*, 1898), with its pseudoscientific justifications for the anti-Semitism long smoldering in German society. Zionism, too, frequently resulted in, and in part arose from, attitudes quite as chauvinistic as those of Chamberlain and his followers. Amid these attitudes Landauer's call for mutual recognition and for not just understanding but appreciation of the contributions all peoples can make to mankind was a beacon of humanity on a sea of bigotry.

Aside from explaining Landauer's attitude toward Judaism, the material discussed above provides the most detailed example for Landauer's use of the term *"Nation."* One sees that *Nation* is not only a situation, but also a path of action. Landauer specifically stated this in "Sind das Ketzergedanken?": ". . . what is *Nation* other than a union of those who, brought together by unifying *Geist*, feel in themselves a particular duty toward humanity? To be a *Nation* means to have a function." [17] The recognition of one's "nationality," however, is not in itself a dedication to the cause of humanity; as in the case of some Zionist Jews, awareness of "nationality" can easily lead to chauvinism. Landauer did not overlook this possibility. He provided a method for putting "nationality" at the service of mankind, a method that was possible only after one had come to understand the meaning of one's own "nationality." The basis of this method was *Geist*.

As stated above, *Geist*, according to Landauer, is inherent in the individual, and the experience of *Nation* is the most obvious way one can become aware of its presence. Landauer made a distinction, however, between individuals having a common historical background, and *Geist* that comes to be an active force in the everyday life of the individuals within a "national" group. Such a group, which is under the influence of *Geist* environmentally as well as hereditarily, Landauer called a *"Volk"* (a "people").* The distinction between *Nation* and *Volk* was not always as clear in Landauer's later writings as indicated here, but his first use of these words as a part of his specific philosophical terminology ("Thirty Socialist Theses") showed a significant difference between them. His statements about *Nation* in that essay have already been discussed. His comments there about *Volk* begin with the astonishing statement, "But *Volk* is something that does not exist. . . ." [18] By this he meant that no example of *Volk* existed in the early

---

* Landauer would certainly reject this use of the words *heredity* and *environment*, but I see no way to avoid this conventional terminology when trying to define more concretely what for Landauer were essentially symbols.

twentieth century. But it had existed in the past, the best illustration being Christianity at the time of its greatest flowering. "Christianity . . . was a *Volk* in the best and most powerful sense: thorough permeation of the economic and cultural community with the bond of *Geist*." [19] It had been the active presence of *Geist* at that time that had created a *Volk* out of the Christian *Nation*, and Landauer insisted that *Geist* must be reactivated as a unifying force between individuals so that "economic community, cultural society, can replace the state." [20] The contrast here between the concept of the state on the one hand and *Geist* and community (*Gemeinschaft*) on the other remained a basic characteristic of Landauer's thought throughout his life.

The idea that *Geist* is the necessary basis of culture in a *Nation* is a salient feature of *Die Revolution*, Landauer's first major work to appear after the "Thirty Socialist Theses"; but the interrelation between *Geist* and *Volk* is most succinctly described in *Aufruf zum Sozialismus*. Here Landauer stated that periods during which *Geist* determines the course of human life always come to an end because the influence of *Geist* is overcome by religious dogma and a literal, nonpoetic use of language. Since *Geist* is inherent in man, however, *Geist* is not destroyed; when its influence is dissipated, it lies dormant within most people. Only in a few, rare individuals —thinkers and artists, individuals isolated from the *Volk*, which no longer reacts to *Geist*—is it still active.[21] From these individuals a new wave of *Geist* might sweep over mankind and create a new *Volk*. The changing influence of *Geist* upon human life, then, is the principal force that determines the history of mankind.

In a period when the prevailing interpretations of history were scientific and materialistic, Landauer's approach represented a radically divergent direction. His rejection of materialism had been presented in *Skepsis und Mystik*. Four years after that, he dedicated the introductory pages of *Die Revolution* to a detailed discussion of the distinction between science and history. For Landauer the task of science is to review our concept of the world by dissolving abstractions into their basic sense data so that the sense data may then be resynthesized into new abstractions more adequately descriptive of the apparent world. The new abstractions differ from the old ones in that the new enable an individual to picture his world in terms of processes, a flow of changes, while the old ones represented the world as a constant state. Processes are the end products of science. History, on the other hand, is the study of processes. In this area, too, the human mind must analyze abstractions (Landauer suggested "Middle Ages," "state," "society" as examples of such historical abstractions), but the fundamental constituents of those abstractions are events and human relationships, not the sense data to which scientific analysis leads: "In short: exact science corrects experience; it leads us from experience to intellectual abstractions. The so-called science of history, on the other hand, no matter how perfectly it is developed, can lead us only back to the first data of experience" (pp. 8–9).* [22] History, he concluded, is not a scientific study.

Synthesis of the processes uncovered in historical study has a tremendous importance to mankind, Landauer contended. For the convenience of memory these processes are grouped together into abstractions—e.g., "church," "state," "community"—but these are more than intellectual abstractions. Men live according to them, and this fact lends them a reality found in no other abstractions; Landauer called them practical forces (*"Mächte der Praxis"*) (p. 9). This means that the study of history has two very contradictory functions: it creates new abstractions on the basis of the human relationships it studies, abstractions that may become actual forces in the life of mankind; but it reduces old abstractions to their basic constituents and so tends to destroy them, not only as memory devices, but as real forces in everyday life. In this sense, history is not only revolutionary, it is revolution. It has two results:

. . . on the one hand, construction of supraindividual systems and higher forms of organization that provide the lives of individuals with purpose and consecration; on the other hand, destruction and overthrow of these same forms when they have become unbearable to the freedom and welfare of individuals (p. 10).

As proof for his hypothesis that history cannot be understood scientifically, Landauer began *Die Revolution* by attempting to formulate a scientific definition of revolution, one of the historical

* All page references in the text here and below to the end of the chapter unless otherwise indicated are to *Die Revolution*.

processes, but soon exhausted the available sense data. He demonstrated by this experiment that our knowledge is not sufficient for us to form an abstraction that will satisfactorily describe the phenomenon "revolution" in all its possible ramifications. If "revolution" is to be understood at all, the understanding must be arrived at by other than scientific means.*

The discussion in *Die Revolution* that follows this futile experiment shows what an important place Landauer's approach to history holds within the body of his work. Consistent with the idea that historical study creates real forces influencing human life, Landauer mantained that history is not fixed and unchanging. The details of history (dates, places, actions) form an almost rigid framework, which varies only when new historical interpretations are applied; but history as a force continues to influence us, and these influences change as our lives change. History influences mankind and the existential interests of mankind influence history: "Of the past we know only our past; of all that has been we understand only that which still concerns us; we understand what has been only as we are; we understand it as our path" (p. 26).

Though Landauer does not specifically point it out, this view of history is identical with the idea, proposed in *Skepsis und Mystik*, that the individual and his forebears are the same being. History develops through the life of earlier individuals, influencing them and being influenced by them. It runs through later generations, modified at each stage by the needs and desires of individuals and to a large extent determining the nature of these individuals. If it differs at all from species-memory and the common background of

---

* In his *Ideology and Utopia* (1936), Karl Mannheim completely misrepresented this abortive experiment that Landauer had considered futile from the start. As part of his "scientific vocabulary" for the discussion of revolution in *Die Revolution*, Landauer used the terms *"Topia"* and *Utopia*. Once he had proved to his satisfaction the impossibility of explaining revolution scientifically, he abandoned these terms; *"Topia"* never again appeared in his writings. On 5 October 1907 he wrote to Mauthner, "I coined the word 'Topia' half in fun as a contrast to Utopia but then found that it was useful in earnest." In another letter, to Ludwig Berndl, 18 January 1910, he made it quite clear that the earnestness concerned only the futile scientific experiment. Mannheim, in his discussion of *Die Revolution*, concentrated exclusively on these two terms, giving the false impression that they are central to the entire book.

individuals, the variation is one of degree, not of kind. History has the same relationship to mankind as does species-memory to the individual and common background to nationality; therefore, it is as significant a factor in Landauer's *Weltanschauung*.

It is indicative of Landauer's philosophic orientation that his interpretation of history leans heavily upon two ideas borrowed from Mauthner. The first of these is a reevaluation of the time structure in which we view historical relationships. Mauthner had suggested somewhat ironically in the *Sprachkritik* (II, 199) that since our knowledge of history spans such a relatively short period when compared with the total time man has existed, we should really consider all this knowledge as contemporary history. Landauer took this suggestion seriously as an insight compatible with his concept of *Nation*. He saw history as divided into three parts: "remote" ("*Fremdgeschichte*"), "vicinal" ("*Nachbargeschichte*"), and "immediate" ("*Die eigene Geschichte*"). In the category "remote history," Landauer placed the histories of all those people for whom no evidence of influence upon the development of our own culture or that of our "neighbors" has yet been shown. The "neighbors," whose record is "vicinal history," were the Greeks, Romans, and Jews. These *Nationen* contributed to our own, the "immediate history," but were neither forebears of it nor models for it. "Immediate history" is the history of Christianity, and must be understood as something unique in itself, a new beginning, a new culture brought about by the impact of the Greeks, Romans, and Jews upon a "rested" people.

The concept of "rested peoples" ("*ausgeruhte Völker*") was the second idea with roots in Mauthner's considerations of history. In the *Sprachkritik* (II, 638 ff.) the theoretical proposal had been made that the composition and distribution of the human race might be inescapably subject to periodic climatic changes, which, because of heat on the one hand and glaciers on the other, would make different areas of the earth habitable at different times. The catastrophic changes that advancing glaciers would bring about in the lives of human groups would limit the term of a civilization to 21,000 years, the time between the maximum extensions of periodic glaciations. If this is true, civilization would have to start all over again as the glaciers begin to recede, leaving behind them small pockets of individuals who had been reduced to a savage or near-savage state by the hardships imposed upon them.

Landauer accepted the possibility of this theory in *Skepsis und Mystik*, quoting it directly from Mauthner. His own use of this material shows, however, that it was the human aspect, not the geological, that impressed him. A corollary of Landauer's belief in the manifestation of the eternal psyche in individuals is that all peoples are equally old. Different times of origin cannot be used, therefore, to explain cultural differences between various peoples. Since we know that cultural levels are always changing, a possible explanation of cultural difference might be that every people experiences a wavelike progression of cultural highs and lows, with the movement of the wave being determined by innumerable and varying factors. So-called primitive people could very well be the epigones of a culture, totally lost in the passage of time, that had equaled or even surpassed any now known. This high period may have been preceded by a host of others, all lost to us, stretching back into infinity, always representing in some form or other the eternal psyche. According to Landauer, the potentiality for a new period of high culture is always present in even the most primitive groups, and "backward peoples" are simply in a necessary stage of rest between two high-culture periods. Once such a group has become thoroughly rested, it is prepared to take part in a new florescence of culture.

It should be stated that this is not a summary but an interpretation of material presented in *Die Revolution*. Landauer did not use the term *psyche* in his discussion of rested peoples; but its use is justified here to show the continuity between this work and *Skepsis und Mystik*. For it is obvious that he had the idea if not the word *psyche* in mind when he wrote in *Die Revolution*: "Human beings all reach back over thousands of years as human beings, but they also existed before they were human beings, before the earth existed, back into infinity" (p. 20).

Were a speculative anthropologist to accept Landauer's concept of rested peoples, he would most likely outline all the possible reasons why a people at the low point of cultural development might begin a cultural ascent. Landauer was concerned with only one such incentive: contact and mixture of a primitive group with one or more other groups on a higher cultural level. The impact of two peoples upon each other does not lead to the destruction of one or the other—Mauthner had emphasized that only languages die out, not peoples—but to a merger of the historical elements inherent in both groups, resulting in something entirely new. The origin of modern Europe, Christianity, was Landauer's prime example:

Christianity, this insignificant, degenerate product of classical decadence and Jewish sectarianism, would have achieved no importance if it had not impinged upon rested peoples [the Germanic tribes] for whom it was not insignificant, but an overwhelming force. Phidias and Sophocles meant nothing to them because these men were pinnacles, representatives of a period of grandeur. A new period grows from decadence and rested privation: from these elements emerges myth, and only where myth develops does a new *Volk* arise (pp. 23–24).

Christianity, it will be remembered, was also Landauer's best example of a *Volk*, a *Nation* under the influence of active *Geist*. For him, Christianity was something very specific that had existed in the past but that existed no longer:

Our presentation will show that the one great era of our history, the era that led to a cultural apex, is the Christian period generally called the Middle Ages; this time of Christianity, however, is past and since then we have not come to a new tranquillity, to stability, to a new summit of *Volk* (pp. 36–37).

He believed the Middle Ages had possessed the necessary characteristic of every great culture:

A level of great culture is reached when manifold, exclusive, and independent communal organizations exist contemporaneously, all impregnated with a uniform *Geist*, which does not reside in the organizations nor arise from them, but which holds sway over them as an independent and self-evident force. In other words, a level of great culture develops when the unifying principle in the diversity of organizational forms and supraindividual structures is not an external bond of force, but a *Geist* inherent in the individuals, directing their attention beyond earthly and material interests (p. 40).

Christianity was the *Geist* pervading the social organization of the medieval period and welding the diverse human functions into a cultural unity. Christianity was the *Mythos* by which almost everyone lived and understood reality. It is significant, however, that *Geist*, according to Landauer, was not the cause of the social organization. Landauer pointed out later that *Geist* was able to influence human life at that time because a social organization existed in which the effects of active *Geist* could be felt (p. 116). This organization consisted of decentralized interest groups established by individuals to meet their own various needs. The groups constantly interacted in a society of societies (*"Gesellschaft von Gesellschaften"*), and in that context of freely determined mutual relationships *Geist* was able to operate as the dominant principle. This principle was a palpable reality for the people of the time:

For them it [Christianity] could be nothing but a santification and transfiguration of a communal life bounding with fresh energy. For these individuals and peoples Christianity was a truth only in relation to their private and public life, to their works, growth, and personal development, which were the preconditions and basis for everything else; if one had told the member of a gild or diocese that these positive, formative, life-encouraging alliances stood in contrast to the true spirit of Christianity, he would not have understood . . . (p. 42).

Landauer realized that elements other than *Geist* might be cited as determining factors of the Middle Ages: feudalism, the Church (in contrast to Christianity), the Inquisition, the administration of justice. To all this he said:

I know. None the less . . . : All history, all understanding is abbreviation, condensation; knowledge does not arise only from looking; it demands overlooking as well, just as life needs forgetting as much as remembering (p. 51).

Landauer's admiration for the Middle Ages never diminished. His later works bore repeated witness to his belief that modern man had reached the high point in his cultural development during that time. Symptomatic of the importance he placed on that period in the development of modern Western man is the fact that he interpreted the entire history of Europe since then as one revolution that had begun when the influence of *Geist* upon medieval society abated.

Landauer viewed the development of individualism, one of the most significant features of the Renaissance, as a factor that ran counter to *Geist* and undermined its hold upon medieval life. Individualism arose as scholastic theologians and empirical scientists destroyed the symbolic meaning of Christianity. The final blow to the efficacy of *Geist* in daily life came with the Reformation and Luther's doctrine that salvation could be achieved only through belief, not through activity. This doctrine was the only part of the Renaissance to reach the common people, and it completed the transformation of Christianity from a symbolic understanding of reality to a series of dogmatic abstractions. Since that time Europe has been involved in a constant struggle to reattain a level of stability such as marked the Middle Ages. This struggle is a long-lasting revolution against dogmatism for the reestablishment of *Geist* as the fundamental principle of human life.

This is the only revolution about which Landauer felt we have any specific knowledge. We cannot come to an objective description of it because we are still taking part in it, but we can recognize various stages through which it has gone; Landauer listed the Reformation, the Peasants' War, the English Revolution, the Thirty Years' War, the American Revolution, the French Revolution of 1789/91, and the Franco-Prussian War. Had *Die Revolution* been written ten years later, he would also have listed World War I. Landauer admitted that his grouping these events into one revolution was an interpretation and that other interpretations were possible, but he felt that his view was the one most consistent with the effect of history upon modern Western man. To Landauer, history was a path from the past leading into the future; and this revolution, the struggle of *Geist* against dogma and abstraction, seemed the clearest indication of the path's direction.

The first phase of this revolution was marked by the change at the end of the Middle Ages from a stateless society to one in which the state was the dominant feature, one in which politics replaced *Geist* as the basis for society. The discussion of this change occupies a central position in *Die Revolution*, but the philosophical foundation for it appears in the "Thirty Socialist Theses." In the nineteenth thesis Landauer presented the view that culture is not a function of the state, but of economic organizations (*Wirtschaftsgemeinschaften*), which can exist only on the basis of *Volk* or *Nation.* The state differs radically from *Volk* or *Nation* in that the latter are natural aspects of human existence whereas the state is an accident of history, a confused mass of purposes with no natural unity or relationship, held together by tradition and force. The twenty-eighth thesis explains the difference by means of a new term that occurs frequently in Landauer's later works: the term *"Wahn."* *

"Wahn" is the word Landauer used to describe the aspirations of mankind, and in this sense it is a fundamental characteristic of human life. In this twenty-eighth thesis he identified *Geist* as a kind of *Wahn:*

> *Wahn* is not only every goal, every ideal, every belief in a sense and purpose of life and the world: *Wahn* is every banner followed by mankind; every drumbeat leading mankind into danger; every alliance that unites mankind and creates from a sum of individuals a new structure, an organism. *Wahn is* the greatest thing mankind has; there is always something of love in it: love is *Geist* and *Geist* is love: and love and *Geist* are *Wahn.*[23]

State, *Volk,* and *Nation* are all examples of *Wahn,* but their effects on the individual differ radically. When, as in the Middle Ages, *Volk* and *Nation* act as the focal point of life, they provide the individual a valid means of transcending his own being. The state cannot do this, for it is *Wahn* of a different kind; it is not a natural characteristic of man and is, therefore, a false *Wahn.* The twenty-ninth thesis tells how the state conflicts with the true *Wahn* of *Nation* and *Volk:*

> The state is a false *Wahn,* because it attaches to locality, territory, geographical area, purposes having nothing to do with locality, having no relationship with each other, achievable only by a small group or comprehensive, independent organizations.[24]

Landauer believed, as stated in the thirtieth thesis, that every purpose demands its own organization (as represented by the "society

---

* The word *"Wahn"*—usually translated "delusion," "madness," or "folly"— has a secondary sense, closer to its meaning in earlier periods of the German language; this might be rendered by "illusion" if a connotation of (justified) hope and expectation is included in that concept. Landauer's usage is, of course, based on the secondary sense.

of societies" in the medieval period) and that the state artificially combines personal, social, and economic aspects of life in one self-contradictory unit. Aside from failing to provide an adequate context in which these various functions can be carried out, the state further hinders them by taking on the guise of a purpose in itself. In supporting this ostensible purpose, the citizens lose contact with their individual purposes, with those things that should be providing the *Wahn* by which their lives are led. This is all restated in a passage in *Aufruf zum Sozialismus*:

The state, with its police and all its laws and its contrivances for property rights, exists for the people as a miserable replacement for *Geist* and for organizations with specific purposes; and now the people are supposed to exist for the sake of the state, which pretends to be some sort of ideal structure and a purpose in itself, to be *Geist*. . . . Earlier there were corporate groups, clans, gilds, fraternities, communities, and they all interrelated to form society. Today there is coercion, the letter of the law, the state.[25]

This modern political state, Landauer asserted in *Die Revolution*, is a product of modern Europe; the states we know of in the history of our "neighbors," the Greeks and Romans, contributed to but did not determine the current political structure. This arose only when the unifying *Geist* of the medieval period began to diminish:

We do not assert that there was no state in the Christian period . . . ; but in any event there was no supreme power of the state, no state as the focus for all other forms of community, but at most a state as an imperfect, atrophied structure amid other, highly various configurations of communal life. There were only remnants of the state from Roman times and small, new beginnings that came to be important only in the period of dissolution and revolution (p. 43).

The four hundred years following the Middle Ages saw a constant increase in the power of the state and a trend toward centralization. This was true even though the basis of state power underwent changes; Landauer described the history of the modern state as having shown three successive tendencies: absolute power in the hands of the princes; absolute power represented in the law; and, finally, the absolute power of nationalism. In all of these stages it was the presence of absolute power that characterized the state.

In opposition to this absolutism there arose, as early as the sixteenth century, a countermovement that showed some signs of *Geist*, but feeble signs in comparison to what had gone before: this was the spirit of republicanism, revealing itself in revolutionary activity, both physical and intellectual. Landauer accorded Thomas More's *Utopia* (1516) the first place in a series of works and activities directed against centralization during the four centuries separating the Middle Ages from his own period. Even when it succeeded more or less in its efforts, however, the republican movement was unable to reestablish *Geist* as the basis of life, for republican efforts were directed against monarchs or ministers or the privileges of nobility, not against the state itself. The republican philosophers did not consider the state an organ of absolutist rule, but rather as separate from it and their strongest weapon against it. Speaking of writers in the sixteenth century, with special reference to the Huguenot statesman Hubert Languet, Landauer said, "For the revolutionary pioneers of that time, state and law were God in man, a unifying characteristic; something which came from all individuals and united them into an entity and a higher organizational structure" (p. 76). As the strength of the commercial class grew, the republican concept of state took on more of an economic aspect; this became especially pronounced after the French Revolution, when the prevailing political philosophy demanded that the state serve as guarantor for the freedom and independence of economic undertakings. The result of this attitude was that state and capitalism came to be all but identical in modern Europe.

While the interests of the state and capitalism were merging, however, another economic situation was coming to light. As the absolute power of monarchs diminished, the state's wealth came to be considered public assets rather than royal treasure, assets whose source lay in the larger community. This view led to the discovery that there was another financial force within the state, a national wealth in addition to a state wealth. This national wealth was the sum of all private business dealings carried on within the state, dealings that bound the individuals involved in them together in a union completely separate from the state: "People had begun to find that there exists a community alongside the state, not just a sum of isolated individual atoms, but an organic solidarity, consisting of highly differentiated groups. . . ." And in language more cautious and tentative than he meant, Landauer went on:

We still know nothing or very little about this supraindividual structure that is pregnant with *Geist*; but one day it will be known that socialism is not the invention of something new, but the discovery of something that has been present and has grown in society (p. 105).

According to Landauer's interpretation, the discovery of the national wealth was for some individuals the discovery of the true society in which financial interests could represent the unifying *Geist*. The various commercial groups were the kind of purposeful units (*Zweckverbände*) necessary to constitute true society. Others wished to combine the independent economic life with the structure of the state. Still using tentative language, forced upon him by his assertion in this work that one cannot comment definitively upon a historical situation in which one is still living, but leaving no doubt that the formulation represented his personal conviction, he suggested that this second group, seeking unification of national wealth and the state, was the politicians and that all political parties subscribe to a union of state and *Nation*. The first, however,

. . . who called themselves socialists, declared: after the discovery of society, the free and voluntary interrelationship of the energies of communal life, the state has only one task more: manifold interlacing of unions, organizations, and societies, which are making ready to replace it and the senseless, unplanned, *Geist*-less individualism of economics, production, and circulation (pp. 107–08).

In this statement is the basis for Landauer's total rejection of the socialist party. He found the concept of a socialist organization operating on the principles of state government as self-contradictory as the idea of a socialist state.

Yet it is certainly not consistent with the nature of politics, Landauer reasoned, for the state voluntarily to take steps toward its own eradication. No, if the centuries-long revolution is ever to succeed, some method must be found to circumvent state power and political structure. Landauer offered such a method, based on the work of Étienne de la Boëtie, a sixteenth-century philosopher and friend of Montaigne, who concerned himself with the nature of tyranny. In *Die Revolution*, Landauer discussed the essay "Discours sur la servitude volontaire" ("Discourse on Voluntary Servitude"), in which de la Boëtie characterized the relationship between the tyrant and his servitor. He maintained that the tyrant's power is granted him by those over whom he rules and that the relationship can be changed whenever the subjugated individuals wish. They need only refuse him their support, and he will fall. Landauer was convinced that an analogous situation existed in his own day, and that the future, though the details could not be predicted, would not be based on the social structures inherited from the past.

It would not because those structures could not support *Geist*. If *Geist* showed any continuing activity during the period since the European Middle Ages, it was within inspired individuals, the artists and thinkers. Among the masses *Geist* was manifest only during occasional moments of revolutionary upheaval, but it could not maintain itself as the motivating force in society much beyond these brief flashes, for they were all politically motivated movements, and political revolution can only be destructive. When problems of reconstruction arose after periods of revolutionary violence, the political revolution was unable to cope with them, and society fell back into a political situation little changed from the pre-revolutionary one. In the face of this, the unifying power of *Geist* subsided, leaving only small echoes of itself among the masses, like the joyous Bastille Day street dances in France.

The path from the past shows where the future must lead. Political devices can never reestablish *Geist* as the guiding principle of human life. Hope for this lies only in a *social* revolution, which Landauer called "a peaceful building, an organizing in a new spirit and to a new spirit and nothing more" (p. 115). Political revolution may be necessary before a social revolution can take place, but the social revolution must be prepared for in advance so that it can take over when the necessary destruction is completed and the task of rebuilding can and must be faced. The preparations must be directed toward the establishment of a new society in which *Geist* can once again assert itself. For Landauer, socialism was both the preparation *and* the social revolution.

When he wrote the "Thirty Socialist Theses" and *Die Revo-*

lution, Landauer was experiencing the isolation of the prophet in the wilderness. Martin Buber later said of the "Theses" that Landauer wrote them "after he had risen from the agitation of the anarchist movement to his own knowledge and mode of expression, to give to his understanding of the proper course of action a form capable of uniting individuals." [26] But there was no organized body of individuals to whom Landauer could direct his words. Since 1900 he had not taken part in the public activities of anarchist groups; the fact that he had risen above them also meant that he was isolated from them. It was thanks to Buber that *Die Revolution* was written. Landauer had met him in 1899, and a warm friendship based on mutual admiration developed. Buber asked Landauer to provide a book on the nature of revolution for a series Buber was issuing, *Die Gesellschaft*. Landauer and Buber agreed that *Die Revolution* was more a call to action than would normally be published in a series dedicated to social psychology, as *Die Gesellschaft* was; but this in no way diminished Buber's appreciation of the book. In 1908, Landauer received a request to donate a copy to the library of the Maria Hilf monastery at Vilshofen in Bavaria; he accepted this sign of recognition graciously, although the Benedictine Fathers were not exactly the group he hoped to influence with his work. Other recognition remained sparse and other outlets for his writing often disappointing. He did not feel moved to contribute to any of the existing anarchist journals, not even one his old *Sozialist* colleague Albert Weidner was trying to keep alive; so he had to continue publishing in the more radical commercial journals such as the *Zukunft* and the *Blaubuch*, and he had to write material acceptable to their editors. This primarily took the form of literary essays, a number of which he wrote during this period.

It is interesting to note, nevertheless, that ideas in *Skepsis und Mystik*, "Thirty Socialist Theses," and *Die Revolution* were plainly reflected in Landauer's discussions of literary figures. Three essays from 1906/07 provide a clear example of this. One dating from 1907 discusses Walt Whitman, who was the subject of no little controversy in the German literary world. There could be no doubt about Landauer's position in this controversy: Whitman's poetry represented everything Landauer expected in the work of a modern poet. The American "seemed to have thought only with his senses," Landauer said;[27] and in *Leaves of Grass*, Landauer saw reflected his own belief that man carries the world within himself. Love was the basis of Whitman's philosophy, Landauer wrote, and the love Whitman expressed for individuals was symbolic of the force the poet felt should bind men together into a new *Volk*. This *Volk* was, of course, the American people—as a people, not as a political organization. In Americans Landauer saw a "rested people," barbarians in his sense of the word, people ready to start on the path to a new era of cultural grandeur. And in Whitman he saw their prophet. It would scarcely be possible to find a better example than Whitman to demonstrate Landauer's image, presented many times in his writings, of the poet as the product of his *Volk* and prophet to them. Whitman absorbed America in all its being, Landauer claimed—even the technological aspect, which had come to be something of an American trademark—and his poetry was a call to the people to build for themselves the society that, as Landauer expressed it, Whitman felt his experience had built in him. "His feeling of self is really a feeling of his *Volk* as himself; one must not be led astray by the mystical 'myself' of his verses." [28] The sympathy Landauer must have felt for Whitman is obvious and explains why Landauer was among the early German translators of Whitman's poetry.

In Landauer's opinion, the Germany of his day also possessed a poet of feeling and *Volk*, similar in many ways to Whitman. That was Richard Dehmel. In the Dehmel essay mentioned in Chapter 3, Landauer wrote of him in terms also applicable to Whitman: "Instinct [*Trieb*] wants to become spirit [*Geist*]; this statement characterizes Dehmel's poetic essence; and everything spiritual—only spiritual, only cultural—wants to immerse itself in the instincts, to descend into the primordial, to become nature." [29] Conversely, Landauer could as well have had Dehmel in mind when he wrote in the Whitman essay, "It corresponds to the particular nature of every creative fantasy that there is something erotic in all feeling and in everything created." [30] Dehmel's eroticism was not as overtly sensual as Whitman's—it was more metaphysical than physical—but at the same time it was not abstracted or sublimated as in other poets' work. Landauer referred to it as an experience of the polarity inherent in being, not a sensual but a metaphysical experience. Like Whitman, Landauer held, Dehmel displayed a strength, a lack of inhibition, and a clarity of purpose that made him able "to lead us to the heights and the depths, through the life of reality, dreams, and ecstasy." [31] Also like Whitman was Dehmel's contact with the Volk and its modern situation, including in his case not only technology but social organization and socialism. If Whitman served his Volk as a beacon for the future, Dehmel stood among his people and wished to spur them on to a new life. For both, the spiritual communion with the Volk was intimate enough so that there was hope, however slight, that their message might be heard and their call followed.

What of the poets, the majority of poets, who were still totally isolated from their Volk? Landauer expressed his concern for their fate repeatedly, perhaps most specifically in his 1907 article on Walter Calé. One result of isolation, Landauer said, is decadence, which he called "complete hopelessness." [32] The decadent poets, of whom he considered Calé the best, do not have the genius necessary to escape from the conditions that surround them. Instead they join together in exclusive groups and thereby further their isolation from society. They are victims of loneliness and "a soft antipathy toward their surroundings, their times, toward existence as a whole." [33] If they cannot manage to live under these conditions, they die. Calé's suicide demonstrated this, as did the poetry of Erwin Kircher, whose work illustrated for Landauer how the conflict between contemporary society and the demands of Geist was destructive to these young men.

Despite his involvement with literary topics and lack of an organization Landauer was in no danger of becoming a "decadent." He kept his eyes on events around him and occasionally had the opportunity to express his attitudes toward them. In 1907 he wrote two articles for the Blaubuch concerning the disarmament debate then going on in the Reichstag in connection with the Second Hague Conference on International Peace. Landauer branded the debate, which suggested the possibility that Germany might be in favor of some arms reduction, a sham; and, indeed, when the conference took place, it was Germany along with Austria and the Balkan countries that stood in the way of progress toward demilitarization. Landauer insisted that the SPD was no less supportive of the belligerent state policy than any other party; his opposition to parliamentarianism remained as strong as ever. Finally, a year later, he found a way, not a practical one, but a possible one, to combat it actively.

5

The
Socialist
Bund
1908–1914

LANDAUER's personality always had a strong effect on people—even those who came to know him only slightly. It was therefore quite natural that he was particularly successful as a lecturer and felt very much at home in that role. Late in May 1908 he spoke before a gathering of anarchists and radical socialists about his concept of socialism. His ideas, presented in a two-hour address, were greeted with obvious interest, for he was asked to return for further discussion. He did so in June, and at the close of his speech read the "Zwölf Artikel des sozialitischen Bundes" ("Twelve Articles of the Socialist Bund"), which he had composed between the meetings. These statements of purpose outlined a program for an organization Landauer felt could serve as the first impulse toward the development of a truly socialist society. Together with the speech itself, which became the basis for his book *Aufruf zum Sozialismus*, first published in 1911, the articles convinced a number of his listeners that his concepts were valid. At the end of the meeting these individuals pledged themselves to work for the attainment of the goals he had proposed. With this pledge of 14 June 1908, the Socialist Bund was created.

The Socialist Bund aimed at a nonviolent social revolution. It was to be the rallying point for those individuals who understood the tenets of the "Thirty Socialist Theses" and *Die Revolution* and who wished to live according to those tenets. Their first principle was a belief in Landauer's vision of the way to create a socialist life for themselves—outside the state, but at first, necessarily, alongside the state. Following Landauer's interpretation of Étienne de la Boëtie's statements on tyranny and servitude, those who joined the Bund agreed to withdraw further support from the state and the capitalist economic system.

Denial of support for capitalism and the state was, however, only part of the plan for the Bund. A social revolution, as Landauer understood it, is a process of building. It really begins when those who have withdrawn from capitalism join in a new relationship, and the structure of the relationship Landauer wished to create was one of small communities that could function for the benefit of all their members, as a family serves all those who belong to it. In such a community and system of communities the oppressed proletarian could develop into what he really was meant to be—a human being:

One begins to be a human being when one works not for wrong purposes, profit and its market, but for genuine human need, for the reestablishment of the submerged, genuine relationship between need and work, the relationship between hunger and the hands.[1]

The state and capitalism would be powerless to prevent this movement, for it could be started simply by taking advantage of the rights and activities allowed the individual within the capitalist state. It could exist beside capitalism at first. As Landauer saw it, only the hesitancy of individuals prevented the establishment of a viable socialist relationship at that time. The Bund was meant for those who wished to hesitate no longer.

The practical organization of the Bund was intentionally kept simple so that it would not become bogged down in bureaucracy. It was to consist of many independent groups, each of which would gather new members and work toward the establishment of small, self-contained settlements of members. The independence of the various groups was emphasized by the fact that there was no central office, no overall director. Landauer saw his function to be that of instigator—not leader—of the individual cells. He took this function quite seriously. By July he was traveling in Germany to speak on behalf of the undertaking, and shortly after the middle of that month received an invitation from a man named Mark Harda to speak in Switzerland. He responded to this invitation in August and found encouragement of a kind entirely unexpected.

Mark Harda, it turned out, was not a man but a woman named Margarete Faas-Hardegger, who as secretary of the Swiss Labor Union Alliance was intimately involved with socialist and anarchist activities in Switzerland. There was something in her personality, in the independence with which she faced the turmoil of an often tempestuous life, that inflamed Landauer's nature in the same way Hedwig had done some years earlier. But Margarete was not hesitant as Hedwig had been. After a speaking engagement in Bern, he spent a few days with her vacationing in the Bernese highlands before a second talk in Zurich. One can imagine that these were days of magical excitement for him—and not only in a romantic sense, for here, far from home, he had discovered a kindred spirit, a person who not only sympathized with and supported his ideas but in a way seemed to have anticipated them. He inspired her with his concept of the Socialist Bund; it was she who made him decide that the *Sozialist* must be revived once more, this time as the organ of the Bund. He returned home, full of memories of her and plans for the future—returned to Hedwig.

For this new love was to have no effect upon his relationship with Hedwig. Margarete had added an important new dimension to his life; but he was unchanged otherwise, and he anticipated that Hedwig would appreciate how significant this new association was for him and rejoice in it with him. Similarly, he made it perfectly clear to Margarete how much Hedwig meant to him. He explained the situation to Hedwig in September 1908, and she did indeed accept it, if not joyfully then at least with admirable understanding. A friendship grew between the two women. Margarete and her daughter had a long, happy visit with Hedwig and Landauer in December of that year, and they won the affection of Landauer's entire household.

This relationship, in all of its ramifications, provides a tangible illustration of Landauer's attitude toward women, love, and marriage. For all the sensuality that runs through his works, he was no advocate of "free love." Often, and most specifically in the two articles "Tarnowska" and "Von der Ehe" ("On Marriage"), both published in the *Sozialist* during 1910, Landauer stated his conviction that marriage is the fundament of society and the basic form for human social life. He rejected the notion of some Communists that polygamy is a necessary aspect of the collective state, but he was equally opposed to the idea of marriage as something to be regulated by the state; in *Von Zürich bis London* (1896) he had taken the SPD to task for not working toward the elimination of state controls on marriage. Nor was the exclusiveness of marriage something that he considered absolute:

When a mature man and a girl grown to great love have united themselves in marriage, their will to partnership and their mutual understanding become so firm that they are inseparably joined, although each one is an individual and can experience things in every sphere, even things that hurt and must hurt the other person in the marriage.[2]

His experience with Margarete exemplified this. He loved her, and sensuality was certainly a part of this love; but his union with Hedwig was never jeopardized in the slightest. It could not be, for marriage, his marriage with Hedwig, was too important. He saw marriage as the situation prevailing between a man and woman who derive their basic reason for existence from the relationship; it is the status of two people whose actions all stem ultimately from their love for each other. It is not a legal convention, but a metaphysical position.

As early as *Der Todesprediger* the emphasis Landauer placed upon the love-marriage relationship as the basis for a true society was clear. A couple, married in the sense Landauer meant, inevitably experiences life as worthwhile; and both individuals are, therefore, interested in the conditions under which they live and in attempts to better those conditions. Improvement of society is achieved when people with this interest band together to work for common goals; ultimate improvement, Utopia, is achieved when everyone is similarly prompted to create it. Thus, marriage is the sine qua non for a true society. And Landauer's hopes for an improvement in social conditions rested largely on the part he expected the feminine principle to play in the future social organization. He saw these hopes reflected in the writings of Martin Buber:

. . . just as Buber is the apostle of Judaism to mankind, he will be the awakener and advocate of the specific feminine manner of thinking without which no renewal and revitalization will come to our exhausted and sunken culture. Only when everything that lives as thought in the spirit of mankind, when all our abstract thinking is immersed in union with the deep chasm of feeling, only then will deed arise from our thoughts, will true life grow from the desert of our logic.[3]

He considered Goethe his predecessor in the emphasis he put on the conciliatory effects of the feminine, not only in the personal sphere as demonstrated in *Faust*, but in the sociocultural, as shown in *Iphigenie*. Landauer came to believe that the failure of women to exert their influence upon social and cultural conditions had been an important contributory factor to World War I, and he was to look to them for assistance in escaping the tragic situation into which the war had plunged the Western world. In 1916 he would write:

At this moment when we men bear almost exclusive guilt for the fact that humanity is besieged by the remnants of its own past and can find no escape of the spirit, but only hopes for an escape based on chance, we truly have no grounds for arrogance and none to refrain from the attempt to allow select women to influence us spiritually and to influence them as well.[4]

Such an attempt would be a bond of the male and female outside the love relationship, but it would be strong enough to awaken the feminine principle in men (for it exists in men—Landauer would expressly state this in a letter in 1915[5]); and it is only when the male and female within the individual are actively combined, as Landauer insisted they were within him, that a new society, a new reality could be established.[6]

As he began work in earnest on the Socialist Bund and the resurrection of the *Sozialist*, he had the kind of feminine support he desired. Other encouragement was not lacking either. Mauthner hailed the Bund's beginning, though he could not bring himself to join the organization. Buber became a member as early as September 1908. The individuals who comprised the Berlin Bund groups volunteered time to begin republication of the *Sozialist*. By the end of 1908 there were ten cells of the Bund, three of them in Switzerland and two in Berlin alone. When 1909 arrived, Landauer was able to draw real hope from the progress that had been made. The movement was small but going in the direction he wished, and that satisfied him. On 13 December he wrote to Auguste Hauschner: "I do not require the belief that the 'goal' will be reached in the foreseeable future, only the belief in the undertaking."

This encouraging outlook was not achieved without personal cost to Landauer; the activities of the Bund set the pattern of his life for the next six years. The speaking and writing he did for his organization conflicted strongly with the normal activities of making a living. As early as November 1908 he wrote to Mauthner of renewed financial problems, and by January 1909 he was personally without funds and had to ask Mauthner to help him. His attempt to free himself from financial worries by having Mauthner arrange a stipend for him—it was hoped that people interested in his work might give monthly donations to a fund for his support—was unsuccessful. He was forced to continue his translation work and to write articles for journals other than the *Sozialist* to maintain himself and his family. He gave some lecture series as well: on Goethe during the last part of 1909; on socialism from December 1910 to April 1911; and, starting in May 1911, on the French Revolution. At the same time, however, he had to provide a great deal of material for the *Sozialist*, oversee the fortunes of that paper, and write the documents necessary to provide a general understanding of the goals of the Bund, especially the *Aufruf zum Sozialismus*. It was only an unshakably firm "belief in the undertaking" that enabled him to accomplish all this.

Central to all these activities was the *Sozialist*. It began to appear as a monthly on 15 January 1909 and was so unexpectedly successful that it became a fortnightly after the March edition. It served primarily as a propaganda organ for the Bund, stating the intentions of the organization and reporting on developments as they occurred. It had a secondary function as well: to comment on the political events of the time from the anarchist point of view. In this regard it was like the old *Sozialist* of the 1890s, but in general, there was little similarity between the two papers: the second one was more definitely Landauer's and reflected the philosophical turn of his mind. His hopes for a better future were built on a very specific metaphysical foundation, and he used the paper to educate others to his way of thinking. The *Aufruf zum Sozialismus* and three pamphlets that the Bund distributed received space, in whole or in part, in the *Sozialist* as well.

When read chronologically, the essays connected with the Bund provide a philosophical history of the organization, for they reveal the series of problems to which Landauer successively turned his attention as he struggled to gain recognition for his ideas. The first two appeared as pamphlets before the *Sozialist* began publication: in October, 1908, *Was will der sozialistische Bund? (The Goals of the Socialist Bund)* and early the following year, *Was ist zunächst zu tun? (How to Begin?)*. This second pamphlet quickly went through an edition of 10,000 copies and was reprinted separately, even though the *Sozialist* was being revived just at that time. A third pamphlet, *Die Siedlung (The Settlement)*, was published in 1910 when plans were being made within the Bund to establish the first colony. And the *Aufruf zum Sozialismus* finally appeared in toto, as a book, in 1911, though Landauer had been working on it since 1908. When one is familiar with the three pamphlets and the many articles in the *Sozialist*, the *Aufruf* diminishes in importance as the high point of Landauer's work; but it is primarily to the *Aufruf* that one must turn for a complete statement of the sociological implications that grew from the philosophical insights of *Skepsis und Mystik* and the historical theories of *Die Revolution*.

The *Aufruf* bears obvious stylistic traces of having first been a speech. It is truly a call, passionate, occasionally propogandistic, sometimes, especially in the section on Marxism, demagogic. It begins with several statements about socialism. Of these the two most significant in light of Landauer's total work are: "I understand socialism as a tendency of the human will *and* an insight into the conditions and ways that lead to fulfillment" (my emphasis), and "Socialism is an endeavor to create a new reality with the help of an ideal" (both p. 1).* This reality had already been discussed eight years before in *Skepsis und Mystik*, where Landauer had spoken of the individual becoming society by making himself one with the world and thus preparing himself for a real social relation-

---

* This and all quotations throughout the chapter that are documented within the text are from the *Aufruf*, except where otherwise specified.

ship with others who had also achieved this condition. The *Aufruf* was a call to humanity to join in that relationship.

The discussion continues in the spirit of *Skepsis und Mystik* and *Die Revolution.* The ideal by which the new reality is to be created exists because the modern period does not provide a cultural situation in which a satisfying life can be led. This ideal is *Wahn,* the image of a new life, pointing the way for those who recognize and suffer from the conditions surrounding them. For these individuals the ideal serves as *Geist,* the necessary prerequisite for the realization of the new reality: "*Geist* is the spirit of community, *Geist* is unity and freedom, *Geist* is the union of humanity . . . where there is *Geist* there is *Volk;* where there is *Volk* there is a wedge, pushing forward, a will; where there is a will there is a way; the adage is true; but only then is there a way" (p. 3). *Geist* together with superstition and a metaphorical use of language were the elements that determined the high point of Western culture. The discoveries of science overcame superstition but at the same time destroyed the other elements, and the scientific knowledge that has superseded them has not been able to replace them successfully as fundamental concepts for human existence. "That is why we call our times a period of decline, because the essential element for culture, the unifying *Geist,* has decayed" (p. 98).

A concomitant of the decline of *Geist* was the growth of the state. The artificial integration of individuals into the state destroyed the natural union of people in relationships determined by *Geist.* Landauer's profound dissatisfaction with his times, their industrial development, nationalism, and drive for progress, is based on this fact:

. . . a unifying *Geist,* I say, that would drive mankind from within to cooperation in community affairs and the production and distribution of needed goods, is not there. A *Geist* that would set all life in relationship to eternity, that would sanctify our senses, that would make everything corporeal heavenly, every change and everything changing a joy, a soaring, wheeling, and rapture, is not there (p. 14).

The most obvious sign of the absence of *Geist* was for Landauer the plight of the industrial workers. Separated from the earth and its products and spiritually isolated from each other despite the closeness of their living conditions, they become victims of alcohol, disease, and poverty. The relationship between worker and employer becomes completely dehumanized through capitalism, technology, and the state. For the state, despite the wishes of the laissez-faire industrialists, continues to play a part in the commercial practices within its boundaries: under the name "social politics" it sees that the most harmful of the workers' circumstances are mitigated. In this way it removes from the shoulders of the industrialists the responsibility for the care of their workers, and the workers then become the victims of increased indifference on the employers' part. Because of this, social legislation cannot basically improve the workers' position. Attempts by workers to better their lot through unions are frustrated by the nature of this society. The fight for higher wages, one of the most important functions of the labor union, is actually a fight of each individual against himself. Landauer quoted Proudhon in this regard: " 'In economic matters, what is valid for the private individual becomes false the moment one tries to extend it to the entire society' " (p. 75). Specifically, rising prices soon wipe out much of the advantage from union-won wage increases, so that even this minimal manifestation of Geist, this basically selfish attempt at unity for a specific purpose, is of relatively little use to the worker in the capitalist state.

This sampling of comment is representative of Landauer's approach to the workers' problems, but he recognized that the absence of Geist is not detrimental to them alone. Capitalist industrial development has not been an unmixed blessing for the entrepreneur, either. His existence is bound to his capital, even though he does not have personal control over his capital. He becomes dependent upon his machines and is compelled to use them at their maximum efficiency even if his product is thereby manufactured at a rate greater than the market can absorb and still return him a profit. He must then reduce his prices to the point where his goods will be bought. A manufacturer may employ thousands of workers to make a product on which he is constantly losing money. To compensate nearly every industrialist must turn to stock speculation with its worries and its constant risk of financial ruin. The troubled entrepreneur who envies his workers symbolizes the fact that the capitalist system brings real joy to no one, only misery to all.

Modern society, however, continues to operate under these capitalist conditions. According to Landauer, they arise from three wrongs: possession of land, money as a means of exchange, and surplus value in the economy. The first has been a familiar objection since the time of Rousseau; but Landauer, unlike the French philosopher, stressed the economic rather than the moral wrong inherent in the possession of land: under the system of landownership the individual who does not possess land is refused the possibility of making an independent living.

The idea that money as a means of exchange is a social evil is related to, if not based upon, the fiscal theories of Silvio Gesell, a contemporaneous Swiss economist who asserted that although circulation of money is the key to a sound and fair economy, the very nature of money encourages hoarding, and so an unhealthy economy. The idea, as Landauer discussed it in the *Aufruf*, is that money acts not only as a means of exchange, but also as a commodity in itself, and as a commodity it has the unusual characteristic of not losing its value as it ages. Therefore, it can be withheld from use for as long as its possessor wishes and still be as good at the end of the period as it was before. Moreover, the value of money increases relative to other commodities, which depreciate with age or are consumed in use. The person with money has a commercial advantage since he may withhold his "commodity" until a favorable time, whereas others risk loss in the value of their goods with the passage of time. The person with money has, of course, the added advantage that his money may draw interest for as long as he chooses to hold it, a situation Landauer interpreted as parasitism. As a means for arresting the pernicious effect of money and the inevitable temptation to hoard it, Landauer advocated Gesell's proposal for a currency that would actually diminish in value with time.

Surplus value, the third of the three capitalist evils, is an economic concept based on the labor theory of value. The underlying hypothesis is that since the value of any commodity is determined by the amount of labor necessary to produce it, the price of any article should be just what it cost the manufacturer to have it made. In capitalist society, however, prices are determined by supply and demand, and the manufacturer usually sells his product for more than it cost him to have it produced. The difference between the true value and the price, or exchange value, is the surplus value and is the capitalist's profit on the article. To the worker this means that he cannot buy the article that he has been paid to produce, because his wages differ from the price of the article by the surplus value; essentially, the capitalist's profit bars the worker from the result of his labor. It is important to note that Landauer considered surplus value a feature inherent in the capitalist system, not something imposed upon it by capitalists. According to his analysis, surplus value is the difference between the price of a commodity and the worker's wages. One might consider either the wages too low or prices too high, but in any case what is significant is the disparity between them.

Landauer did not blame the wrongs of the capitalist system solely upon the moneyed class. He felt that any social system determines the actions of all who live within it and that the system is, in turn, perpetuated by the actions of all citizens. Workers play as great a role in the capitalist system as the capitalists, and the workers' suffering will end only if their complicity ends. "Emancipation is possible only for those who prepare themselves internally and externally to step outside capitalism, who stop playing a role and begin to be human beings" (p. 129). How far-reaching and revolutionary this statement was can be appreciated only when one remembers that in Landauer's theory state and capitalism are inseparable entities. Landauer was urging the acceptance not only of a different economic system, but of a totally new social organization. His alternative to capitalism was socialism, and socialism and the state remained for him irreconcilable enemies.

He knew what he wanted in place of the state. Periods when Geist has flourished, he wrote, are marked by a simple social structure and relatively primitive conditions. A return to an earlier situation that was culturally better is not possible, but a return of Geist could create a new situation that would satisfy our needs. It would have a social organization simpler than the modern one but would incorporate the results of science and technology to which we are heir. The return of active *Geist* as the determining factor of social organization would lead to a new *Wahn*, a new guiding principle for life, "the reality of social creation, leaving unimpaired the complete spiritual independence and diversity of individuals" (pp. 101–02).

Landauer's vision of the social structure necessary for the creation of this new reality was firmly in his mind long before the publication of the *Aufruf*. As early as 1900 he had expressed his belief that the goals of anarchism might be achieved by small groups living in anarchist settlements (*Siedlungen*).[7] This same idea is evident in the *Aufruf* when he defines the basic structure of the new society as "the union of communities with independent economic organization and mutual trade relationships" (p. 130). The size of the individual communities must be limited so that members can all be in close contact with each other. This will allow the warmth of the one natural social unit we now have, the family, to be expanded to encompass the entire community. *Geist* will be for the community the unifying power that love is within the family. These communities then will be tied together by economic factors to form the *Volk*, the economic community, the cultural unit, the social organization Landauer had described in 1906 in the "Thirty Socialist Theses."

The economic system Landauer visualized for the communities had three principal points. Within this system the individual would not work for money or for a market but for his own needs: "Reestablishment of the relationship between work and consumption: that is socialism" (p. 145). In this way the worker could obtain the true value of his work, for the evil effects of money as a means of exchange and the possibility of surplus value would be eliminated. Exchange of goods without the use of money is the second principle. This does not mean that individuals must necessarily exchange their products directly with other individuals. An organization will be set up for the purpose of expediting exchange, "like the Exchange Bank Proudhon described" (p. 139). The purpose of this will be a completely equitable system of exchange.

The third principle, fundamental to the others, is the use of mutual credit in place of capital. "Capital," in Landauer's view, is an artificial abstraction comprising two real values: land and human relationships. Land and human relationships are the basis for any economic system, whereas capital is nothing more than the "possibility to produce certain products in a specified period of time" (p. 138). In the capitalist system possession of money functions as capital. It represents the possibility of obtaining land and the products of the land (raw materials, tools) necessary for the manufacture of a product, and it allows the capitalist to withstand the period during which the product is being made without as yet providing a return on investment. In a moneyless society credit would take over these functions: credit and mutual trust would be the capital. Since everyone would be working for his own needs and since everyone would have the same needs, since no one would have special advantages, nor suffer from a disadvantageous trade agreement, necessary materials would be furnished by those in control of them so that a product could be manufactured. In return they would receive the finished product in amounts equal to the value of the goods they provided. The claim that workers in the capitalist system lack the capital to better their position is true, but not in the fiscal sense usually meant: "They lack the capital of capitals, the one capital that is reality, reality, although it is not a thing: they lack *Geist*" (p. 140). It is *Geist* that will unite people into the kind of economic community where mutual credit is possible; the mutual credit will be a clear manifestation of *Geist*. If this is to be brought about, however, arrangements for the other aspect of capital must be made. It is necessary to obtain land upon which this financial and social system can be established: " 'Land and *Geist'*—that is the watchword of socialism" (p. 140). *"The struggle of socialism is a struggle for land; the social question is an agrarian question"* (p. 142).

These views would at first glance seem to align Landauer with the so-called *Völkisch* Movement, a collective term for a number of sometimes quite influential organizations active in Germany from the late nineteenth century into the Nazi period. Their basic tenets were a rejection of modern industrialization and a belief that the true German spirit could thrive only in a nonurban context. But this superficial similarity with part of Landauer's social philosophy is the only point of tangency. The *Völkisch* Movement was thoroughly authoritarian in its structure, advocating a natural aristocracy of leaders to whom other members were expected to maintain unwavering loyalty. It was also strongly conservative in political orientation and a rallying point for anti-Semitism. Like Landauer, the theorists of this group wrote of *Volk, Nation,* and *Geist,* but in their understanding of these terms the individual lost all significance. The ultimate, tragic extreme of this line of thought was Nazism. There is no better evidence for Landauer's basic humanity than the difference between what he meant by *Volk* and what the Nazis meant by it.

There is quite obviously a tremendous difference as well between Landauer's socialism and Marxism, with its emphasis upon the industrial worker and materialism; and Landauer found it appropriate to include in the *Aufruf* an exhaustive confrontation with Marxist theory. His concept of *Geist* as the factor determining the nature of society contrasted most sharply with the scientifically framed economic determinism Marx had espoused. Equally incompatible were their attitudes toward history. Marx's scientific approach had tried to fit history into the evolutionary ideas prevalent at that time—Marx had considered dedicating *Das Kapital* to Darwin—by defining economics as the arena in which human beings fight the struggle for survival, the struggle that, as Darwinism asserted, underlies all life. Such a union of science and history was, as we have seen, unacceptable to Landauer, and he completely rejected the notion that a natural law capable of accurately predicting the future might be established on the basis of historical events: "Because for us human history does not consist of anonymous processes nor of many accumulated little happenings and omissions among the masses; for us the bearers of history are persons . . ." (p. 44). The future is not irrevocably determined by the past, because the will of individuals does not allow them to be controlled by the superficial occurrences of daily life. They act on the basis of their own being, which derives its character from a historical development unhindered by the "events" of history. The failure of the Marxists to recognize this, their emphasis on economic conditions as the exclusive driving force of human life, isolates them from true socialism. The only concept they have in common with the socialists, Landauer asserted, is the labor theory of value, but they cannot use this insight for the betterment of society, because they accept it as the prime factor of human life. Their materialistic interpretation of life and history stands in the way of the foundation of a new, better society. Marxism is "the plague of our time and the curse of the socialist movement!" (p. 5).

In *Paths in Utopia* (1950), Martin Buber suggested that part of Landauer's specific contribution to the theoretical development of socialism was "his direct insight into the nature of the State." [8] One might say that Landauer's rejection of Marxism was based largely on a difference of opinion regarding the nature of the state. This becomes clear in *Die Revolution*, where Landauer discusses the discovery of a national wealth as contrasted to the state wealth. Two divergent attitudes toward this discovery led respectively to the modern state political structure and to socialism. Another attitude was possible, however:

In addition there were also a few isolated individuals of a third direction, who stood to one side and, with a bitter smile on their lips and a spark of good joy and hope in their eyes, thought more than they said: the way to complete dissolution and obviation of the state leads through the absolute, democratic, economically based state.[9]

These, of course, were the Marxists. Consistent with the theoretical nature of the discussion in *Die Revolution*, Landauer sought to combat this third attitude with a broad, theoretical statement: "Since there has never been something positively absolute, however, they were most likely not quite correct; they only expressed the unspeakably slow movement in these our times." [10] In the *Aufruf*, Landauer turned to the details of Marxist philosophy.

The idea that socialism is an evolutionary development of capitalism is an error, Landauer believed, for two reasons. First, the combination of capitalism and state interests prevents the workers' condition from becoming as desperate as Marx had predicted, because the state, by its legislative processes, restricts or ameliorates the exploitative actions of the industrialists, thus providing a minimally satisfactory economic situation for the proletariat. Second, the continued growth and centralization of industry does not provide the workers with training in or understanding for the concept of communal work, as Marx had suggested it would. It is true that great numbers of workers must combine their efforts in the service of modern industry, but this is no more a striving for some beneficial, common goal than the work carried out by a group of slaves in a cotton field. These two consequences of the steady growth of industry—the collateral growth of misery for the workers and the experience of common work that industry provides the workers— are, Marx had maintained, the two roots of socialism in the capitalist system. But what they actually lead to, Landauer argued, is the constant increase in the power of the centralized state and a growing production for a world market that does not take into consideration the needs of the consumers, i.e., the workers. Instead of promoting *Geist* as the unifying force in human life, the Marxist cultivates ever-increasing industrial productivity. Marxism originated with the use of steam for power and the ensuing industrial centralization; steam fathered Marxism. "Old women prophesy from coffeegrounds. Karl Marx prophesied from steam" (p. 48).*

Landauer went on to say in the *Aufruf* that the history of the period from the publication of *Das Kapital* (1867) to the appearance of the *Aufruf* (1911) showed that Marx had been wrong in his predictions. He had overlooked the involvement of the workers themselves in capitalism. Everyone who lives within the system depends upon it. This situation cannot give rise to a socialist movement, but serves only to solidify the position of the centralized state and its industrialist patrons. This had been fully recognized even within the Marxist camp and had led to the revisionist movement, which no longer desired the establishment of socialism: **

---

* It is interesting to note that the historian Werner Sombart (1863–1941) criticized socialist theory (including Marxism) for its practice of predicting future situations on the assumption that production will always be increasing.[11] The similarity between this and part of Landauer's attack on Marxism is obvious. Ironically, Sombart quoted a section from the introduction to the second edition of the *Aufruf* (p. xii) as verification of this tendency on the part of the socialists. He took the quotation out of context: Landauer did not make a general statement of belief at this point. He was discussing the specific situation at the end of World War I, and the stress in this statement is not on the value of production itself, but on the part it can play in the reestablishment of *Geist* in society.

** The revisionists, led by Eduard Bernstein (1850–1932) insisted that socialism would evolve from capitalism and opposed the official revolutionary stance of the SPD. Though the party refused to accept revisionism as its doctrine, the "conservative" attitudes of the revisionists were predominant in it after 1906. (*See* Carl Schorske. *German Social Democracy, 1905–1917*, Cambridge, Mass., 1955.)

"The revisionists are skeptical epigones who see that the generalities drawn up [by Marx] are not consistent with the newly developed realities, but who no longer have the need for a new and completely different total understanding of our time" (pp. 110–11). Revisionism is not the answer, however, to the problems of the workers; for the capitalist system can never be adjusted to operate for their benefit, nor will the adherents of orthodox Marxism convince the workers that they should attempt to change the economic system in which they live and are so deeply mired.

According to Landauer, Marxists also fail to take into account the spiritual poverty of the proletariat. They define a proletarian as someone who, no matter what his financial status, does not own the means of production necessary for his livelihood; this makes a consideration of any spiritual aspects unnecessary and inappropriate. Landauer was equally clear about what he meant by proletarian: a person who lives the life of a proletarian, that is, a person whose life is devoid of culture. Money is not the only determining factor. Some individuals, especially professional men with minimal incomes, do not belong to the proletariat, because they possess a cultural awareness; and some workers, despite an income generally sufficient for a culturally oriented life, can still be counted among the lower class. Marxist doctrine claimed it was the proletariat that would transform society into a socialist system, but Landauer was convinced that the proletariat could do nothing because it lacked Geist: ". . . the proletarian is the born philistine . . ." (p. 53). Marxism flatters the working class by telling workers they are revolutionaries who will bring about a new order. But, Landauer asserted, they will not, for they remain attached to and dependent upon the capitalist system, and this situation will never allow the Geist necessary for revolution to infiltrate the masses. The longer the workers wait for the historical moment when the revolution will be initiated, the longer the time before Geist will be allowed to reassert itself in the life of the people; if they wait long enough, the people may become so spiritually weakened by the miseries of their present life that they will no longer be receptive to Geist: "We have said that socialism is not inevitable as the Marxists believe; now we say that if the people continue to hesitate, the moment may be reached when socialism can no longer come to *that* people" (p. 112). That is, if action for a renewal of society is not taken soon, Western civilization will be replaced by that of a healthy—i.e., a "rested"—people; if there are no healthy people to succeed us, mankind will end.

Landauer maintained that action could be taken immediately; there was no need to wait for the revolution: "Socialism is always possible whenever a sufficient number of people want it" (p. 61). Socialism would help the workers obtain the cultural condition necessary for a happy life, not by establishing a dictatorship of the proletariat, but, as Landauer often repeated, by eradicating the proletariat. Instead of the theoretical rigidity imposed upon the masses by Marxism, Landauer offered an opportunity for a vital life, a poetic freedom for constructive action:

. . . we are poets; and we want to eradicate the science-swindlers, the Marxists, the cold, hollow, spiritless men, so that poetic vision, artistically motivated creating, enthusiasm, and prophecy find the places where from now on they must work, create, build; in life, with human bodies, for communal life, work, and cooperation of groups, communities, peoples. . . .

. . . we poets want to create with life and want to see who the greater and stonger practitioner is . . . (p. 34).

This quotation is an example of the impassioned language that Landauer used to spread his gospel and to call the people to the better life he envisioned. The *Aufruf* had more substance, however, than just passion and theory. Included in the details of the poetic practicality he wished to achieve is Landauer's view that, although socialism would not evolve from capitalism, socialist concepts could aid the workers' plight within the capitalist system. He claimed that Marxists tended to resist ideas for improvement of the workers' situation, believing that such improvement would delay the coming of the socialist state; but Landauer insisted that as long as the capitalist system remains, the workers will have to strive, using such socialist devices as cooperatives and unions, toward a more adequate standard of life. Landauer had supported the establishment of consumer cooperatives for a long time; he mentioned them in *Von Zürich bis London* as one of the things the workers found attractive in the anarchist program. In the *Aufruf* he proposed organizations in which the workers would pool their resources to provide necessities at relatively low prices. In this way they would actually benefit from the higher wages gained for them by their unions.

The unions themselves are of great value to the workers, he held, and not only in the fight for higher pay. Shorter working hours, better working conditions, a system of emergency financial aid: unions are the workers' means to all these ends. And unions could also launch a campaign against the alcoholism prevailing among the workers. This would be especially important in a time when the workers have more free time because the unions' fight for shorter hours has been successful. Properly used, this time could be the vehicle by which the workers would be introduced to a new understanding of culture and a new feeling of solidarity with their fellows; both are not only good in themselves but necessary in the struggle for the establishment of true socialism.

The union's primary weapon, the strike, is also discussed in the *Aufruf*. Landauer urged the use of the general strike, but a general strike of a new kind. It should take the form of work, work for one's own benefit rather than for the capitalist market. The structure of the Socialist Bund was to make this possible. The first phase of the strike Landauer advocated would be organizational: people should band together in independent, autonomous groups, which later would serve as cadres for eventual settlements. Aside from gathering new members, the prime task of these groups was to procure land upon which the settlements would be established. Since it would be necessary at first to contend with the capitalist system, the land would have to be purchased, and the obvious means toward this end would be for the groups to act as cooperatives, pooling whatever resources they had. Outside resources might also be acquired from wealthy people sympathetic to the movement. After the land was obtained, the groups were to found the settlements, making and growing as many of the things they needed as possible, exchanging products within each group and among the groups by some scheme of barter. The workers would need help for this, because they have no knowledge of agricultural procedures. They would have to unite with farmers willing to join them in the cooperatives. The farmers had to be shown that this would not be, as they feared, a scheme to take their land away:

The farmers do not have too much land, but too little, and one should not take from them, but give. They, as everyone, must first of all be given the spirit of cooperation and community again; but it is not so buried in them as in the city workers (p. 149).

The settlements of the Bund were to be founded in association with rural villages where the age-old tradition of communal and community property and work is still a memory, if no longer an actuality. This memory is the last general manifestation of *Volk*, and those who are ready to revitalize the *Volk*, who feel the *Volk* within themselves, can lead all the rest of the population in that direction by providing them with this example:

That is the task: not to despair of the *Volk*, but not to wait for it. He who wishes to satisfy the *Volk* within him, he who unites with others like himself for the sake of this unborn bit of life and this urgent vision of the fantasy, to create in reality whatever can be realized of the so-cialist dream, he leaves the *Volk* to return to the *Volk* (p. 147).

An extremely important aspect of this proposal was Landauer's attitude toward ownership and property. In *Die Siedlung* (1910), he made clear that he did not reject the principle of ownership: "All culture has always been based on property, and there is no objection to property, whether it is community or private; *the objection is to having no property!*" [12] What is necessary, Landauer stressed, is a means by which society can prevent one individual or family from depriving others of property, and a system for assuring that everyone has an equal share. To achieve this, Landauer suggested a periodic redistribution of goods and, especially, of land among the members of a community. He returned to this problem in the *Aufruf* and, recalling the Hebrew tradition of the jubilee year, wrote:

Possession is something different from property, and I see in the future the fullest blossoming of private property, gild property, community property; property not just in regard to consumables or the simplest tools, but also in regard to ownership of the means of production, so superstitiously feared by some, of houses and of land. No final security arrangements for the thousand-year empire or for eternity are to be established here, but a great and encompassing accommodation and creation of the will to a periodic repetition of the accommodation (p. 136).

What Landauer was calling for here was not merely a new attitude toward society, but a new attitude toward life. A short, challenging paragraph from *Die Siedlung* states this very succinctly:

The piece of nature that belongs to all, land, can be reattained only when the piece of nature that we are ourselves becomes different; when a new spirit of agreement, of renewal of all conditions of life comes over us.[13]

In this society the individual would help sustain the self-sufficiency of his community and his own emotional vitality by working not at one but at all the various tasks his settlement required. Work in the fields would be rotated with work in the shops and small community factories. Running through and united with this life would be vigorous intellectual and artistic activity, led by those especially talented but relished by all. How significant a part this aspect was in Landauer's vision of his new society becomes clear in the early pages of the *Aufruf*, where he calls upon artists and thinkers to join in the movement and thus pay back the debt they owe their *Volk*:

It was individuals, inwardly mighty ones, representatives of the *Volk*, who gave birth to *Geist* in the *Volk*; now it lives in inspired individuals, who consume themselves in their might, who are without *Volk*: isolated thinkers, poets, and artists who without support, as if uprooted, seem to stand on air. . . . All the concentration, all the form that lives within them, powerfully painful, often stronger and larger than their body and soul can bear, the innumerable figures and the color and swarming and thronging of rhythm and harmony: all that—listen, you artists!—is stifled *Volk*, is living *Volk*, that has gathered within you, that is buried within you and will arise from within you (pp. 6–7).

As early as the "Thirty Socialist Theses," Landauer had defined the artist's service to society as religious: the creation of things that do not serve life but are life, things which represent the luxury necessary for a culturally satisfactory life. Through the years he had asserted repeatedly that in the capitalist system creative individuals were "wage slaves of the spirit." The Bund offered the intellectual and the artist an opportunity to reunite themselves with a culturally inspired society.

The attitude toward work that was to prevail in this new society was admirably suited to the needs of creative people. The advantage these individuals would share with all others was the right to determine for themselves the amount of time they wished to spend at work and the intensity of the effort they found desirable to put forth. The requirement of earning a living would, of course, still be upon them; but they would decide their own needs and the best way to satisfy them: some would work with great intensity so that the span of their free time would be increased. Others would derive as much satisfaction from the work as from other activities and be willing to labor at a leisurely pace. If the society were informed with *Geist*, there would be many in this latter category, for work was meant to be a pleasant part of life. After the *Aufruf*, Landauer wrote two articles on this subject, "Der Arbeitstag" ("The Workingday") for the May Day celebration of 1912 and "Arbeitselig" ("Joy in Work") in 1913. Both essays state that the capitalist system inspires hatred of work, because work is not considered by the workers to be part of themselves, but only a means of supporting themselves. Landauer insisted that all elements of life should be united in one satisfying whole:

Actually work and enjoyment, even work and sleep, are not such mutally contradictory things that they would have to exclude each other. They merge together and are separated only by degree. Work, sleep, and enjoyment are united in the concept of play. Work is the play of energies for the purpose of manufacture and distribution of goods. . . . Proper sleep is a purposeless continuation of the play of energies, an hours-long, gracious and light movement in dream. . . . [14]

In socialist society the creative individual, as well as everyone else, would be able to develop this kind of unity in his life.

But Landauer did not define in detail what the position of the artist within the new society would be. In the "Thirty Socialist Theses" he considered the question of whether the artist should concentrate only upon his own work or should also take part in the physical work of the community; the question was left unanswered there, and six years later he still would not answer it. Julius Bab wrote a letter to the *Sozialist* criticizing certain aspects of the *Aufruf*. Landauer responded with the essay "Antwort auf einen kritischen Brief" ("Answer to a Critical Letter," 1912), which is in part concerned with this problem. There Landauer asserted only that in a socialist society art would no longer be considered a commodity, but rather a luxury and a religion. Landauer could not foresee more because the *Geist* that would pervade the society would determine the artist's place, but the character of the *Geist* cannot be known until the society is established, so the duties of the artist within the society cannot be predicted.

Landauer might have gone on to say that the position of the artist would not be finally fixed even after the new society had been created, because the *Geist* would not always remain the same. Repeatedly he stressed that his vision was not a Utopian absolute; there would never be a finished, perfect socialist society. This is given as a first principle in "Sozialistisches Beginnen" ("Socialist Beginnings," 1909), which introduced the idea that socialism is not a goal but a way of acting. It concerns the affairs of and the relationships among men; as Landauer wrote in *Die Siedlung*, there is no final answer to the problem of human relationships:

Neither among men nor anywhere else in nature is there a finished structure, something perfect and self-contained. Only words, images, signs, and fantasies are perfect and finished. Reality is in the movement, and *real socialism is always just beginning, is always something moving.*[15]

Landauer was working to create something that was real and living, and experience had shown him that a rigid and unchanging society is inimical to true vitality. It becomes evident in the *Aufruf* that the revolution he was calling for was not the first step in a new way of life, but was, like socialism, the new way of life itself: institutions always become rigid and always require revolutionary revision.

Unless taken in the context of Landauer's total social philosophy, this idea appears to be a condemnation of everything that has become established or will become established and seems to support the charge of the sociologist Karl Mannheim that Landauer found no value in the "historical and institutional." [16] There is in Landauer's writings, however, ample evidence to show that he possessed a strong regard for tradition. A letter of 26 February 1916 to the writer Hans Blüher contains one example:

As little as I lose something of my humanity by demonstrating it, as little as the light of the spirit burns down when it shines, as little as in nature a species must disappear in order for a new species with other forms and conditions of life to develop, just so little must an old living force be "overcome" for the sake of a new one. Rather, the new one will have no pure existence if it does not stand in holy tradition.

A similar statement can be found in the "Thirty Socialist Theses," where tradition is discussed in terms of *Wahn:*

There is nothing more worthy of veneration than old *Wahn,* even when it is moribund or in the way; there is nothing more powerful than old *Wahn* that is still living and goes on from generation to generation; and there is always something ugly about new *Wahn* that is cheerless, encroachingly expansive, and uncertain, like young dogs and young grape vines.[17]

It is obvious, then, that Mannheim's characterization of Landauer's thought is inferior to Martin Buber's interpretation that Landauer "united the conservative and the revolutionary spirit. . . ."[18]

The *Aufruf* contains a long passage describing the tradition Landauer revered and meant to use in his new society. There he spoke of "the gentle reality of lasting beauty in the communal life of mankind" (p. 87). Tradition lends a beauty even to obsolescent things like the state and the military, a beauty that cannot be found in innovations, however inspired, for in these tradition is lacking. That which is to be created, therefore, should be something with roots in the past:

May our Bund be a union of striving life and the eternal powers that merge us with the world of being; may the idea that drives us—idea: that means Bund—unite us above the transitoriness and separation of superficial temporal events with the concentrated and firm elements representing *Geist.* Let this be our socialism: a creating of the future as if it were something that had existed through all eternity. May it come not from the stimulation and the wildly reacting vehemence of the moment but from the presence of *Geist,* which is the tradition and heritage of our humanity (pp. 87–88).

Buber penetrated to the essence of Landauer's thought about tradition in a sentence that serves both as summary and interpretation: "He who builds, not arbitrarily and fruitlessly, but legitimately and for the future, acts from inner kinship with age-old tradition, and this entrusts itself to him and gives him strength." [19]

It is hard to say what effect material of the kind Landauer presented in the *Aufruf* and the *Sozialist* might have had in a period when the *Geist* of his philosophy prevailed in society; but *Geist* did not prevail when he was writing, and the effect was as might have been predicted. Among anarchists there were, to be sure, a few who heard and were attracted to Landauer's call: by April 1911 there were twenty-one groups in the Bund, including one in Paris and another without territorial base but consisting of those who desired to found a settlement in the immediate future. Some of these groups had only a dozen members, but the four in Berlin amounted to well over one hundred people, and there were others outside the Bund who were interested in its progress. But there were difficulties, within the organization as well as from outside. By June 1909 the accusation came from Switzerland that the *Sozialist* was on too high an intellectual plane for the workers. Landauer admitted in letters from this period that he had not yet found the language to use in speaking to the common man,[20] but he gave himself unstintingly to the cause, and he demanded sacrifices from others as well. He answered this attack by saying that the workers must learn to think. He was equally unbending toward his colleagues and almost mercilessly rejected contributions from Margarete, Mühsam, and even Buber when he felt that the quality of their work was not satisfactory.

The establishment's recognition of the Bund followed traditional lines: the public press ignored it and governments brought proceedings of various kinds against it. Mühsam stood trial for "conspiracy" in 1910, a charge arising from his leadership in the Munich group of the Bund. Both Landauer and Margarete appeared as witnesses; Mühsam was acquitted, but a high police official told him in private that he would never stop persecuting the Bund. In Berlin an antiwar document was confiscated from the *Sozialist* printing office in 1911, released after two trials in which police spying was an important element, reconfiscated in 1912, and never officially released in its entirety.

There were other anarchist organizations, too, and antagonism among the various factions was rampant. One group, centering around the Leipzig journal *Der Anarchist*, generally gave friendly recognition to Landauer and the Bund; but accusations of intellectual isolationism and indifference to the true principles of anarchism came even from this source. In Berlin a man named Bernard Zack, who had written a few times in the first *Sozialist*, founded in 1911 the Vereinigung der individualistischen Anarchisten based primarily on the philosophy of Max Stirner and John Henry MacKay. The short-lived journal of this group was as much concerned with the dispute between Zack and Landauer over the meaning of the term *anarchism* as it was with the actual furtherance of the movement. Yet another group, the Anarchistische Föderation, was Marxist oriented, believed in the expropriation of property, and wanted nothing to do with the Bund other than to attempt an occasional disruption of the meetings it sponsored. Landauer's response to all this was not conciliatory, but he acknowledged that views other than his were possible and encouraged those who found them more attractive to follow them. This rift in the anarchist camp was certainly one of the most discouraging aspects of Landauer's life during these years. He recognized that unity was impossible, but he felt more and more that it was needed, needed to combat a specter that was haunting Europe—not the one Marx and Engels had written of in the *Communist Manifesto*, but the even more devastating specter of general war.

Since the end of the nineteenth century, there had been a peace movement in Europe, and although many respected individuals participated in it, it had little success. In the German Reich in particular it was considered at best unpatriotic to hold pacifist sentiments. During the period when Landauer had been trying to propagate the idea of a new society based on a new view of reality and de la Boëtie's concept of the tyrant's dependence on his subjects, Wilhelm II, Germany's greatest patriot, and his government had been edging the country toward war. Most Germans followed him; when the question of German nationalism versus an antiwar stance was put to the voters by Chancellor von Bülow in 1907, the

SPD, campaigning against proposed new taxes for armaments, received a stinging defeat. From then till the beginning of World War I, the party had constantly to adjust its tactics so as to avoid accusations of being unpatriotic. Its antiwar program was thereby weakened, while military posturing became ever more a part of German governmental policy.

Other countries responded in kind. National interests and colonial jealousies foiled all attempts to conclude international agreements aimed at halting, or at least slowing, these developments. Throughout the period from the beginning of the century to the war, Landauer spoke out from his position of relative isolation, trying actively to stem what proved to be inevitable. In the "Thirty Socialist Theses" he stressed that war is an instrument not of *Nationen* but of states, and he rejected it as he did all other elements that contributed to the power of traditional governments. The reinstituted *Sozialist* gave him an opportunity to carry on a consistent campaign against the bellicose actions of those governments.

The Austrian annexation of Bosnia and Herzegovina in 1908/09 prompted Landauer to write the essay "Der Krieg" ("The War") in April 1909. In this article he sounded the alarm that the troubles between Austria and Serbia over the annexation were not to be dismissed as a local affair and that a war in the Balkans would be of vital concern to every German. In light of events five years later this essay was remarkably prophetic.

The war did not come in 1909, but another crisis with serious international implications broke out two years later when the German government sent the gunboat *Panther* to Agadir, Morocco, ostensibly to "protect German interests." This was actually an attempt by Germany to disrupt French plans for taking control of that country. An earlier disagreement over the future of Morocco had led to an international conference in 1906; now all the perils inherent in that situation came to life again. In the essay "Marokko," Landauer warned the Germans that they must be aware of what was going on around them with—since they did not oppose it—their tacit consent. Once again war was averted. France retained control of Morocco, and Germany received some other French colonial territory in Africa as indemnity. But the tensions had been high and the danger great, and Landauer now moved to prevent a recurrence of such a danger.

In September 1911 the *Sozialist* published an article by Landauer entitled "An die deutschen Arbeiter" ("To German Workers"). It called attention to some successful strikes in England as an example of how workers could influence government. Noting that the unions and the SPD were too enmeshed in bureaucracy to lead the workers in this type of effort, this essay urged the workers to take the initiative and arrange for an international meeting at which plans for concerted action might be made. This article was reprinted as a pamphlet; its impact was reinforced by a public meeting on 19 September at which Landauer spoke to a gathering of between six and seven hundred people, outlining a way in which individuals might take action to prevent the state from involving them in war. This speech was the basis for the pamphlet "Die Abschaffung des Kriegs durch die Selbstbestimmung des Volks" ("The Abolition of War through the Self-determination of the People"). It called on the workers to strike against war preparations, an act meant to convince the government of the will of the people.* Such an undertaking would be successful even if international cooperation of workers had not been prearranged, for foreign workers would follow the lead of their German colleagues. It would be more effective, however, if an international workers' organization would be established first; this would assure concerted action in the antiwar program and would also lead to success in other matters of concern to workers. The final result would be "freedom in joint action." [21]

The unity of purpose already existing among the workers was the principal theme of "Vom freien Arbeitertag" ("A Free Workers' Convention"), published in the *Sozialist* on 1 October 1911. The essay cited as one example of this unity the prevailing antiwar attitude. It is the duty of the socialists, it urged, to convince all working people that there would be no war if workers would not allow it. Recognition of the power this unity would

* Though an international workers' strike against war had been debated in the congresses of the Second International since 1900, the German delegations (SPD) had consistently, and successfully, opposed it.

give them would make the workers ready to act jointly in other areas. A nonbureaucratic international workers' organization is necessary to determine common goals and to act to achieve them. As a first step workers should hold an international meeting (*Arbeitertag*), independent of the unions and socialist party organizations, to begin planning for the future. It would be a future with hope, for the possibilities inherent in the proposed international organization would go far beyond the basic purpose of preventing war:

Something of great significance will have happened, a decisive step on the way to true society, to true *Volk*, that is, to socialism, will be made when the workers create the form for some sort of independent action, the form for free alliance and lasting participation.[22]

The workers' meeting itself would point the way to socialism by its demonstration of unity and its call for a general strike against preparation for war. This would bring the workers into direct conflict with capitalism and so be the first step toward the rejection of the capitalist state and thus toward the establishment of socialism.

This rejection was an absolute necessity, Landauer felt, for the state could never function as anything but a war machine. He asserted this in a *Sozialist* article of December 1911 entitled "Rede von der Reichstagsgalerie" ("Speech from the Reichstag Gallery"), insisting that even the social democratic delegates, despite antiwar statements, were government functionaries rather than representatives of socialism and the workers. One of those delegates, August Bebel, head of the SPD, had made a speech in the Reichstag warning that war would lead to the downfall of bourgeois society. Such a downfall was, of course, just what Marxist philosophy called for as the prerequisite for the final realization of socialism. Bebel's opposition to war, therefore, was based on bourgeois rather than socialist values; in Landauer's eyes Bebel was not a socialist at all, only a parliamentarian. The true socialist knows, Landauer concluded this article, that the worker opposes war because he has nothing to gain from it and more to lose than even the bourgeoisie, for it is finally the worker who must support

war and suffer its consequences. Only the workers, by taking affairs
into their own hands, can oppose war and at the same time establish socialism.

A few people listened to him. Committees were established in
Berlin and Leipzig to plan the workers' meeting. A third committee in Cologne was set up later. One must suppose, however,
that the members of these groups were closely associated with the
Bund and that little of Landauer's message reached a broader
public. The police were interested, of course. The comedy of the
confiscated pamphlet began in December 1911, when a police spy
on the *Sozialist* staff stole some copies of "Die Abschaffung des
Kriegs" from the printing office. The police charged several members of the staff with distributing inflammatory material, but were
forced to admit that no distribution had taken place; they had
"received" their copies before any were shipped from the office.
Charges were dropped against the people, but the document itself
was tried and found guilty of being dangerous. This decision was
reversed on appeal. Distribution was started, and again the booklet was confiscated and the staff members charged. Again the
charges were dropped against individuals while the document was
found guilty. Again there was an appeal. What the final dis-
pensation was is no doubt buried deep in the records of the German federal courts; the message in the document was distributed
in the meantime in the pages of the *Sozialist* in Berlin and the
Anarchist in Leipzig. The police need not have bothered. The
workers' meeting was never held.

Landauer kept up his efforts. Antiwar articles continued to
appear in the *Sozialist* up to the outbreak of hostilities; he tried,
on the one hand, to expose the actions of the German government
that were precipitating war while, on the other hand, to convince
his readers that individuals are responsible for the acts of their
governments. Even the assassination of Archduke Franz Ferdinand
was used by Landauer as a symbol of the need for peace and a
demonstration of the fact that wars are fought between states, not
peoples, but that people are misled by states into believing in war.
Three essays of July 1914 were dedicated to this interpretation of
the events at Sarajevo: "Die Erschiessung des österreichischen
Thronfolgers" ("The Murder of the Austrian Crown Prince"),

"Ein Protest in Volksliedern" ("A Protest in Folksongs"), and "Veitstag" ("Saint Vitus's Day"). The latter two articles were tributes to the Serbian *Volk*, endangered in its freedom by the machinery of state politics.

Landauer marked the advent of war with a simple letter to his friend Ludwig Berndl, like a sigh of defeat: "There is nothing more to hope, and nothing to fear; it is here." [23]

6

The
War

1914–1918

WHILE nearly every German man of letters, even Rilke, rejoiced at the outbreak of war, Landauer continued as best he could to work for peace and the development of the Bund, two tasks representing a single goal. His attitude, however, showed the disappointment he felt that his earlier efforts had not had greater effect. He felt isolated again as he had before the founding of the Bund. Dehmel supported the German war effort. Kropotkin attacked it, not on the grounds that all war is evil, but because he felt Germany to be specifically at fault for the conflict. Even Mauthner expressed more concern for the fate of Germany than for the lot of mankind. To Landauer the war marked the total failure of the German *Geist*.

From the discouragement and the feeling of defeat Landauer experienced when the war began grew the determination to gain from the holocaust whatever good for mankind possible. A personal and moving demonstration of this is found in three letters to Hugo Warnstedt, the one-time editor of the Leipzig *Anarchist*, which had ceased publication in 1913. Warnstedt was in the army by October 1914, but he was plagued by his conscience and considered refusing to fight. On 24 October, Landauer wrote him that the war, once begun, had to be fought, and that people of Warnstedt's generation could gain valuable experience for the future by serving in it. In another letter of encouragement, written on 27 November, Landauer said that the time was not yet ripe to sacrifice oneself: the sacrifice would be for a hopeless cause. He stressed that the few Germans who sincerely supported socialism could not be replaced: ". . . since we are needed we must live in order to have an effect." In the third of these letters, 22 June 1915, Landauer explained the basis of his own will to carry on:

[Now because of the war] one can see quite certainly who and what sort of forces, especially in Germany, brought this dreadful misfortune upon mankind—there will be a reckoning, and people are looking for the place to begin building anew. Let us do our part to live if we are called upon, in great things or small, to be guides and helpers. A man does not live for happiness, but for the task he chooses. For the sake of that task everything, really everything, must be borne.

A public statement of these views was carried in the *Zeit-Echo* sometime during 1914 under the title "Aus unstillbarem Verlangen" ("From Unstillable Desire"). The original article was censored; and the full version, reprinted in the collection *Rechenschaft* (*Reckoning*, 1919), does not indicate what part or parts Landauer was forced to omit in the first publication. What he wanted to present in 1914, as the complete text shows, was his repudiation of the state and his desire to have social structure reorganized so that *Geist* would become the directing force in life. He pictured the war as the prelude to the hour

when this monster, the war of other people, falls clattering to the ground and, after a moment of magical transformation and rejuvenation, arises as my war for achievement and change.

. . .

. . . The time is now coming when we must make and build concretely, politically, economically what the poets have always swirled into images, what the prophets have always desired and displayed. The time is now when the reality shows itself to be impossible and when the impossible wants to become reality.[1]

Some means of carrying on his work remained available to him. The *Sozialist* was not forced to discontinue until April 1915, although its effect was reduced. Its audience grew smaller as young men interested in Landauer's ideas and the Bund went into the service. (The immediate cause for suspension of publication was that the printer, who had donated a tremendous amount of time to the paper, was drafted.) Also, military consorship was threatened after July 1914, so the paper had to be restricted to material acceptable to the authorities, mostly pieces with a social message from earlier periods of the German literary tradition. Yet Landauer continued his attempts to influence those people he could reach. If socialist activities had not been able to prevent war, then at least they could be used to help innocent victims of the conflict. In the article "Der europäische Krieg"("The European War," August 1914), he urged communities to establish shelters and soup kitchens for the homeless and hungry and to take common action to provide clothing for those who had lost their own. A letter of 6 February 1915 suggested growing food on lawns and street borders, a project requiring community effort. Such undertakings would not only ease the burden of the war upon its victims; they also would provide a school where many people could learn the benfits of common effort. Landauer never pointed out this second aspect, but only a military censor would have failed to see it.

Landauer's international contacts with other socialists provided a context in which more direct work toward peace and toward influencing the nature of the peace seemed possible, but nothing positive developed from these attempts. Shortly before the outbreak of war, Landauer had taken part in the efforts of some Dutch, Scandinavian, and German socialists, including Buber, to establish an international association bent on preventing hostilities. The French writer Romain Rolland was also invited to participate, but could not. When the war came, Landauer wished to keep the group together to promote the cause of peace. But differences of opinion and the national interests of some members made all strivings in this direction futile, and he withdrew from what little there was left of the organization in the summer of 1915. He tried for awhile to work with some of its members on a less formal basis and was in contact with the industrialist Walter Rathenau, hoping to enlist him in a concerted effort to reestablish peace. All these attempts failed, as did plans Buber was trying to develop for an Austro-German peace group. Landauer's desire to exert influence in neutral countries by having some of his writings published there also came to nothing. During the hostilities, as a token of their objection to the war, he and his family refrained from celebrating Christmas, a holiday which for them, although not a religious observance, was a joyous family festival. But Landauer's deep, sincere desire for peace and justice among men still could find no way to impress the world at large.

Despite the war, many of Landauer's activities continued more or less as usual. The Neue Freie Volksbühne, now united with the Freie Volksbühne, planned to carry on its work as long as conditions permitted; and Landauer, still a member of the artistic committee, was an active participant in the efforts to keep the theater alive. He still gave lectures on literary topics and worked at translations (e.g., Tagore's *King of the Dark Chamber*, 1915), though he felt his productive power to be at a low ebb. He wrote to his friend Berndl on 16 August 1915 that it was his "mission and hope" that kept him from despair, but he sometimes was hard pressed to find reason to hope.

There was one area, however, that seemed to promise a positive development in social understanding. From letters written by young men at the front and from various other indicators, Landauer concluded that the new generation showed a better, more realistic understanding of politics and social relationships than earlier ones had; that these young people, who were now bearing the brunt of the tragic situation to which the old state-capitalist social structure had led, were growing together into a solid group that could be the basis for a new society. One piece of evidence for this tendency was an institution set up in 1915 around the student Ernst Joël and the magazine *Aufbruch*, which he edited. According to Hans Blüher, the purpose of this group was to provide a meeting ground for students and workers. Most of the members were young people, but Landauer was not the only older man attracted to the meetings. Blüher, then twenty-seven, spoke there, though he was not concerned with the organization's program of educating workers;[2] and Kurt Hiller, a well-known literary figure, was interested in the undertaking.

Nothing of lasting importance for Landauer's work grew from his association with this group, but it led to one interesting contact. Hans Blüher had been an early and enthusiastic member of the Wandervogel movement, a youth organization initiated at the

beginning of the twentieth century by a young man named Karl
Fischer. Fischer's intention had been to train young German boys
away from the stifling traditions of the middle class and toward a
life of independence and freedom within the great traditions of
the German past. Blüher's experience with this organization led
him to adopt an elitist philosophy that held that the great ac-
complishments of the human race are due to a few great individuals and that the majority, inferior and envious, constantly
attempt to destroy the great ones: human life is a struggle for
power between the great and those who dream of being great.
Blüher also held that erotic elements play an important role in all
human activity and that the highest expression of the erotic is the
Männerbund, the alliance of men in friendship among themselves.

Blüher built a career around expounding these views. He was
a strong Prussian nationalist, a monarchist, an antifeminist and—
despite his denials—an anti-Semite. Landauer, on the other hand,
was an apolitical internationalist and an anarcho-socialist opposed
to Wilhelm II and all other monarchs. He believed the feminine
spirit to be essential for the rebirth of mankind; and he was a
Jew. His faith in his convictions and visions was unassailable, while
Blüher's own self-assurance, as expressed in the first edition of his
autobiography *Werke und Tage* (1920) smacks at times of advanced megalomania. It seems inconceivable that they could have
had any relationship other than one of deep mutual antagonism.
Yet Landauer followed the development of Blüher's career with
interest, and Blüher confessed in both versions of his autobiography that Landauer's personality left a definite mark upon him. In
the second version (1953) (completely rewritten—Blüher had
retracted the first version soon after its appearance) Blüher discussed his association with Landauer at length. From this discussion emerges a fact that neither man seems to have recognized:
their social philosophies, as different as they were, had one element
in common, one that set them together, apart from the main-
stream of social thought; for the foundation of both men's thinking was the individual, rather than institutions such as capitalism,
socialism, or state. The very different attitudes they held about the
nature of the individual accounts in large measure for the vast
differences in their conclusions, but this one point of tangency

may have been the thing that made an exchange of views possible. Blüher called their relationship "a good proof of the fact that things of the spirit, if only they are purely cultivated, are able to bridge even the most extreme antitheses." [3] It is a surprising tribute to Landauer's personality that Blüher, who insisted that all intellectual Jews are isolated from Eros and are, therefore, lacking in one of the most important elements of human life, should find such purity in Landauer.

Both Landauer and Blüher published articles in the *Aufbruch* during the short life of the journal; for Landauer it was a convenient outlet for his writing after the *Sozialist* ceased publication. In its first issue (1915) the *Aufbruch* published an essay entitled "Stelle Dich, Sozialist" ("To Your Post, Socialist"), in which Landauer presented a bare outline of his socialist program and a demand that a start be made toward its realization. He insisted that, though the conditions of the times were oppressive, they were not necessarily an impossible obstacle to such a beginning; socialism calls for the individual to rise above the times. Another issue contained most of "Von Sozialismus und der Siedlung" ("On Socialism and Socialist Settlement"), a revised version of the "Thirty Socialist Theses." Also in the pages of this journal appeared an article, in the form of a letter to a Swiss professor, in which Landauer attempted to counteract some of the nationalist propaganda current in Germany at the time. It bore the title "Zum Problem der Nation" ("On the Meaning of *Nation*").

By November 1915 the group that published the *Aufbruch* found itself in trouble with the authorities. Blüher had already broken off all contact with it after having decided that its actions had a touch of high treason. After four numbers the *Aufbruch* was forbidden, and Joël was expelled from the University of Berlin, ostensibly because he had been engaged in commercial activities as editor of *Aufbruch* but actually because of the radical policies the journal and its editor supported. Landauer was involved in a public protest in Joël's favor, and the proceedings developing from this protest indicate that Landauer's name was something to be reckoned with in the Berlin of 1915, for the university judge mentioned him (erroneously) as the "driving force" behind Joël. Joël enrolled in the University of Heidelberg even before his case in Berlin was settled; the organization he headed dissolved when he left Berlin.

About the same time, Landauer was considering another means of influencing young people. A poet named Rudolf Leonhard approached him with the idea of founding a school independent of the state and in competition with the University of Berlin. Landauer had long been interested in educational reform; a number of articles on that subject (not written by Landauer) had appeared in the *Sozialist*. Blüher, Joël, and others were also interested in this "Free Academy," and discussions went on, in person and by letter, concerning the proposed curriculum and, more significantly, the proposed student body and faculty. The various proponents of the plan were not entirely in agreement on these matters (e.g., Blüher did not wish to accept women students); and eventually the project had to be adandoned, though Buber later claimed that the failure was not due to disagreement among the involved parties, but to the war.[4]

For the war remained the great burden. At the end of 1915, Landauer contemplated a revival of the *Sozialist* but then, sure that the paper would be suppressed at once, gave up the idea. He took part in the beginnings of several movements with pacifist overtones, but none of them got beyond the first stages. The immediate political future seemed bleak: he could see within the government no effort to combat the war policy; and, with the isolated exceptions of the SPD leaders Eduard Bernstein and Karl Liebknecht, he felt that the official socialist party was as bad as the capitalist-backed groups. A government ban in March 1916 forbidding distribution of the *Aufruf* and other Landauer works within the state of Prussia increased his pessimism and sense of helplessness.

Since he was prevented from doing anything immediately effective within Germany, Landauer made one attempt to have a direct effect upon political thinking outside the country: he sent a letter to President Woodrow Wilson, one of the few political leaders for whom he ever expressed admiration. It was dated Christmas 1916 and bore the title "Friedensvertrag und Friedenseinrichtung" ("Peace Treaty and Peace Conditions").[5] In the name of permanent peace, Landauer urged Wilson to work for the establishment of a postwar international congress that would have binding control over armaments and the constitutional rights of individuals. Landauer was especially interested in the second point; for he felt that if these rights were secured, the citizens of every country might then be held personally responsible for the actions of their government. He also called for openness and truth between states and the employment in the service of peace of those good human qualities brought out by the war. Work must now begin toward real peace, Landauer said; and he pledged Germany's assistance in that work, offering assurance that the Germans would accept both their past guilt and their responsibility toward mankind that the great works of German artists symbolized. This letter was smuggled out of Germany approximately four weeks before Wilson's "Peace without Victory" speech of 22 January 1917, which anticipated the "'Fourteen Points" and included ideas very similar to those expressed in Landauer's letter. There is no evidence, however, that the letter ever reached Wilson; the incident serves only to illustrate the parallels between Landauer's thinking and that of individuals outside Germany who were seeking a practical formula for peace.

This letter is typical of Landauer's activities between 1916 and 1918 in that it is concerned not with the present but with the future. He could do no more about the war, but he could try to prepare mankind for the period after the war, and he set about doing that in the one way that remained open to him: through literature. He lectured and wrote a great deal during these two years; one might say they were the harvest of a lifetime's concern with literature. It is important to realize, however, that this was not a withdrawal from the problems of society into art. The hero of *Der Todesprediger* had temporarily turned away from a world that disgusted him and had given himself over to aesthetic satisfaction. Such an escape was impossible for Landauer, whose personality and intellect had become permeated with the idea that art is the expression of *Volk* in the individual artist and that it is the artist who keeps *Volk* alive during periods when *Geist* and *Volk* lose their hold on society. Landauer had once defined a cultured people as one whose art is of a social nature,[6] and he saw the isolation of art and the artist from contemporary society as an important sign that *Geist* was lacking. His most earnest desire was for a social explosion that would introduce the revival of *Geist;* to his mind literature was a part of that revolutionary explosion. As Buber put it,

Everything that Landauer thought and planned, said and wrote—
even when it had Shakespeare for subject or German mysticism, and
especially all designs whatsoever for the building of a socialistic reality
—was steeped in a great belief in revolution and the will for it.[7]

It is revolution alone, Landauer insisted, that would make it possible for *Geist* to reassert itself in society, and as wartime conditions forced him to concentrate ever more intensely upon literary activities, he wrote: "The consequence of poetry is revolution.
. . . "[8] In the 1892 essay "Die Zukunft und die Kunst" ("The Future and Art") he had suggested that the times were not suited to the production of true literature and that social action was more appropriate than artistic creation. By 1916, however, he had come to the position that artistic creation *is* social action.

Like so much else in Landauer's writings, this idea is founded primarily upon *Skepsis und Mystik.* The artist works on the basis of the reality his own being represents. This reality is as constant as the universal psyche of which it is a part. What separates the artist from the masses is his awareness of the universal as it is reflected in the transitory; his problem is to express the universal. In the artist's life, experience and memory have equal value and force: experience continues to affect him with its initial intensity as long as the memory of the experience remains. Because the artist is to an unusual degree aware of the universal, he is also aware that his memory is not only an accumulation of his own sense experience, but a manifestation of the universal as well. In the ability to combine sense experience with the awareness of self as a manifestation of the universe Landauer recognized the true artistic spirit.[9]

It must never be forgotten that the difference between the artist and the masses is one of awareness, not of essence; for the artist, like everyone else, is the product of his *Volk.* Every individual is as much a part of the universal psyche as any other, but most people are not conscious of the relationship. The artist has the power in his creative ability to awaken this consciousness in others. Art is a creative process whose effect is to call forth a creative response in the beholder.

In his *Shakespeare* (published posthumously in 1920), Landauer stated that the highest achievement of the artist is the expression through his works of his own inward personality.[10] He reasoned that since the creative influence of art is exerted through *Geist* and the artist is the repository of *Geist*, it is by means of his personality that *Geist* can be restored to the masses. The *Volk* can come to see its own reality in the reality of the artist, in the *Geist* that is his reality. The artist is often misunderstood by the masses, Landauer had written in 1907 in his essay on Walter Calé, because the masses do not understand themselves to be a *Volk*, and it is to the *Volk* that the personality of the artist speaks. This personality must not become disgusted with the masses and must always continue to speak. In his essay "Martin Buber" (1913), Landauer blamed creative people, the guardians of *Geist*, for the failure of the masses to respond: "We are not yet doing it well enough, we are not yet pure and strong enough, we ourselves, we have not yet spoken the conquering word that melts the mass and sets it in motion." [11] The search for this word, this word that will infuse the masses with *Geist*, was for Landauer the essence of literary endeavor, both original and critical.

It was in criticism that Landauer best demonstrated how his views of art, especially literature, applied to him personally. Though his own fiction received some favorable comment from associates, he eventually gave up his original belief that fiction was his most fruitful means of expression, and by 1910 was convinced that he was better able to present his ideas in other forms. Bab suggested a reason for this:

He was a prophet and not a poet, because he was not enraptured by the fantastic possibilities of life, because he compared: he compared this possible grandeur with the baseness, the great misery, the humiliation of existence, and he became enormously incensed over the difference, over the raggedness of life. For him the success of the most sublime artistic life became with pressing immediacy the most wrathful call to revolution.[12]

In a letter written 18 October 1912 to the poet Emanuel von Bodman, Landauer offered his own explanation:

Call to Revolution
The Mystical Anarchism of Gustav Landauer

I think I am something unusual and do not fit into any category. That comes from the fact that I am neither an agitator nor a poet, but a synthesis of both, which has no name. The poetic elements are there, to be sure, but there is something that does not want to be a poet. Do not misunderstand: I would like to be one, but "it" in me does not want to.

The part in him that was poetic, however, could not be stilled completely; from the year 1908, but especially after 1915, it expressed itself in an ever-increasing flow of literary criticism.

This was a compromise between the poetic and the nonpoetic in his nature, a compromise inimical to neither, because the same sociometaphysical philosophy was fundamental to both. For Landauer, the critic was not simply an intermediary between the artist and public; he felt that criticism itself was a creative activity. In 1902 he had taken Bab to task for failing to achieve a creative approach in an essay written that year about Dehmel. Criticism, according to Landauer, was only valuable "when [the critic's] personality forms something new from the given material." [13] Sixteen years later he gave a more complete statement of his philosophy of criticism in the introduction to a fragmentary essay about the dramatist Georg Kaiser, reprinted in *Der werdende Mensch* (*Emerging Mankind*):

Between him and me, between the poet and his critic, there is a difference only of degree. We want to let our essence, our unsaid and unsayable, stream into the hearer as into something equal and identical to what we are—but we must first allow the stream to break up on things and obstructions, to become words and images. And so I will speak, when I talk of Georg Kaiser, just as one must: through images coming to me from the outer world, through the picture that I make for myself of this poet, and thus I will, whether I want to or not, speak of him with my own being, speak with him of myself, of my fantasies, feelings and thoughts, my wishes and designs for our Volk, for our humanity, for our society, for the relationship between our inner and outer worlds (pp. 349-50).*

Just as the artist creates from his own reality, the critic must judge a work of art on the basis of the reality his own being represents, and he is, therefore, as much an interpreter of the universal psyche as is the artist himself.

* All page references here and throughout this chapter are to this collection.

Indicative of Landauer's conception of literature was his life-long respect for the medieval German mystics, especially Meister Eckhart, and the German romantics; he saw in the works of these writers a metaphysical understanding paralleling his own. He described mysticism as an attempt to get outside of life and watch the universe in the hope of discovering God (p. 9). He admired the attempt, but he did not think it could lead to the discovery of reality as the mystics desired. He felt that the creative process is the same, whether in the hands of man or God, and that man must, therefore, consider himself as a character in a divine work of art. God is known by this work, but man's attempt to find Him in the universe is as if Faust and Margarete were to try to discover Goethe by reading *Faust*. Only those who are capable of searching within themselves, above all the poets, can discover what God is, for they create the gods from within themselves and place them before mankind (p. 235).

Similar to the desires of the mystics were the longings of the German romantic writers. They, too, "sought to express the world spiritually" (p. 18); and they, too, often used the traditions of Christianity. Some of them wanted simply to revive Christianity; but the more significant effort was their attempt to employ Christian mythology symbolically, as a new key to reality. Only after they failed in their search did some of them accept the dogma of the church in place of the symbols of religion.[14] The realization of the new reality was not achieved by the work of the romantics, for mankind was not yet prepared for it. It is still not ready:

. . . we too may yearn for that which the romantics so wanted to establish: a science that would be a joy like a rhythmic art; a religion that would reveal the deepest essence of reality and still would not represent the complete conquest and constraint of the spirit, but would be suffused with playfulness (p. 89).

Though the romantics were not successful in establishing this science and this religion, they did point out how to do it. Romantic irony, which did occasionally allow characters to step from the confines of the work surrounding them, is, in a larger sense, what mankind still needs. It is only through such irony that humanity can extract itself from the mundane world and experience eternity (p. 9).

In modern literature Landauer looked to Tolstoi as the best example of the metaphysical understanding for which the romantics yearned. He called Tolstoi, Rousseau, and Strindberg "representatives of the time and exhorters against it" (p. 137). What distinguished Tolstoi from the others was that his reason was the reason of the prophet and the saint. All three were concerned with what is useful for mankind, but for Tolstoi the useful was the eternal, the things of the soul. Landauer cited the story *Kreuzer Sonata* as evidence of Tolstoi's conviction that God and the world exist in the individual, the same conviction that underlay the metaphysics of Eckhart and the romantics. They all strove to make this conviction a reality for mankind. To Tolstoi, the realization (*Verwirklichung*) of the world, of God, in the individual was what gave life meaning. It was the way to "the infinite, which is the only reality" (p. 208). Tolstoi advocated a life that rejected the senses, because they cannot lead to an understanding of the eternal. In place of reason based on the senses he proposed reason based on belief. He was "a genius of action, not in the things of the marketplace, but in the things of true life" (p. 201).

Tolstoi's efforts to bring about human understanding were, like Landauer's, unsuccessful. The great Russian did not live to experience the war and the defeat of his principles it represented, but Landauer, living that defeat every day, was intensely aware of it. In his deep sorrow over the failure of *Geist*, especially German *Geist*, he turned his attention to several writers whom he felt were the best representatives of German *Geist*. One of them, the dramatist Georg Kaiser, was a contemporary, but the other three spoke to Landauer from the past. Two of them were towering figures of the German literary tradition: Goethe and Friedrich Hölderlin.

A hint of the Goethe who emerges from Landauer's criticism is given in his writings on Tolstoi. There Landauer maintained that Goethe's great contribution to literature was his rejection of reason based entirely on the senses and sense data: Goethe offered feeling in place of dry rationality. Unlike the romantics, whom he resented because they refused to profit from his experience, Goethe did achieve a new vision of reality and thereafter strove to make this vision meaningful to all mankind. He insisted that mankind must find its salvation in this world and in itself, as was clear, for example, from his poems "Grenzen der Menschheit" ("Denn mit Göttern soll sich nicht messen irgend ein Mensch") and "Das Gottliche" ("Der edle Mensch sei hilfreich und gut"). Landauer quoted a prose passage from Goethe, too, in which the poet affirmed that mankind must be directed back to the earth, and in this affirmation Landauer saw a significant moral: "Such words of exhortation, which summarize Goethe's work, express simply and far-reachingly the realization [*Verwirklichung*] we owe him." [15]

Activism like Tolstoi's was present in Goethe's vision also, hidden beneath "der Weisheit letzter Schluss" that Faust comes to understand at the end of his life. The need for action in the struggle for reality was the insight that Goethe left mankind. Even his aesthetics was a call to action, as Landauer illustrated with material from the poet's *Campagne in Frankreich:* ". . . the beautiful is when we see the principles of life in their greatest activity and perfection, whereby we, incited to reproduction, feel ourselves equally alive and thrust into a state of most powerful activity" (p. 142).

Landauer insisted that the activity Goethe espoused was in part social and political. Most of the evidence for this he drew from miscellaneous statements of Goethe, recorded by visitors to his home, statements revealing that the poet wanted to create a lasting effect on mankind, but not in a literary sense. Several times Goethe expressed dissatisfaction because in Germany creative work led only to art and philosophy, not to improvement in human circumstances. In one such statement Goethe complained that German art and philosophy were removed from the natural springs (*Naturquellen*) that should nourish them. Landauer interpreted: "The natural springs are the lively drives and the active life, which, together with the *Volk* and its movements, create actualities of society from events of emotion and of thought" (p. 141). Because he found no following in Germany with which to act upon his sociopolitical desires, Goethe was forced to turn these desires into poetry.

Even in art Goethe saw the possibility of exerting an influence upon society. Among foreign literary people, especially Frenchmen, he found some who were socially aware, and there are several reports in the recorded conversations of his hopes to establish with these writers a supernational *Bund,* a union he called "Weltliteratur." Upon this organization, which was to give leading positions in society to intellectual leaders (*führende Geister*), rested Goethe's social hopes. The idea of this *Bund,* Landauer believed, was the inspiration of the never-completed poem "Die Geheimnisse," a fragment of which, entitled "Zueignung," is used as the dedication to Goethe's collected works ("Der Morgen kam; es scheuchten seine Tritte . . . "). Insights into the nature of the society Goethe wished to create can be gained from several of his works. *Wilhelm Meisters Wanderjahre* provides a complete outline of it, envisioning a social structure based on the adjuration in Meister's "Wanderlied": "May your efforts be in love/ and your life be the deed." * The society that emerges at the end of *Das Märchen* is an amplification of this precept. In this society, as Goethe himself said, "Love does not rule, but it builds, and that is more" (p. 152). It is more because in this process of building, of forming the fabric of human life, mankind follows the course nature prescribed for it and thereby lives in harmony with its own reality. Landauer presented a letter of Goethe, published under the title "Aufenthalt in Dornberg," to show the poet's conviction that the constancy of the world lies in the activity of successive generations, not in the efforts of individuals. Nature taught Goethe this lesson. Since he saw man as an integral part of nature, ethical behavior consisted for Goethe of acting as nature decrees, so that

the sublime statement of a wise man is realized that says: the reasonable world is to be considered a great, immortal individual that incessantly performs what is necessary and thereby elevates itself to mastery even over the caprice of fortune (p. 13).

To achieve this outlook, the individual must find the meaning of his life in his own part of this eternal process, in his own contributions to society. Landauer used Goethe's words to illustrate this: "The individual is not sufficient unto himself; society remains the first requirement of a true man" (pp. 149–50). Society is man's need; love is his way of fulfilling it.

* Und dein Streben, sei's in Liebe,
  Und dein Leben sei die Tat.

In the poem "Wiederfinden," Goethe spoke of love bridging the gap between being and God opened up by the primordial act of creation. This same idea occurs as a fundamental element in Hölderlin's poetry. Landauer asserted that Hölderlin, despite his own unhappiness, never lost faith in love and believed that even unrequited love was good, because love in any form represented for him the connection of the individual with the unending stream of humanity. In Hölderlin's poem "Menons Klagen um Diotima," the beloved, as Landauer believed, is not an individual, but love itself. Hölderlin found consolation for his personal failure in love by considering himself a part of a humanity, which, if it had a proper place for the artist and his creations, would reflect a divinely directed universe, sped on by *Geist* (p. 182). The poem "Die Liebe" demonstrates Hölderlin's urging to his contemporaries to create such a world.*

As a protoype of the society he wished to see established, Hölderlin pointed to the world of ancient Greece. "Der Archipelagus" gives an example of how love can be put to use as a social instrument. His poetry repeatedly bemoans the fact that such a society exists no longer; against the spiritless activity he saw around him he advocated nature, *Geist*, and *Volk* as an ideal unity. Yet, in contrast to some other poets of the time (e.g., Byron), but like many of the German romantics, Hölderlin did not allow his admiration for the ancients to blind him to the possibilities of the modern world. In this regard he was truly a national poet, for it was from the Germans that he expected a spiritual renaissance which would lead the world into a new era of peace, freedom, and beauty. Landauer specifically mentioned "Germanien" and "An die Deutschen" as poems exemplifying this. To these he might well have added "Gesang des Deutschen," in which Hölderlin referred to Germany as the new Greece.

As in Goethe's case, however, Hölderlin's ideals were forced to remain poetry; there was no *Volk* that could live by them in his time. His isolation from the masses led him to express the fate of

---

* Wachs' und werde zum Wald! eine beseeltere,
Voll entblühende Welt! Sprache der Liebenden
Sei die Sprache des Landes,
Ihre Seele der Laut des Volks!

inspired individuals, geniuses, in terms of nature and to show how much such individuals are, as he was himself, a part of nature. Landauer's discussion of "Der Rhein" is a convincing demonstration of this. The genius in this poem, the Rhine River, discovers himself—or, one might say, discovers his reality—in the existence chosen for him by nature, an existence in which love is a basis, but not a restraint. The poem unites nature, love, the genius, and society into a whole that symbolizes for Landauer the import of Hölderlin's entire poetic vision:

Love and peace, *Geist* and *Volk*, beauty and community: for him all that belonged together as a unit; and his beloved, his own ability to love, like the woman to whom he gave his love, were once again a unity and the symbol for the universal love that he felt to be something present in us, in itself unrestrained but disastrously suppressed, something natural, the power of being; this love should pervade the fine, free life of society and make an end of conflict and vulgar servility (p. 187).

With this summary Landauer provided both a specific image of Hölderlin and an illustration of his own critical method. There can be no doubt that the critic as much as the poet is present in this statement.

Landauer's comments on Hölderlin were first presented in the lecture "Friedrich Hölderlin in seinen Gedichten" ("Friedrich Hölderlin in His Poetry"), prepared during 1916 and published as a pamphlet the same year.[16] Most of his remarks about Goethe were made in the long essay *Ein Weg deutschen Geistes* (*A Path of the German Spirit*), written 1915/16, in which Landauer tried to show the responsibility German culture placed upon the Germans. For this purpose he chose to relate Georg Kaiser to Goethe and, in a short but sensitive discussion of the Austrian writer Adalbert Stifter, poet of the eternal, gentle flow of nature, to establish a continuum between them with Stifter as a spiritual link. It was Stifter's purpose, Landauer said, to show the process of education by which his characters learn to understand that flow and become part of it, thereby submitting to the unifying *Geist* requisite for a new, better humanity.

Georg Kaiser's work interested Landauer greatly. He called Kaiser the poet of the "new deed," and on 23 April 1918 he wrote in a letter, ". . . there is no greater, no more powerful, no purer dramatist living now than Georg Kaiser." He likened Kaiser to Shakespeare, and asserted in his Shakespeare essays that Kaiser's style was a further development of the form toward which Shakespeare had struggled but had only achieved in his last work, *The Tempest*. This style was the fulfillment of an aesthetic ideal: "that the drama [*Schauspiel*] ascends to a play of the intellect [*Denkspiel*], which knows the heaviness of earthly things only as a coarsely burlesque scherzo and which already understands heavenly melancholy." [17] The writer Hans Franck, reporting a conversation with Landauer from this period, wrote that Landauer expected Kaiser to create "the new ethos." [18]

In *Ein Weg deutschen Geistes*, Landauer discussed a perfect example of this: Kaiser's play *Die Bürger von Calais*. The "new deed" the play called for was a betrayal of the old order, of the conventional world. Whoever would perform it must dedicate himself unwaveringly to the central purpose of life, the unification of the self with the community, community not in a political but in a metaphysical sense: the community of the universe. The "new deed" is not political, it is a mythological—i.e., religious—fact. Kaiser's own list of people who had influenced him, quoted by Landauer in his "Fragment über Georg Kaiser" ("Fragment Concerning Georg Kaiser," 1918), shows how deeply metaphysical his inspirations were: he mentioned Schopenhauer, Dostoevski, Nietzsche, Hölderlin, and Plato (p. 355). From these sources of inspiration and his own personality he created a drama that proclaimed a new reality, the same reality for which Landauer constantly strove. As Landauer interpreted,

. . . true dedication to the works of this earth carries us beyond time and life and the things of this earth into the empire of secrets, where one is nothing and one is everything, where everything transitory has been only a metaphor, where we know why we—in our self-determination and freedom, which was not arbitrariness, but a link in the invisible chain of unity through *Geist*, a cresting and ebbing impulse in the rush of the universal spirit—why we have lived, and how we live on without end.[19]

So closely was Kaiser's drama related to Landauer's own philosophy that Landauer, in an essay in the journal *Masken* preliminary to the premier of Kaiser's *Gas* at the Düsseldorfer Schauspielhaus in 1918, offered nothing more than excerpts from his own *Aufruf zum Sozialismus.*

At that time Landauer was the editor of *Masken,* an organ of the Düsseldorfer Schauspielhaus. His appointment resulted from his association, going back to 1916, with the staff of the theater. He had been invited to speak in a lecture series the theater sponsored. The title of his first talk was "Goethe in seinem Verhältnis zu den Mächten der Zeit" ("Goethe in Relationship to the Forces of the Time"). He chose that theme because Goethe was an excellent cover for views that in any other context would have been forbidden by the censor.[20] The public response to this lecture was not overwhelming, but the members of the theater were very impressed and invited Landauer for a second speech. During 1917 his contact with these people grew closer; and by November of that year, the possibility of Landauer's joining the staff was being discussed. The prospect was appealing to him for several reasons. In May 1917 his personal circumstances had dictated that he move from Berlin to the home of Hedwig's deceased parents in Krumbach, Swabia. This meant that he was cut off from activities at the Volksbühne in Berlin. He would have preferred continuing his work with that organization but that was impossible, and so the offer of a salaried position in Düsseldorf was too attractive not to be seriously considered. Since Landauer believed strongly in the theater as one means to preach the important gospel of a new society to the people, he was eager to be in a position from which he could influence the policy of a stage.

The Düsseldorfer Schauspielhaus was no insignfiicant, provincial theater. Under the direction of Louise Dumont and Gustav Lindemann it had become one of the leading theaters in Germany, a theater operated according to principles thoroughly sympathetic with Landauer's own ideals. The directors considered the theater not a profession but a mission; and they demanded from their coworkers the ability and dedication that missionary endeavor requires. They contended that the dramatic poet's message reaches the people in a living dimension not available to the lyric or epic poet, and so remains a part of the people after other art forms have been rejected; of all art forms the theater is most representative of the people. Louise Dumont, whose creative works commanded Landauer's full respect, used in two of her speeches a quotation from Shakespeare that reflects this point of view, but in more universal terms: " '. . . the theater, whose purpose from the beginning was and is to show to the century and the body of the time the print of its character.' " [21] Kurt Loup, the chronicler of the Düsseldorfer Schauspielhaus, pointed out that because Louise Dumont believed this, she considered her work in the theater an opportunity and an obligation to effect beneficial changes in the ethical outlook of the public. This partly explains why she responded in kind to Landauer's admiration for her, since he was equally firm in his belief that the theater was a means to the reawakening of *Geist* in the German *Volk*. One suspects his influence in the speech Dumont gave on New Year's Day 1919, "Käme ein Wanderer," in which she called for a revitalization of what is essentially German by "service to *Geist*" ("*Dienst am Geist*"). Toward this end, she said, the artists of the theater must work in the true spirit of cooperation: "The much misused word 'socialism', understood in this way, in its deepest meaning of mutual help in a common work, would in this way be born to deed." [22]

During the first years of his association with the Düssedorf stage, Landauer indulged his interest in drama in another way as well. Beginning in 1916 he wrote a series of essays on August Strindberg and some of his works. These were meant to be chapters in a book on the Swedish playwright. The book was never completed; but the four essays—one on Strindberg as a poet, and one each on *Historical Miniatures*, *A Dream Play*, and *The Spook Sonata*—appeared separately in various publications and all four were later compiled in the collection *Der werdende Mensch* (1921). When he began to write about Strindberg, Landauer turned his attention first to later works, ignoring the naturalistic ones with which Strindberg had started his career. This is characteristic of Landauer because of his antagonism to naturalism as a literary movement. It was not the Strindberg of *The Father* or *Miss Julie* who captivated him, but the one who denied the causal relationship between events, whose work, because of the new form this denial created, was, Landauer thought, freed from the lies of the senses and so demonstrated a higher truth "than the sphere of logical understanding" (p. 286).

Despite their new form, Strindberg's later works, Landauer thought, explored the same problem that had concerned him in the earlier ones: the conflict between the spiritual and the sensual. This was not an abstract or remote matter for Strindberg; he lived this dichotomy and suffered from it. Eventually he came to see it as the fundamental principle of being. He was tortured by his knowledge that the spiritual was mired in the physical, a knowledge that led to a horror of life and a feeling that life was meaningless. Yet in his later works these feelings were combined with a hope for salvation, a hope that a new and valid reality might somehow be within reach of mankind. In contrast to Ibsen, who was concerned with the individual, Strindberg's interest was in "'the path of mankind and the meaning of history" (p. 274). He did not attempt to create a new reality, but to expose the reality behind the superficial aspects of life.

To achieve this exposure, Strindberg frequently used a dreamlike atmosphere, "a dematerialization of the natural world" (p. 288). The dream, however, is not an indiscriminate collection of symbols. The experiences of the characters on the stage remind the audience, not rationally, but emotionally, of life as they know it. As they see the certainties of this life dissolve before their eyes, they are led to a new awareness of reality; the viewer recognizes that he is like a figure in a dream that is dreamed by some power greater than himself. Conflict between the spiritual and the sensual always characterizes that reality and makes it horrible. Strindberg, as Landauer puts it, was a Christian of the Old Testament. In his work the New Testament exists only as a feeble hope "for those who have conquered" (p. 336).

One must not overlook the hope, however tenuous, in Strindberg's writings. He did seem to find some unity between mankind and the transcendent: "His consolation was . . . that he perceived a correlation between the stark logic of thought and the logic of events, just as there is behind all dissension an unfathomable but sometimes brightly shining unity" (p. 261). When Strindberg wrote in his story "Richtfest" ("The House-Raising Party"), "The first and last illusion of a man is to seek salvation through woman; why, no one knows" (p. 293), it was probably, Landauer conjectured, a statement of desperation, for Strindberg always connected the feminine with the physical in contrast to masculine spirituality. In the *Historical Miniatures*, however, Strindberg had Voltaire wonder if vulgarity is not necessary for humanity, and in *A Dream Play* he depicted a poet who derives his poetic energy from mud. The *Historical Miniatures* even allows woman a function in the salvation of mankind: in a discussion of Aspasia, the companion of Pericles, the conclusion is reached that woman is bad only in her sexuality. As midwife to the thoughts of men, she can play a valuable role. It is in the *Historical Miniatures*, too, that Landauer finds the best formulation of Strindberg's answer to the problem of meaning in life, expressed in the story by Pope Gregory the Great (540?–604) : "That is how the world is, that is how life is; but if it is like that, and if you see it is like that, there remains only— to live it, and to consider the living of it a matter of honor, until death comes and frees us" (p. 276).

Nevertheless, even the loveless Strindberg offered something more attractive than the cold duty here urged upon mankind. The Hyacinth Girl of *The Spook Sonata* and Indra's daughter in *A Dream Play* both are capable of love, though the love is destroyed by the meanness around them. And Strindberg seems to have had some idea that love could provide value to the life that the human being is honor-bound to lead. A glimpse of this is caught in the coal carriers' scene in *A Dream Play*; but a more specific statement, very much in line with Landauer's social philosophy, occurs at the end of the *Historical Miniatures*. After the French Revolution, when Napoleon has become leader of France, an aristocrat and his old servant discuss the revolution, and the servant, the voice of mankind fighting its way upward through history (as Landauer saw it), reveals what for him was the greatest event of the revolution: "the united labor of all people and classes for the festival of brotherhood on the Field of Mars" (p. 283).

Landauer was strongly impressed by the contrast between Strindberg and Hölderlin. Both were isolated geniuses, but Strindberg lacked the love which sustained Hölderlin. In the same category as the Swedish playwright Landauer placed Friedrich Nietzsche.

Call to Revolution
The Mystical Anarchism of Gustav Landauer

Nietzsche represented the antithesis of Hölderlin in approach to the basic problem that concerned them both, the position of the spiritual individual in a nonspiritual time. Whereas Nietzsche seems ever to be struggling upward toward the spiritual, Hölderlin appears to be a part of nature, not in titanic conflict but in harmony with the forces around him: a soft, descending movement like flowing water characterizes both him and his work. The Olympian height from which Nietzsche looked upon the world, on the other hand, was achieved through struggle; and Landauer was not convinced that the heights Nietzsche reached were really as sublime as the author of *Also sprach Zarathustra* believed them to be:

He who looks down, not like the sinking sun, but upon low places, like one who knows them well, all too well, with arrogance, disdain, irritation: he must just have made his way up. If Nietzsche considers himself in his loftiness to be a god, he always strikes one as a *dieu parvenu* (p. 155).

Landauer thought that Nietzsche's desire was to explain the spiritual in terms of experience, that he attempted to define *Geist* and the problems associated with it as a social phenomenon based on "Ethos" and "Ethnos." This was, of course, unacceptable to Landauer, who did associate *Geist* with society, but only as a force that transcends the society and that can inspire it from outside, not as a product of it. He felt that Nietzsche lacked the poetic insight necessary to fathom the nature of the problem he faced: "And so the attempt of Nietzsche, whose spirit had too little profundity, whose intellect was too bright, must in the end be called not powerful, but violent. . . ." [23]

Much of what Landauer wrote about Nietzsche appeared in the Hölderlin lecture, and it is indicative of Landauer's rich and many-sided personality that he could devote himself simultaneously to a consideration of these two so different intellects. An even better example is to be seen in the fact that while Landauer was writing his Strindberg essays, he was also translating excerpts from a poet who might well be thought the one most unlike Strindberg in attitude, Walt Whitman. These translations from *Leaves of Grass*, published along with Landauer's Whitman essay from 1907 under the title *Gesänge und Inschriften (Songs and Inscriptions*, 1921), were prompted by Landauer's long admiration for the American poet, who seemed to speak the same language as this German anarchist. Throughout the war years Landauer was also deeply involved with the works of another poet with whom he felt intimately related: William Shakespeare. From a series of lectures given during 1916 grew two large volumes eventually published under the title *Shakespeare, dargestellt in Vorträgen (Lectures on Shakespeare)*.

Julius Bab illustrated the similarity in the personalities of Shakespeare and Landauer, a similarity symbolized by the words of Miranda in *The Tempest*, "How beauteous mankind is!": "This deep faith in humanity, this deep astonishment, like Miranda's, over the unimaginable divine possibilities of the human soul, this united Landauer with Shakespeare. . . ." [24] A letter to his friend Ludwig Berndl, written 16 January 1918, offers a glimpse of Landauer's own attitude toward his work on Shakespeare:

You are quite right that the book is also concerned with me and my deepest self; but one comes to me in it only by way of Shakespeare, whom I believe to know in intimate friendship as no one else has known him. I do not say that arrogantly; I would not allow myself the right to write about him if I did not feel this urgency.

The specific details of his approach to Shakespeare are outlined in a letter of 13 June 1917 to Adolf Neumann, a member of the publishing firm to which Landauer offered the Shakespeare book. Landauer stated that his intention was to reveal Shakespeare's personality through his dramas and sonnets; his study of these had brought him to a unique position:

I believe that the decisively new thing in my work is freedom. Certainly not in a political sense, directed toward conditions; nothing was further from Shakespeare; freedom rather in the human, the private sphere, especially in the relationship that is Shakespeare's perpetual problem, between drive [*Trieb*] and spirit [*Geist*]. Freedom from formulas, from conventions, both theoretical and moral.

Shakespeare was not meant to be a philological study. As in all his work Landauer was concerned here with the problem of reality. The answer he sought in Shakespeare was to the question of the meaning and the task of life. It was the present, the life of the present that concerned Landauer, and he wanted to make Shakespeare speak to the present and reveal the realities of that life. It is in this light that Landauer's *Shakespeare* must be understood.

In the process of presenting Shakespeare from his own point of view, Landauer rejected most of the work done by professional philologists. They reject him as well, and quite naturally, for they insist on treating *Shakespeare* as literary interpretation and ignore Landauer's philosophical intentions. The Whitman translation suffered the same fate. A review of *Gesänge und Inschriften* in the *Beiblatt zur Anglia* for November 1922 goes into great detail about the translation errors (and there are many) that Landauer made; the reviewer, Gustav Noll, gives a word of admiration only for the introductory essay. Dedication to philologic detail blinded Noll to the realization that, despite the inaccuracies, the translations catch the spirit of Whitman's verse and are beautiful and powerful. Noll had no eye, either, for the message Landauer found in the poems and wanted to pass on to the masses, not as a source of literary pleasure, but as an insight into reality.

A certain M. J. W. (not further identified), in the *Literarisches Zentralblatt für Deutschland* (12 March 1921), offered the same kind of criticism of the Shakespeare book. He praised, somewhat sarcastically, Landauer's enthusiasm for Shakespeare, but primarily wanted to warn the public that the book was philologically unreliable and to take Landauer to task for writing disparagingly at one point about Schiller. In a review for the *Deutsche Vierteljahrschrift für Literaturwissenschaft und Geistesgeschichte* (1928), the noted German Shakespeare scholar Levin L. Schücking provided a classic example of how Landauer's book was often misunderstood. He begins by commenting that the book had found a large audience in Germany and that the author was to be respected: "Indeed, one meets here a deep, sincere personality with rich feelings and a strong imagination. There is no lack either of the capacity for independent observation, for ingenious weaving of new relationships." [25] Then follows a sentence that serves as transition from Landauer's book to the world of philology: "But is that enough for his task?" Schücking complains that Landauer did not understand Shakespeare in the context of Elizabethan times, which is precisely what Landauer, as the introduction to the book makes clear, did not want to do. Schücking reveals himself the victim of his own "scientific" proclivities when he justifies his rejection of the *Hamlet* essay: "For an explanation of so complicated a figure as especially Hamlet, one really cannot hope to succeed with nothing more than healthy human understanding and a volume of the text." [26] Here there is a hint of why Landauer generally rejected the findings of professional philologists. He once wrote about *Hamlet*, "there is nothing to explain, it is all totally clear, necessary, natural, self-evident." [27] A work of literature made an intuitive impression on him. He admitted in this same letter that he was never immediately aware of the basis for the impression and added, "I feel very clearly how my understanding later seeks reasons." Schücking did not tell what he thought *is* necessary for an explanation of Hamlet's personality, but one suspects that he felt Shakespeare had written exclusively for Shakespearean scholars.

In any event, Schücking could approach Shakespeare only as a Shakespearean scholar and could not make his outlook flexible enough to appreciate Landauer's concepts. He strongly asserted that Shakespeare could not be understood politically and that Landauer was wrong even to attempt it. But Landauer did not attempt it, as, once again, the introduction to *Shakespeare* plainly shows. He did, indeed, speak of Shakespeare as foreshadowing a new society, but in his usage this is a metaphysical, not a political, term. It may be that Landauer did not make this clear enough within the Shakespeare book itself, but however explicit he might have been, his point would not have been understood unless the reader had been able to view the entire book from Landauer's standpoint.

Some people were able to. In 1921 the *Zeitschrift für Deutschkunde* published a review of the Shakespeare book that offered an interesting contrast to Schücking's opinions, and did, in fact, compare Landauer's book with one by Schücking. The reviewer, Julius Stern, identified as "professor in Baden-Baden," was a regular contributor to this journal and called upon this fact to introduce his discussion of Landauer's work:

If I was able in my reports of last year to call Schücking's book the most important contribution to the solution of character problems in

Shakespeare, I can now report on a much more outstanding achievement in the field of Shakespearean exegesis. It is the two-volume work by Gustav Landauer.[28]

Stern, who was probably not specifically a Shakespearean scholar, even finds Landauer's philological discussions interesting and valuable, and states that the book makes entire libraries of Shakespearean studies superfluous. The most significant aspect of the review, however, is that it showed its author understood the book the way Landauer meant it to be understood: "What gives [the book] its special quality is the deeply and purely human, and therefore in the noblest sense unlimited, nature of the entire conception." Stern's willingness to accept Landauer's criterion for the book led him to an appreciation of it that went far beyond the normal terms of literary criticism: "In sum: a work that, because of its subject, its sheer humanity, its lively form and purity of style, belongs among the highest achievements of the culture of our time." [29]

There were many other favorable reviews, but the one that would perhaps have pleased Landauer most was by the author Stephan Zweig in the *Frankfurter Zeitung* of 19 July 1921. On first reading, Zweig, who never knew Landauer personally, found more of interest in the book than he could underline and make notes on; the impression was overwhelming, and he felt the book to be a masterpiece. And, as Landauer had wanted, Zweig discovered within the book the personality of the author, a personality for which he felt the highest admiration:

In these lectures I can imagine the speaker in a university as a leader of youth and at the same time as a leader into the essence of life, the speaker for whom philology on the one hand and fine language on the other are only points of transit to a philosophical eloquence as in classical antiquity. . . .

These words, written after the war and after Landauer's death, seem an echo of the hope Landauer expressed in 1917 that *Shakespeare* would have a definite effect upon criticism, the theater, and the schools.

In the last paragraph of *Shakespeare*, Landauer admitted that his approach to the subject was a personal one and that his own times had colored his view of the great Elizabethan poet. He accepted this as justified, for he had shown throughout the book that the problems of Shakespeare, who stood between the individualism of the Renaissance and the unifying influence of Christianity, were the same problems that faced the world in the second decade of the twentieth century. The same question of freedom, not transcendental freedom but freedom in this life, plagued both periods. Shakespeare's personality represented freedom, but his works showed that mankind did not have it:

Shakespeare showed the constraint and the captivity the more clearly because he showed his own freedom; because through him we shudderingly perceive that we are our own turnkeys, our own slaves, our own murderers, and because we see through him the complete clockwork of the inner mechanism with which we make our hearts our own torture chamber (I, 240–41).*

To demonstrate this, Shakespeare created creative individuals (*formende Menschen*), people who are not products of their environment but who must nonetheless react to it, to "this terrible world of wrath, wickedness, lust, and greed" (II, 123). They are not the pawns of outside influences; their positions in the world and their personal fates are determined largely by the extent of their submission to drives (*Triebe*) within themselves. The tragedies are concerned with individuals in whom the senses and their associated drives become the central force in life. Those who achieve freedom from their personal drives survive in spite of a hostile world. This is the wisdom of Shakespeare, a wisdom as applicable in Landauer's day as in the poet's own: "The ascending path from drive to spirit [*Geist*], Shakespeare's difficult and dangerous path, is also the way from war to peace, from death to life—I believe it, no matter how long and tortuous this path may be" (II, 394).

In Landauer's Shakespearean criticism love is seen as the opposite of the drives, and the balance between them represents the conflict between good and evil. The love called for is love in all its aspects, including the sensual—it is this total love that gave Romeo and Juliet the "divine force of humanity that we call freedom" (I, 3). But the love often succumbs to various drives, and the result is tragedy. In *Troilus and Cressida*, Shakespeare showed

---

* All references here and below through p. 163 are to *Shakespeare*.

the beneficial nature of friendship, a manifestation of love, and demonstrated how it could be extinguished by the destructive effects of sex as drive, destructive not only to persons but to entire societies. In *Antony and Cleopatra* the question of love is central, but is complicated by many other factors arising from the personalities of the protagonists. The sonnets, too, present a picture of the struggle among love, friendship, and sensuality. In *Othello* one sees the tragedy of a man whose life is so controlled, so dominated by reason, that he cannot trust love, cannot allow it to approach him. The passion that is released in him, untempered by love, is as destructive as raw sexual passion. In all of these works it is not passion nor reason but the proper relationship of the two, the whole individual, that is Shakespeare's concern.

To this problem *King Lear* adds another, related one: the power drive. Lear's demand for outward appearance in love and insistence upon personal power in life alienate him from the love and life he desires:

It is a profound insight of Shakespeare . . . that he bases the power drive upon a delusion that bears the other name "lust." As far as selfish lust is removed from eternal love, just this far does the greed for power deviate from ordered understanding among men . . . (II, 115).

Lear's insanity is only a reflection of his earlier life. He possesses enough personal strength to recognize and overcome the forces that have been driving him and turns from the political expediency of Goneril and Regan to the true love Cordelia represents. Thereby he is cured of his insanity. His death, in contrast to that of Macbeth, who suffered from the same drive, is preceded by his personal liberation from the destructive forces within him. Macbeth, urged on by Lady Macbeth, remains to the end the victim of the drive for power. For him it grows more and more to be the central force in life, until in the end his submission to it becomes a duty. Macbeth is overcome eventually by individuals (Malcolm, Macduff, Siward) who have developed a constructive harmony between spirit and flesh. This is especially obvious in Macduff, who, by generalizing his personal grief and putting it at the disposal of his people, becomes a hero in Shakespeare's war against the destructive drives within the individual.

Measure for Measure calls on sex and the power drive to demonstrate the hypocrisy that often confines mankind:

Measure for Measure shows us power and the misuse of power; the relationship of the true individual to the role he plays in office; the grand juridical pose; shows us the man who lives in an idealistic framework of words that collapses as soon as the storm of drives arises . . . (II, 4).

In this case, however, another matter of great concern to Shakespeare is added to the plot: the proper organization of society. The play condemns the present organization by showing how the state wrongly attempts to regulate the personal affairs of individuals as if it were something more than a sum of individuals, a superhuman structure with a superhuman knowledge of an absolute right. Landauer's interpretation of this play bears the influence of Mauthner's theory of language and his own conviction that the artist is always in search of his *Volk*. He felt that Shakespeare had demonstrated in several works besides *Measure for Measure* his inability to find *Volk* in the political society that surrounded him. *The Tempest*, for example, is an extremely personal statement of the isolation Shakespeare felt under the prevailing social conditions, and in Landauer's eyes this isolation is also the basic factor in the tragedy of Hamlet.

Hamlet is a philosopher, suited to a world other than the one in which he lives, but forced by circumstances to act in a world he mistrusts and disparages. The drive that bedevils him is thinking. When he thinks, he is unable to act, because his thoughts correspond not to the world around him, but to a better one, which he creates in his thoughts:

Hamlet is humanity. . . . His inability, when he thinks, to do the usual, the force of his criticism, and his spontaneous deed show us the place where we stand, not as a resting place, but as something that has become and is becoming; we see where he came from and where he is going, and we with him (I, 254–55).

The world refuses him an opportunity to be effective in the organization of society; his desires go counter to the accepted standards of society, for he craves a republican reorganization. This is the necessary outcome of his thinking, because he, like the artist, dwells in the "realm of *Geist*," and *Geist* longs for a human situation, a republic, not political but social, in which it can assert itself. The murder of Claudius is symbolic of the struggle the entire drama represents: "the fight of the intellectual against the world that wants to crush and suppress him" (I, 215).

This highly unusual interpretation brings Hamlet close to the figure of Brutus. Brutus, too, is primarily a philosopher, and his life is bound to the world of his philosophy rather than the world around him. The spirit of republican Rome still lives within him; he is unable to see that it no longer exists beyond himself. Cassius can interest him in politics because both men possess a strong desire for freedom, a freedom that is "not always far from jealousy" (I, 158). Because the Roman *Volk*, which they believe they represent, no longer exists, their actions lead to a freedom valid only for the privileged. The spirit of their undertaking is republican; its results are tyranny. *King John* presents another side of this problem, "the eternal struggle between politics and humanity" (I, 114). In *Coriolanus*, too, one sees the great individual breaking upon the reef of state. All these plays involve individuals who lose their personal freedom to some internal drive, usually, though not always, a thirst for power. Robbed of freedom, they become the victims of the world around them.

Yet, Shakespeare did not believe that the victory of the destructive drives within the individual is inevitable. *The Tempest* shows individuals who have overcome such drives: "Shakespeare, having become mild and mature, sought a means of expressing the resignation and renunciation in superiority and serenity, and when he had found it, he wrote no more" (II, 287). But it is not only in this last play that the possibility of achieving personal freedom is demonstrated. As early as *Romeo and Juliet* tragedy is transcended, when the two families, stunned by their personal grief, finally unite and so escape the hate that has driven them. *The Merchant of Venice* portrays a range of people from Shylock—an all but hopeless victim of his own lusts—to Portia, priestess in the kingdom of the spirit. A mood of loftiness and triumph unites the entire drama, affecting all the characters and even promising that Shylock—whom Landauer considered a representative of an oppressed people and, therefore, not responsible for his condition—could, under other social circumstances, escape from the tyranny of his drives. *Measure for Measure* does not end tragically because the duke tries to reform society by love rather than preserve it by terror.

In the last plays, *Cymbeline, The Winter's Tale,* and *The Tempest,* Shakespeare began in earnest the task the German romanticists later tried to undertake: "to transform the attitude of man toward the individual life" (II, 241). The new technique Shakespeare used in these dramas itself symbolized the hope he cherished that destructive drives within the individual and society might eventually be overcome. His new idea was ". . . to have the tragedy reach its peak and its conquest, not in the traditional violent death of the ancient classics, but in the renewal and enhancement of life" (II, 240–41). Landauer saw both *Cymbeline* and *The Winter's Tale* as experiments with this new style, which culminate in the ending of *The Winter's Tale,* where a new generation, free from the conventions and the force of destructive drives, is announced. Polixenes and Perdita have found in their love for each other the proper relationship of the physical and the spiritual and are, therefore, safe from the jealousies that for so many years had devastated the lives of their parents. They are free individuals, natural and noble in their freedom (II, 268). The most perfect example of this freedom and this nobility is, of course, Prospero, who has become a master of the world because he has achieved a true understanding of and compromise with it: "In his Prospero, Shakespeare de-Christianized mankind and formed a free man, who in purity, in nobility, in beauty, and with a good conscience because in goodness, magnificently rules the elements" (II, 283). From his position of understanding he is able to resign himself to the forces of existence. He has shown by his own actions—his spiritual rather than physical revenge for the wrong that had been done him—that the true power of humanity lies in its spiritual resources. Ferdinand and Miranda offer a hope that his lesson can influence the life of the future, but his awareness of the forces of nature—the eternal structure of the universe—allows him to forgive those who cannot profit by his example, for this life is not real, and the wicked can have no effect upon reality.

This is Shakespeare's "final wisdom" and is stated all but directly by him to his audience through the person of Prospero. An even more personal statement of the same belief is provided by the sonnets, as Landauer demonstrated. According to Landauer the two loves of the sonnets are outward representations of the forces, spirituality and animal drives, Shakespeare felt at conflict within himself. His works were attempts to express this conflict, to give it an articulated form in language and, thus, to transcend it and reach a new reality of life. The sonnets provide the opportunity to observe the process through which Shakespeare suffered and his final victory over the conflict that threatened to consume him. In the end he achieved a "superior serenity," like Prospero's, that allowed him to accept this life and at the same time to recognize it as a curtain behind which the true reality of nature is hidden.

During 1916, Landauer, suffering from his isolation and lack of opportunity to deal immediately with problems of the times, was forced to turn toward the past. On 31 August 1915 he had written to Hugo Warnstedt, ". . . the great men of all times and all peoples must serve us as living comrades . . . , especially as long as the supposedly living contemporaries fail. For me the dead are living, just as many too many of the living are dead." It was therefore in a mood of desperation that the Shakespeare lectures were first conceived. As he worked between 1916 and 1918, however, preparing them for publication, the mood changed; a new attitude seemed to be coming alive in the intellectual climate of Europe, an attitude that suggested that the message of Landauer's *Shakespeare* would perhaps find a willing reception. The United States entered the war in April 1917, and Germany's position worsened steadily. Perhaps partially as a result of this, more people were becoming interested in Landauer's writings. He received many requests for copies of his *Aufruf*, and by December 1917 he was planning a new edition of it, to be supplemented by reissue of some other writings. Both the second edition of the *Aufruf* and a collection of antiwar essays, mostly from the *Sozialist*, appeared in 1919. The latter book, called *Rechenschaft*, is a challenge to others to say where they stood before and during the war. Landauer never left any doubt about his position, and in a letter of 13 December 1917 to Leo Kestenberg, a publisher and the musical director of the Volksbühne, he was able to say in a tone of satisfaction and hope that those who were search-

ing had found him during the war. He had been pleased by the
Russian Revolution in March 1917 and was convinced that a German revolution was approaching: not until after the war, and
perhaps not immediately after the war, but a revolution, his revolution, was sure to come, and he intended to take part in it. When
Auguste Hauschner wondered if Landauer was thinking of becoming a Swiss citizen, he answered on 2 January 1917 that he could
think only of the work to be done in Germany, work in which he
wanted to participate. By the end of that year it appeared that his
firmness of purpose would be rewarded, and he would have his
chance. As the demand for his works continued to grow he wrote
again to Kestenberg, 16 October 1918: "The whole world is
searching for a socialism that can be achieved without infringing
upon freedom; for cultural socialism that issues not from class conflict but from humanity. . . ." During the ten months between the
two letters to Kestenberg, Landauer's vision of the future grew
more firm, but it was a vision that had changed in one essential,
personal way; for on 21 February 1918 Hedwig died.

Landauer had gone through much of his life as an isolated
figure, standing outside the political and social events that were so
important to him. Throughout their marriage Hedwig had been
the one person he could count on to share completely his hopes, his
dreams, and his sorrows. Other people had sooner or later disap-
pointed him. His relationship to Margarete Faas-Hardegger, so full
of love at first, had become within two years at best a distant
friendship. His close bond with Mauthner had been frequently
attenuated, especially during the war years; Mauthner had held
steadfastly to his position that the fate of Germany was the most
important consideration, and he had unquestionably resented Landauer's attitude that Germany as a state stood in the way of a
better future. But Hedwig understood this and agreed with it. In a
poem, "Mit den Besiegten" ("With the Conquered"), written in
the summer of 1915, she had aligned herself with the defeated peoples and called vain and shameful the victory achieved by force.
She had meant this poem for the Germans. She and Landauer both
had placed much of the blame for the war upon their own country-
men, who had allowed a militaristic government to determine their
actions. Landauer had come to look upon the war as a deserved

trial for Germany, a cleansing to remove the "principle of evil" from the world.[30] Hedwig had been his staunchest comrade in advocacy of this belief as in all else. Now he was really alone for the first time.

The unexpectedness of her death made it all the more shocking for him. It resulted, evidently, from a weak heart made still weaker by the strains and deprivations of wartime living, and was preceded by a short attack of influenza, which itself was taking a great toll in Germany at that time. Landauer suffered ill health for months afterward, from undiagnosed causes that were no doubt associated with his grief. It was fall before he was able to resume serious work: the book on Shakespeare, his translation of Whitman, the Strindberg essays, all lay untouched during the summer months. His first literary effort after Hedwig's death was a report entitled *Wie Hedwig Lachmann starb* (*How Hedwig Lachmann Died*), which was printed privately and sent to close friends. (The war intruded even upon this personal affair; during April 1918 Landauer's mail was held up for two weeks by some unknown authority, delaying the distribution of this booklet and temporarily preventing sympathetic friends from reaching him. Bab said that Landauer was one of the best-watched men in Germany during the war;[31] this arbitrary, unannounced stoppage of his mail supports Bab's contention.) He also contemplated the publication of Hedwig's letters, but this project never was undertaken. In April he gave lectures in Düsseldorf and Frankfurt, though he seems until the last minute to have been unsure whether he would be able to go through with them. Negotiations concerning a position with the Düsseldorfer Schauspielhaus continued during the summer, and he eventually accepted responsibility for the morning lecture series the theater sponsored, a task he could carry out from his home in Krumbach. He was still in contact with the Volksbühne, too, although he was not at that time taking an active part in its affairs. He seems, indeed, to have been no more active at anything during that summer than was necessary to make a living.

By September, however, he was feeling well enough to be able to work again. He suggested in a letter (30 September 1918) that developments in the war situation that indicated an impending cessation of hostilities might have had something to do with his recovery. There can be no doubt that the new interest in his writings and the promise for the future that interest implied helped to alleviate his sorrow somewhat. By October he felt sure enough of himself to make an important decision concerning his own place in that future, and he accepted posts as editor of *Masken* and as producer (*Dramaturg*) of the theater. He initiated the search for an apartment in Düsseldorf suitable to house him and his daughters; and though there remained some small points of disagreement with Gustav Lindemann, Landauer assumed his new duties while still in Krumbach. For the first time in his life, at age forty-eight, he had a position he felt ideally suited to his talents and desires. But Landauer was never to move to Düsseldorf.

Throughout the war Landauer's hope that a revolution would soon come continued to grow, and, in the belief that revolution can succeed only if it is prepared for in advance among the people, he did what he could to help prepare for it. Since 1912, along with his other work he had been translating and editing letters by many individuals, known and unknown, from the period of the French Revolution. These were finally published under the title *Briefe aus der französischen Revolution* (*Letters from the French Revolution*) in 1919. He hoped that this collection would prove valuable as a guide to the future; for, as he said in the foreword, it allowed the reader a glimpse into the hearts of individuals living in that unsettled time, revealing their desires and their missteps, and providing a pattern for failure that, when understood, might at last be avoided. And he continued to call upon artists and intellectuals to assume their proper role as leaders in a revolutionary movement, a revolution of the spirit. In *Ein Weg deutschen Geistes* he had said that the poet (he was speaking there specifically of Goethe but believed in a general application of the idea) symbolized the future that would be built upon the eternal traditions of mankind:

. . . certain and of decisive importance is that genius, after a shorter or longer entanglement in its milieu, spreads its wings and, in the growth of its *Geist*, lives and forms in advance the coming history of mankind. . . . We understand art only when we comprehend its service to mankind.[32]

In 1918, in the essay "Eine Ansprache an die Dichter" ("An Address to Poets"), he spoke directly to the poets, saying that in the midst of a disastrous war and a society bound up in political attempts to cope with social troubles, the poets must stand as leaders in the movement for change. It is for them to direct society toward the desired ends and to prevent these ends from becoming rigid and static.

These works, his *Shakespeare*, everything he wrote contained the message of spiritual revolution, but he worried that that message was not enough. The social organization in which his contemporaries lived, the state structure, seemed to have blinded them to the possibility, proclaimed in that message, of a complete life; in fact, the seeming impossibility of changing the social organization left them with little other than criticism of prevailing conditions as positively valued activity. The state had placed itself between the individual and the goals *Geist* would have set for him. Shakespeare had provided a demonstration of this in *Coriolanus*. Landauer had expressed his fear in the essay "Zum Gedächtnis" ("In Memoriam," 1914)[33] that the state's war propaganda, which urged everyone to consider himself a part of the state, would destroy the awareness of artists and intellectuals that they were parts of a whole far more meaningful and real than the state. The state stood in the way of the individual's battle for humanity. Thus it was that when the state was attacked by the revolution that swept Germany in 1918, Landauer, even though he felt the time was not ripe for a successful revolution in Germany, saw in the movement a hope that the time was approaching when the meaning of Shakespeare and of all the great poets could be heard and understood by humanity. He left his Shakespeare manuscript and went to help usher in that era.

7

The Unavailing Revolution

November 1918– May 1919

THE German revolution of 1918/19 came too late. During the 1890s Landauer had dreamed of an uprising led by workers who supported the anarchist movement. He had called for a general strike and revolution in his speech to the Anarchist Congress at Zurich in 1893; and, as he wrote in the afterword to the second edition, he had meant *Der Todesprediger* to be "a harbinger of that great revolution . . . that the people of the end of the nineteenth century had, by oversight, forgotten to wage." [1] Because that revolution, the particular revolution Landauer wanted, had not come about, Europe had begun the twentieth century still in the grasp of traditional state politics and had been led not to revolution but to World War I. The revolution followed.

It began as a mutiny of naval forces in northern Germany on 3 November 1918 and within a few days had spread to various parts of the country. On 7 November it broke out in Munich; the Bavarian monarchy was overthrown without a struggle, and a relatively obscure socialist named Kurt Eisner found himself, at least for a time, head of a provisional revolutionary government in Bavaria. As in the other areas of Germany, the Bavarian uprising was not what Landauer desired; it was not basically a movement to initiate a new way of life, but rather a frenzied reaction against the old one. Not the state, but the hopeless conditions into which the state had led its people, was the cause; the eradication of these conditions was its primary goal.

Landauer had no part in the events of early November, and he remained worried that they did not constitute revolution of the kind he desired. They represented for him not a change, only the possibility for change. Yet even the possibility was encouraging; and by 11 November he felt, as he wrote to Mauthner on that day, that he must take part. His state of mind and expectations are revealed in another letter of the same day to Auguste Hauschner: "I am in great joy, although I know what is coming now. I will be needed now, and perhaps even now not listened to." It was not confidence of success, therefore, but a feeling of necessity which prompted him to take part in this revolution. He felt that his presence was needed to push events in the direction he desired, for there were few others whom he could trust as leaders of the new movement. He acted in the faith that the spirit or revolution would provide motivation for building a new life, motivation that years of socialist propaganda and activity had failed to create. A possibility for *Geist* to reassert itself was there: ". . . that now, who knows when, religion will come upon the peoples: this movement is a beginning for that." [2] When Eisner requested, on 11 or 12 November, that Landauer come to assist the Munich revolution, Landauer obeyed the call.

There are as many different characterizations of Eisner as there have been attempts to write about him. His personality and his intentions are hopelessly blurred in the flurry of pros and cons that discussion of this revolution still evokes. One statement bearing the stamp of impartiality is an editorial from the *Frankfurter Zeitung*, written just after Eisner's assassination on 21 February 1919:

We were at odds with him in many things. But that has never prevented us, and today when he has fallen, the victim of a crime, it should especially not prevent us, from acknowledging what he was: a man with the contradictions of a man, a man with his errors, his weaknesses, and his mistakes, but, all things considered, a man with a burning will for truth, with an unlimited belief in that which he considered right and good, a courageous man, prepared to make sacrifices, a fanatic of idealism with the power of heart to pull up others from the dreary materialism of the time to his belief and his ideas.

Landauer's willingness to accept Eisner's leadership in the revolution suggests that there is some truth to this characterization.

Eisner, born 1867, had spent most of his life in socialist activities. From 1898 until 1905 he had been the editor of the official party newspaper *Vorwärts*, succeeding Wilhelm Liebknecht in that position. It is probable that he and Landauer had known each other at that time, though a close contact is hardly to be supposed, since Eisner had then represented the official party viewpoint. Later his position in the party was challenged, and when a serious conflict arose between him and Karl Kautsky, one of the most powerful SPD leaders, Eisner lost his editorial post and his position in the party. (Later, in 1917, Eisner was one of the founders of the Independent Socialist Party [USPD].*) After living in Nuremberg for a few years, he settled in Munich in 1910 and played an active but by no means prominent role in Bavarian political life. By 1918 Landauer was on cordial terms with Eisner and his second wife, Else. Shortly before the revolution Eisner was in prison, awaiting investigation because of his activities in a general strike against the war (January 1918), but he was released so that he could participate in an election campaign that was in part intended to forestall possible revolutionary disturbances in Bavaria. But the disturbances came.

The beginning of the Bavarian Revolution showed signs of the spontaneous revolutionary spirit Landauer often wrote about, but its leaders seem to have been taken by surprise. On 7 November 1918 a mass meeting, primarily of union members, was held on the Theresienwiese in Munich to demonstrate against the war and the conditions of life brought about by the war. Before it was over the meeting had become a revolution. It met no resistance: the ministers of the Bavarian government did not know what to do about it. Eisner had held consultations during the previous days where plans were laid for expanding the meeting into a revolt,[3] but it seems unlikely that the leaders of the movement had anticipated such a complete success. On the evening of the

* A splinter group containing the more radical, antiwar numbers of the SPD.

seventh, Eisner, encouraged by demands from workers, formed the Revolutionärer Arbeiterrat (Revolutionary Workers' Council), abbreviated RAR, with himself as chairman. The RAR, however, was not the official government. That was established by Eisner on 8 November. It was a socialist cabinet in which he was president and Erhard Auer, a leader of the SPD in Bavaria, served as interior minister. There was soon a many-sided power struggle, for the members of the RAR were in general opposed to the cabinet, and the cabinet ministers themselves were at odds over the goals of the revolution. Eisner represented a relatively radical social program that the SPD group, led by Auer, opposed. The SPD faction wished to continue the traditional political and capitalist structure of bourgeois society, and its members acted for the most part in consonance with the political right. The cabinet generally operated according to the accepted practices of a parliamentary government, using many officials inherited from the Bavarian monarchy. The RAR, on the other hand, set out at once to restructure the government. Throughout Bavaria it founded local councils of workers based on the workers' callings. It also helped establish local soldiers' and farmers' councils and made provisions for all these groups to be represented by a Central Council in Munich. This all occurred early in November and led to a situation in which three semi-governing bodies—the cabinet, the RAR, and the Central Council—were working simultaneously and, at least in part, independently.

Because of illness, Landauer was unable to go to Munich until 16 November, though Eisner was eager to have him and contacted him during the first few days of the revolution. Landauer did not become a member of the cabinet, but served in both the RAR and the Central Workers' Council, a division of the Central Council. His work consisted primarily of promoting the revolution by writing and by speaking to various groups, especially to returning soldiers. His letters from November 1918 reflect the ideas he wished to disseminate. He stood strongly against national elections and a new German national parliament, though he feared the necessity of signing a peace treaty would force an election upon the German people. He wished to prevent the old political parties from recovering their power and the bourgeois press from regaining control of people's minds. Events in Berlin did not seem to him to be significant; hope for the future lay in south and west Germany, where some states, epecially Bavaria, were establishing independence from Prussia. He envisioned an eventual federation of independent German republics in which Prussia would have a place, but definitely not the leading one. He did not desire state control of industry nor the "dictatorship of the proletariat." All of these ideas were set down in the pamphlet *Die vereinigten Republiken Deutschlands und ihre Verfassung* (*The United Republics of Germany and Their Constitution*), which appeared in Frankfort on the Main in December 1918.

In Eisner, Landauer recognized a man who shared his goals. Eisner was hard pressed, however, by less radical members of his government; opposition was especially bitter to his plan to publish prewar documents demonstrating Germany's share of guilt for the war. By early December strong demands and, later, armed demonstrations were made for the election of delegates to a Bavarian parliament (Landtag); Eisner resisted this, feeling as Landauer did that the establishment of a traditional legislative body would be dangerous for the revolution. His position was made all the more difficult by individuals and groups, on both the left and the right, who constantly maneuvered to gain their own political ends. On 4 December the organizers of a reception for the returning Bavarian "King's Own" ("Leibregiment") greeted the troops with militaristic and nationalistic speeches that were obviously antirevolutionary. Landauer was informed of this situation and had to hurry to the celebration to speak on behalf of the revolution. On the night of 6 December, Erich Mühsam, leading workers and soldiers, took over the Munich papers and imposed censorship. Eisner moved quickly to overrule this unofficial act by leftists, who, in theory at least, were his followers. About the same time the council system came under attack from the right: an unsuccessful attempt was made by police fiat to restrict the power of local councils. Landauer spoke against this at a meeting of the Landesarbeiterrat on 8 December, stressing that the fears of the right were unjustified:

In bourgeois circles the dictatorship of the proletariat is spoken of so fearfully. We of the revolution do not dream of perpetuating the proletariat, the privation, the deprivation of rights, the subjugation. We do not dream of helping the proletariat to domination or dictatorship; the intention of the democratic-social revolution can only be to abolish the proletariat once and for all (II, 308, n. 1).*

The members of the right were not convinced. Plans were made by Auer and other right-wing socialists for a city militia. At a 30 December meeting of the Provisional National Council, the revolution's temporary substitute for a parliament, a group of leftists including Landauer and the dramatist Ernst Toller offered proof that the militia was to be used for counterrevolutionary purposes. Auer and another important official then withdrew their names from the scheme, and it collapsed. After defeating this attempt to undermine its power, the Provisional National Council decided that stricter measures were necessary for the realization of socialism and the containment of capitalism and imperialism.

One such measure advocated by Landauer was government-authorized control of the bourgeois press. He felt that the capitalist newspaper monopolies, hiding behind freedom of the press, suppressed public opinion and published mendacious antirevolutionary propaganda (II, 298). When censorship was finally imposed after Eisner was assassinated on 21 February 1919 (the papers were forbidden to appear from 21 to 24 February, and thereafter only under government surveillance), Landauer greeted it with the statement, ". . . we now have a beginning of freedom of public opinion" (II, 389). In the lifting of this censorship on 11 March 1919 he saw a victory for counterrevolution (II, 391).

The behavior of the papers during and just after the revolutionary period tends to justify Landauer's opinion. The stories that were circulated about the members and actions of the various revolutionary governing bodies reached the ridiculous. The best example is the report spread throughout Germany that women had been "socialized"—placed at the disposal of revolutionary males— by the Council Government, established on 7 April 1919. Such reports, as farfetched as they were, impressed readers and damaged the revolution. The Munich papers were no better than others when not under revolutionary censorship. After an attack on the press delivered by Eisner on 13 February 1919 before a meeting of

* All textual page references here and below are to the *Briefe*.

174

the Bavarian Workers', Soldiers', and Farmers' Councils, the Munich papers refused to report the activities of this important body any further. The attitude behind the actions of the Munich press is revealed in the *Bayerische Staatszeitung* for 4 May 1919, the day Munich fell to the military forces of the Berlin government: "The workers must free themselves from the fog of lies that arose from a weeks-long suppression of freedom of opinion, from a weeks-long, unscrupulous official press sham of the Council Dictators."

The "press sham" referred to was Eisner's paper *Neue Zeitung*, first issue 20 December 1918, representing the revolutionary government's point of view: but that organ, too, was torn by the dissensions within the governing bodies. Landauer refused to serve as editor of it for fear of becoming entangled in political squabbles. He wished to fight the newspaper situation by starting the *Sozialist* again (the first issue was to be 1 March 1919), but the venture never progressed beyond the planning stage.

During January 1919 two new developments further confused the attempts to form a stable revolutionary government. Elections to the Bavarian Landtag were held by traditional parliamentary election procedures on 12 January. Landauer was against these elections throughout, though he himself was a candidate from Krumbach. He knew he had no chance of being elected, but he felt that his candidacy was the best course for him at the moment because it gave him an opportunity to speak to the electorate about his ideas for a new social structure. As had been expected, the election results were extremely discouraging for those who supported the more revolutionary plans of Eisner. Of the parties running, the Bayerische Volkspartei won 58 seats; SPD, 52; Deutsche Volkspartei, 22; Bauernbund, 16; Nationalliberale Partei, 5; Unabhängige Sozialdemokratische Partei (Independent Social Democrats; USPD), Eisner's group, 3 (II, 358).

The other significant development was the increasing power of the Spartakisten (Spartacists, Communists) in Munich. On 1 January 1919, under the leadership of Max Levien, a Russian-born German Marxist, a proletarian group called the Vereinigung Revolutionärer Internationalisten (founded by Mühsam, 30 November 1918) joined in a coalition with a Communist group in Bremen

175

and became the Communist party cell in Munich. Landauer, who was, of course, not connected with this organization, continued to oppose Marxist doctrines. As their power increased, however, he felt it necessary to include the Spartacists in the plans for a full realization of the revolution. In a letter of 10 January he urged Eisner, in anticipation of the coming elections, to win them over. He made this demand publicly in one of several meetings held on 14 and 15 January to form a united front of the SPD and the USPD. The proposal met with strong opposition, and Landauer explained his position:

I am not a friend of force, but a friend of misled, honest men. And that is what many workers are who were drawn to the Spartacists, like butterflies [*sic*] to a light. Let us form a union of all socialists! A new socialism must arise from the precept of justice and the need of the moment (II, 361, n).

Nevertheless, unity with or without the Spartacists was not to be achieved. The Communists made unity even less possible by refusing to cooperate with other groups. By the end of January, Landauer was very discouraged. Eisner, he felt, had weakened his position beyond hope by making concessions to other members of the cabinet. The elections had fully destroyed his power. The murders in Berlin of the Communists Karl Liebknecht and Rosa Luxemburg, murders over which many Bavarians rejoiced, filled Landauer with disgust. On 15 January he wrote his daughters that he was not sure how much longer he would stay in Munich. Ten days later, in another letter, he gave vent to his frustrations by suggesting that the Germans were not capable of a revolutionary renovation. This same letter, however, bears witness to Landauer's determination, for he followed this indictment of the Germans with the statement, "I will draw just one consequence from all this bitterness, to do my duty still better than before" (II, 368).

February brought no change in the antagonisms and machinations among the various factions. Levien was arrested on 9 February for making an inflammatory speech. Landauer and others protested strongly and planned a mass demonstration in Levien's behalf for Sunday, 16 February. Levien was freed on 11 February, but preparations for the demonstration went ahead, now to serve "general purposes" ("*allgemeine Ziele*"), as Landauer put it (II, 380). Opinions about this meeting differ. Mühsam maintained that it was directed specifically against Eisner and that Eisner tried, rather unsuccessfully, to gain control of it.[4] Arco-Valley, Eisner's assassin, considered it, in the words of his defense counsel, "a triumphal procession of Bolshevism, led by Prime Minister Eisner!"[5] Landauer, who was certainly not anti-Eisner as Mühsam was, and who had a leading role in the demonstration (it was he who brought to Eisner the demands of the Workers' Councils), felt the affair was a success. He estimated the crowd to be 80,000 (II, 382). The *Bayerische Staatszeitung*, in a short report of 17 February 1919 that did not mention Landauer, said 20,000. In a speech before the Bavarian Workers', Soldiers', and Farmers' Councils on 13 February (the same session in which Eisner's attack on the press brought the papers' refusal to publish the further proceedings of this body), Landauer had described the purpose of the coming demonstration as being "the sign of our firm will to manifest the position of the Councils in the realization of socialism" (II, 382, n).

This meeting of the Councils was an important one for Landauer and the revolution. Although the elections for the Landtag had been held the previous month, no date had been set for its convening; Eisner evidently was putting off such a session as long as possible. Other members of the cabinet took advantage of Eisner's absence from Munich (he attended an international socialist congress in Bern during the early part of February) to arrange for the Landtag to meet on 21 February. The more radical individuals in and around the government then felt it necessary to combat the damaging effects that the Landtag would have upon the revolution. In his speech on 13 February Landauer spoke strongly in favor of a council government instead of a conventional parliamentary one. The *Bayerische Staatszeitung* reported on 18 February 1919:

He condemned ballot box democracy, which does not express the clear will of public opinion. The democracy of all creative forces always working visibly, not the dictatorship of the proletariat as such, must be a determining factor in the life of the people.

At another meeting of this group on 18 February, Landauer spoke of the dangers of renascent capitalism and warned that German capitalism could recover from the war with help from the capitalist systems of the victorious countries. Despite his efforts and those of other revolutionaries, the Rätekongress (Congress of Councils) voted to give its powers to the new Landtag.

The revolution might have ended there. Eisner, with only three seats in the Landtag, could not have stayed in power, and control of the government would have passed into the hands of the right or a right-center coalition. But on his way to the first session of the Landtag, Eisner was shot down in the street. Shortly thereafter a man named Lindner shot and seriously wounded Auer in the Landtag as revenge for Eisner's death. The Landtag adjourned, and the Central Council of the Workers', Soldiers', and Farmers' Councils recalled the Congress of Councils.

A period of confusion followed during which, behind the ceremonies attendant upon Eisner's funeral, each faction struggled for advantage. On 26 February, the day of the funeral, Landauer spoke once again before the Congress of Councils, demanding that power be kept in the hands of the councils. Two days later Mühsam appeared in the Congress of Councils and, on behalf of the RAR and the Spartacists, demanded that the Congress proclaim a council republic (Räterepublik). A vote was taken, and the proposal was defeated 234 to 70 (II, 387, n. 2).* Landauer was among those who voted against the proposal; both Mühsam and Buber, the latter directly quoting Landauer, have indicated that he felt the time was inappropriate for such a step (II, 387, n. 2).

After this vote the Congress decided to keep the Landtag out of session for awhile and to function itself as a provisional national council from which ministers would be selected and an executive committee formed. During the next week the problems of organization became truly hectic, for some of the appointed ministers refused to serve and went to Nuremberg, where the leaders of the SPD, the USPD, and a farmers' party, the Bauernbündler, formed a new plan, the "Nuremberg Compromise." This called for a socialist cabinet to be elected and confirmed, not by the Congress of Councils, but by the Landtag, which was to be recalled for the pur-

* Ruth Fischer's assertion that a council republic was proclaimed by that vote is in error. Ruth Fischer, *Stalin and German Communism* (Cambridge, Mass., 1948), p. 101.

pose. Landauer objected to this surrender of power by the Congress; but the SPD majority of the Congress overrode his objections, and on 7 March an agreement was accepted in which control was placed in the hands of the new government as proposed. Representatives of the councils were given freedom to attend ministerial sessions in an advisory capacity and had the right to call referendums in cases of disagreement with the ministers. Once again, Landauer objected and suggested that, if the plan was to be accepted, numerous changes should be made in it. Once again he was voted down. After voting in favor of this governmental arrangement, the Congress of Councils adjourned.

The Communists refused to have any contact with this government. Landauer, despite his disappointment, carried on his efforts for the establishment of a new social structure. Several of his letters from this period contain statements attesting to his inner calm and his intention to do what the times demanded of him. He continued to express a strong interest in the formation of a council government, but he asserted in a letter written 20 March but never sent that there would have to be a provisional dictatorship before his contemporaries would be able to accept such a government. The danger inherent in this idea, that uncontrolled power of a dictatorship might lead to misused power, did not escape him:

This course can be followed only if the leaders are as pure as they are strong; this is the point where every revolution is in danger of the most far-reaching corruption. But mankind cannot avoid its fate of having to prepare good from the material of evil . . . (II, 403–04).

In the meantime political developments were more or less in accordance with the Nuremberg Compromise. The Landtag met on 17 and 18 March and elected a cabinet, ignoring the choices made earlier by the Congress of Councils. Johannes Hoffmann (SPD) was named president. After that, however, things did not go quite as the groups on the right had expected. The Landtag formed a Committee on Socialization to study the prospects of socialization in Bavaria. Within a few days this committee established a Central Office for Economic Affairs (Zentralwirtschaftsamt) under the direction of Dr. Otto Neurath, who was to prepare and carry out a program of socialization. For this he was given extraordinary powers, and he was not slow to use them. What was perhaps his most radical suggestion was made before the RAR on 25 March, where he proposed that the Communists, who were not in favor of the Hoffmann regime, take a gift of land in Bavaria upon which they could try out their proposal for collectivism, independent of and unhindered by the government. He pledged government assistance for three years to help the settlement get established. Letters of Landauer written on 26 March indicate that he liked this scheme; according to Mühsam he urged acceptance in the RAR meeting (this may have been at a second meeting on 31 March).[6] The Communists did not reject the proposal, but insisted on the right to agitate outside their "reserve." Neurath went back to Hoffmann to discuss this aspect.

Right-wing elements of the government were shocked by Neurath's plans and eager to consolidate their own power. Machinery was set in motion to recall the Landtag for 8 April. It was intended that the fully assembled body, dominated by the SPD, would overrule the extraordinary powers given Neurath by the Committee on Socialization. Those who supported a council government felt that action had to be taken to head off this move. The action took the form of a new revolution: the proclamation of a council government in opposition to the Hoffmann cabinet.

The precise events leading up to this proclamation are difficult to unravel. Mühsam maintained that Landauer was among those who planned it from the beginning.[7] Buber has presented evidence that Landauer had no part in the earliest stages of planning, though his name was used by at least one of the instigators, giving the impression that he was an active participant from the outset (II, 412–13, n. 1). The first impulse came on 4 April from officials of workers' and soldiers' councils in Augsburg who sent to the Central Council in Munich a resolution calling for the proclamation of the Council Republic. Whatever Landauer's part had been before, he was now fully involved in the undertaking. New ministers were appointed by the Central Council; it was then, for the first time, that Landauer was given a cabinet position: Provisorischer Volksbeauftragter für Volksaufklärung (minister of culture).* The dram-

---

* This was the first and only time Landauer held a cabinet post. Contrary to the frequently stated view, he did not serve under Eisner as a cabinet minister.

atist Ernst Toller was named president. It was at Landauer's insistence, according to Mühsam, that the entire cabinet was named provisionally, final selection to be made by the various councils throughout Bavaria.[8] This meeting of the Central Council was followed by another the same evening, 4 April, at which the attempt was made to win the Spartacists to the plan. But they still refused to cooperate because members of the SPD were to take part in the new government. Thereupon the SPD members of the Central Council managed to obtain a delay of forty-eight hours before the proclamation was to be issued.

On 5 April, Dr. Wadler, who was commissioner of housing in the new government, publicly announced that the proclamation was pending. On 6 April the Central Council met again, still without the Spartacists. Landauer and Mühsam secured the appointment of Silvio Gesell as minister of finance. The newspapers were taken over that night, and the Council Republic was proclaimed the following morning. It was Landauer's birthday. He had no delusions about the possibilities for the future. On the first day of the new government he wrote to Mauthner: "If I have a few weeks' time, I hope to accomplish something; but it is quite possible that it will be only a few days, and then it was a dream." No more now than before did he believe in the sudden dawning of Utopia. Buber quotes a report of a speech before a general meeting of councils, 11 April, in which Landauer made this very plain: ". . . our present task is not to consider the past few days or the future of coming years, but to direct our sights, calmly and firmly, upon the future of the next few days and there to stand our ground" (II, 414, n. 1).

The few days of this government were hectic ones. Hoffmann fled to Bamberg with his ministers and established a government in exile. The Berlin government expelled Bavaria from Germany and sent troops to help Hoffmann. On 8 April farmers' groups opposed to the new regime ceased sending food to Munich. Within the city problems of unity plagued the young Council Republic. The Communists continued their refusal to collaborate, although they took part in government sessions as advisors. On 11 April the Works' Councils (Betriebsräte) in Munich called a general meeting of councils, hoping to provide a basis upon which the necessary cooperation of all groups could be achieved. All that was accomplished was a fruitless reorganization in which the Central Council relinquished its power to the Works' Councils. The Communists remained intransigent. A very few steps were made toward socialization: the occupation of banks was probably the most significant. Amid this turmoil, on the night of 12 April, a putsch was attempted by right-wing elements. Several members of the council government, including Mühsam, were arrested and quickly sent out of Munich. After heavy fighting workers, led by the Communists, managed to defeat the putsch on 13 April; but during the night of upheaval the government took on a new character. The council structure was maintained, but the Communists were now in control.

Although Landauer managed to escape arrest during the putsch, his official contact with the government was over. In his short term as minister of culture he had started to revise the school system, a project for which he had much enthusiasm. It appeared that he had at last the opportunity to establish a free school system, free in his own sense: a school system within the structure of a truly republican state, a state of a new and better kind. And that was not his only plan for education. As early as November 1918 he had stressed the need for schools (*Volkshochschulen*) in which workers, provided additional free time by the introduction of the eight-hour working day, could achieve an understanding of culture previously denied them (II, 308). His plans for these projects and his hopes for a total, beneficial reorganization of society collapsed when the Communists assumed power.

Somewhat surprisingly, Landauer sent the new government a message on 16 April, greeting their accession and offering his services. This was not an acquiescence to the politics of force that the Communists advocated, but rather an attempt to attain a position from which he might combat or at least mitigate that force. The Communists recognized this; his offer of service was not accepted. On the same day he wrote to the Executive Committee (Aktionsausschuss) a condemnation of the Communists' actions and goals. This ended with the statement,

. . . I have no intention of disturbing the difficult work of defense that you are directing. But I lament most painfully that it is only in the smallest part my work, a work of warmth and progress, of culture and rebirth, that is now being defended (II, 421).

There was little he could have done, even had he been given a post by the Communists. Troops from the Berlin government had partially isolated Munich by 16 April. The little support the Council Republic had received from rural areas soon collapsed. In Munich everything was sacrificed to the defense of the city, and the strict measures instituted by the Communists for this purpose led finally to a new political upheaval. Toller and several others resigned on 26 April. On 27 April the Communists lost a vote of confidence in the Works' Councils, still nominally the sovereign bodies of the government; and a new executive committee, which Toller headed, was formed. But the newly founded Bavarian Red Army remained in the Communists' hands, so they in fact retained power. Attempts made on 28 April to negotiate with the Hoffmann government were rejected. As the danger of attack from the soldiers supporting Hoffmann became imminent, the dictatorship of the Red Army was proclaimed (30 April). On 1 May the battle for the city began.

Few details remain of Landauer's activities during the three weeks between the Communist take-over of the government and his death. There are no letters after 16 April. Buber reported in the epilogue to Landauer's collected letters that Landauer had frequent discussions with friends in Munich trying to find a way to avoid bloodshed. He offered his services to the Executive Committee formed on 27 April; he was told he would be called when needed. The call never came. Friends urged him to flee and offered him assistance, but after some consideration he decided to remain. He was arrested on 1 May at Eisner's house, victim of an anonymous denunciation. Threatened with immediate execution, he defended himself before the officers who held him, and they decided to send him the next day to the Stadelheim prison. Upon his arrival there, however, an officer arbitrarily set a group of soldiers upon him, and he was beaten to death, one of over six hundred people killed by the invading troops. The council government died two days later.

8

Brutus

THE history of Bavaria between 7 November 1918 and 4 May 1919 provides a classic case of the problems to which revolutions are heir, problems that Landauer had frequently discussed in his writings, most completely in *Die Revolution,* later to some extent in the *Aufruf zum Sozialismus,* and still later in the foreword to *Briefe aus der französischen Revolution.* In the Bavarian experience the revolutionary spirit pervaded the masses at the beginning and the uprising was spontaneous and popular. But the movement lacked direction; even among the leaders there was no agreement on what goals should be achieved. The revolution was political, therefore, not social. As confusion and bickering over a course of action increased, the revolutionary spirit died out among the masses and the revolution became a creature of a few prominent personalities. Torn by dissension within and threatened by military attack from without, it finally became a tyranny as bad as or worse than the one it had replaced and so ceased to be a revolutionary movement. The troops from Berlin did not defeat the revolution, only structural vestiges of it.

The specific details that explain the failure of the Bavarian Revolution corroborate this theoretical pattern. Though Eisner supported the radical idea of a council republic from the first, he was unable to make it a reality because of opposition from the old po-

184

litical parties, which, together with many of the workers and soldiers, demanded a continuation of former parliamentary procedures. It is true, as the Communist agitator Paul Werner charged,
that the Council Republic finally established on 7 April 1919 was
the work of a few individuals who organized it and was neither
sanctioned nor supported by the masses.[1] The fact—pointed out by
both Werner and by Ruth Fischer in *Stalin and German Communism*—that there was little heavy industry in Bavaria may partially explain the lack of popular enthusiasm in Munich for a government seemingly designed to meet the needs of a labor proletariat. By the same token, firm support from the rural areas could
not be expected either. Something of the public attitude during
the first (non-Communist) Council Republic may be seen from
an advertisement that appeared on 10 April, just at the time the
new regime was trying to establish its influence, in the *Bayerische
Staatszeitung*: "Wanted: capitalist to support expansion of an
undertaking concerning a great technical invention. The invention
has been reported to the patent office and can be seen in opera-
tion." The revolutionary spirit descended once more upon the
Munich workers after the abortive right-wing putsch, but it was
too late then; the Communists to whom the workers were forced
to turn for leadership suppressed that spirit in the name of protect-
ing the revolution.

There can be no doubt that Landauer recognized these difficulties. As has been seen, he worried even before the revolution
began that the masses would not be ready for it. Six days after his
arrival in Munich he wrote to Buber that the revolution was in
trouble and could survive only by a miracle.[2] On 13 December 1918
he stressed in a letter that the staunchest enemies of the revolution
were the workers who belonged to political parties and unions. In
a letter of 3 January 1919 he referred to himself as a prophet in
the wilderness, and at the end of January he wrote: "I am already
nearly as alone as before the revolution; I see at work only helpless
folly and commonness." * Yet he stayed in Munich despite his
awareness that success was not to be expected. One must ask why,
in the face of constant disappointment, Landauer continued, for

* All letters are from the *Briefe*. Textual reference to their specific date is complete documentation.

as long as he was allowed, to support the cause of a hopeless revolution that seemed not even to have been working toward the stateless society he had advocated all his life.

This question demands two answers, one for the period up to Eisner's death, the other for the time thereafter. The attempt by Rudolf Rocker, anarchistic writer and editor, to provide a single explanation for Landauer's actions is not satisfactory:

Precisely because Germany had lost the war [Landauer] believed with all the fervor of his great heart that the time of change was dawning, the new rebirth, when the forces that had heretofore served the Moloch of destruction would now unite in the creative work of a new social and cultural structure to lead mankind along new paths toward new goals.[3]

Landauer's letters show that he was not at all certain the time for a rebuilding of society had come. But he did believe that the *possibility* of a transformation of human relations was at hand, and he was convinced that Bavaria offered the most likely setting for it. Of all the states in the German Reich, Bavaria was and had been least under Prussian domination and, thus, was the one most likely to assert its independence of the old state system. On 22 November 1918 he expressed to Buber his certainty that, even if a new national legislative body were created, Bavaria would remain autonomous. On the same day he wrote to Leo Kestenberg that the revolutionary activities in Bavaria were "exemplary."

Landauer's belief in Eisner as a leader made him feel even more that Bavaria was the place for him to work. That these two men shared the same fundamental philosophical approach to solving social problems is evident from Eisner's words in a speech he made on 17 December 1918: "*A politician who is not at the same time a poet is also not a politician. The poet is the prophet of the future world.*" [4] Landauer fully supported Eisner's plan to publish documents pertinent to the beginning of World War I and several times during the early stages of the revolution wrote that he and Eisner worked well together. Landauer's growing disappointment with Eisner concerned not the man nor his basic aspirations, but his failure to keep his principles pure, uncompromised by the ideas of bourgeois politicians and traditional parliamentary procedures.

Even after the elections of 12 January 1919 Landauer hoped that Eisner would continue to work in the councils when he left the cabinet.

Having recognized a kindred spirit in Eisner, Landauer knew from his years of experience as a social innovator the problems Eisner would face as he attempted to build a new form of society. Few others would understand him or support his plans, and because of this Landauer knew how important his support might be. He no doubt had Eisner's position in mind when he wrote to Kestenberg that he felt his own place was to help lead the revolution. With Eisner as his chief, Landauer was willing to risk the uncertainties attendant upon it. In the foreword to the second edition of the *Aufruf*, dated 3 January 1919, Landauer pointed out how right he had been when he said in this book that the people were not prepared for revolution; now that it was upon them they did not know how to build within the framework it provided. He and Eisner at least knew the direction they wished to go; Landauer did not consider it their task to anticipate all the details—and the dangers—of the undertaking. He had made a general pronouncement about this years before in the *Aufruf* (1911) and again in the essay "Die Abschaffung des Kriegs" (1911): "The solitary thinker who in burning love for the right and the good envisions some great project is not responsible for achieving certainty in the details of its realization. That is provided by the execution, by every step." [5] But the steps would have to be taken; the expectation of the Marxists that socialism would necessarily arise as a new stage of history remained for Landauer as empty a promise during the revolution as before. It was up to individuals to create the necessity, and he was one of the few individuals—Eisner was another—who had understood it and worked for it for a long time. For years he had maintained that a socialist society could be initiated whenever a few people were ready to begin it. Eisner had taken the first step, and that was incentive enough for Landauer.

Eisner's assassination did more than remove the official leader of this drive for a new society; it symbolized how far away that society still was and how improbable were the chances for its attainment at that time. Bab has suggested it was anger over Eisner's death that caused Landauer to continue the struggle; [6] the full reason for his determination to stay in Munich, however, is more complex. It lies buried deep in his personality. In *Die Revolution* he had written, ". . . when a man of tranquil *Geist* cannot help but take part in the chaos of the times, he will have to be a rebel." [7] Later, in *Ein Weg deutschen Geistes*, he said, "The consequence of poetry is revolution, the revolution that is building and regeneration—for him who does not know that, the poets have never really lived." [8] In the case of Landauer, who was a man of *Geist* and for whom the poets lived with the greatest intensity, there was no turning back once he became involved in the external aspects of a revolutionary movement. Landauer had always been a revolutionary, but this was the first time he was able to influence the course of events personally and directly from a position of political power. If the outlook was dismal, it was, at least, an outlook. On 14 October 1918 he had written to Mauthner:

. . . true politics, the politics that go back to Laotzu and Buddha and Jesus, is not the art of the possible but the "impossible." What is happening today is nothing but "impossible" things, except that these "impossibilities" are realities.

And on 27 November 1918 in a letter to Georg Springer, the director of the Freie Volksbühne, he had repeated a sentiment that recurs in his letters over the years:

. . . when we are not concerned, as in the war, with obsolete insanity, but with reasonable things, then no fight and no abyss is too great for me. . . . I always say: humor is the appreciation for the unendingness of time; it does not occur to me to desire a finished result; I will always see something beyond the end; I am concerned with the process, and we are at last in the process.

These two statements describe the state of mind that drove him to continue his efforts in support of a hopeless cause.

Compounded with this was the feeling that time was short. Eight years before, in the *Aufruf*, he had written of the degeneration of the proletariat over the past sixty years and warned that if the decline were not halted, they would soon no longer be capable of building a socialist society. Now the start had been made, but the development was hindered, on the one hand, by the bourgeoisie and, on the other, by the Spartacists, both certain by their

methods and their goals to suppress these beginnings and the concomitant awakening of the workers. He seems to have felt, too, that
he personally had little time left to combat this suppression. On
Christmas Day 1918 he wrote to Auguste Hauschner that he felt
as though he were only "on leave" in this world for the sake of his
children and the revolution. One commentator mentioned that, in
the foreword to the second edition of the *Aufruf*, Landauer anticipated his approaching death;[9] the words which close this foreword,
though they no more than repeat the philosophy Landauer had
represented all his life, do have an unusually prophetic air:

What is so important about life? We soon die, we all die, we do not
live at all. Nothing lives except what we make of ourselves, what
we undertake with ourselves; achievements live; not the creature,
only the creator. Nothing lives but the deed of honest hands and the
workings of pure, genuine *Geist*.[10]

Was this revolution the deed Landauer wished to accomplish?
Bab suggested that Landauer's involvement in the revolution was
partly a turning away from "that . . . purely spiritual renewal"
he had always advocated.[11] Blüher maintained, and quoted letters
to prove, that during the revolution Landauer became a proponent
of force and violence.[12] The letters he quoted show Landauer's attitude toward the press and reproduce a statement from a letter to
Landauer's friend Carl Vogl, 23 November 1918, in which Landauer suggested that land in Vogl's area ideally would be divided
among the workers. In context this particular example of what to
Blüher seemed ruthless rulership turns out to be only a theoretical
statement of ideals, not a demand for expropriation. An evidently
intentional misrepresentation is made by Blüher in quoting a letter
of 27 November 1918 to Hugo Landauer. In it Landauer wrote,
"The great obstacle is the trained workers who do not even consider changing their calling. Since they do not want to hear, they
will have to feel. Reason triumphs only through necessity." What
Landauer meant by "feel" is that the force of circumstances must
take effect before the necessary changes in society can be achieved,
not that political or physical force should be used on recalcitrant
individuals. This is Landauer's own interpretation; Hugo misunderstood the letter, and Landauer, rather exasperated, explained in his

next letter to him (2 December) that he had been predicting what
would come, not proposing a course of action. Blüher, who seems
to have read the collected letters very carefully indeed, could have
overlooked this second letter only by intention. He also overlooked
a statement written 16 January 1919 to Landauer's daughter Charlotte: "It is because of my conviction, because of my wishes for
mankind, that I resist the methods of violence and revenge, that I
continue to work for the energetic but peaceful building of socialism. . . . I continue on my way as before."

Landauer hoped to make the revolution his way. He had always advocated helping the masses by the means at hand, even
when those means were not in themselves immediate steps in the
direction of the socialism he wished to establish. His early support
of consumer cooperatives, his work with the Volksbühne in Berlin,
his propaganda for an *Arbeitertag* (Workers' Convention) to prevent war: all of these are examples of his willingness to face the
problems of the moment with answers of the moment. And all
demonstrate that his final goal, the free socialist society inspired by
creative *Geist*, was never lost sight of in the pressures of the moment. The Bavarian Revolution was another such means to this
end. If it was itself not directed toward the establishment of socialist communities where true freedom would exist, it could, nevertheless, serve to prepare people for the eventual acceptance of that
idea by restructuring society on the basis of councils in which the
individual would actually have a voice in the decisions of government. The financial basis of the state would be reformed in accordance with Gesell's fiscal theories. The local councils that had
emerged from the revolution would become the foundation of the
new society, the society of independent socialist settlements. As the
revolution made people aware that local councils were capable of
representing individuals adequately, and as trust in the councils increased, the realization would also grow that land held
by individual council members would bring increased benefits to
them and to society as a whole if it were held in common. On this
land the socialist settlements would be founded. A hope for these
developments is implicit in all the political machinations with
which Landauer was involved. On 17 March 1919 he wrote that his

intention was to prepare the foundations for the true community by his work in public office; and a letter to the clerks of the Ministry of Culture, 12 April 1919, provides what might be called his "official attitude" toward the revolution:

By "Council Republic" is to be understood nothing but that what lives in *Geist* and strains toward realization is carried out as far as the possibilities allow. If we are not disturbed in our work, this process is no act of force; only the force of *Geist* will flow from the mind and the heart to the hand and from the hands [*sic*] into the institutions of the outer world.

If doubt remains that Landauer was living up to his ideals during the revolutionary period, his continuing activities in support of the arts and their message to the masses serve as a forceful counter to it. Throughout much of the time between November 1918 and his death, Landauer was in Krumbach, fulfilling his office as editor of *Masken* and working with Dumont and Lindemann (through the mails) on the program of the Schauspielhaus. In a letter to Mauthner on 11 November 1918, shortly before going to Munich, he had equated his obligation to the Schauspielhaus with his intention to work in the revolution; his literary activities were for him an integral part of that work. The program he proposed for the Schauspielhaus and for the Volksbühne was meant to show audiences the "eternal aspects" in their present situation and to provide them with insights for the task of preservation and renewal these "eternal aspects" demanded of them. To that end he wanted Germans at the close of the war to see and hear Aeschylus' *Persians*, Kaiser's *Bürger von Calais* and *Gas*, Beethoven's Ninth Symphony. To Georg Springer at the Volksbühne he wrote on 27 November 1918:

Now there should be energy and power in the house; it must lead as if with trumpets in this time without censors! . . . Speeches of fire, of fervor, which unite the deepest impulses of the private heart with the public life, and tumult should be made in this room.

This demand might be taken as a characterization of Landauer's life: a combination of the private and the public, of the individual and society, a combination so complete that the difference between intellectual and artistic work, on the one hand, and active participation in the affairs of life, on the other, completely vanishes in a personality like Landauer's.

In 1918, Mauthner, under pressure of contract, reluctantly allowed his memoirs to be published; he felt that he and his work were of no importance in that time.[13] But Landauer could not and would not accept this view. In a letter dated 10 July 1918, he reminded Mauthner that it was his work and that of others like him that justified the belief that a new society was possible. In making this statement Landauer was acting in consonance with an assertion Mauthner had made years before in the first volume of the *Sprachkritik*, the work so fundamental to Landauer's *Weltanschauung*: "Our thoughts, especially those that are important for us, that seem to us the great ones, come from our will, from our disposition." [14] Landauer's will, and therefore his thinking, never varied from the direction set in *Der Todesprediger* and *Skepsis und Mystik*; whatever the external circumstances, the views contained in those two early works remained the basic principles Landauer applied to the problem of being in all its ramifications.

Some of those principles were little more than echoes of ideas earlier writers had presented. Landauer's theory of socialism was certainly not original; he was heir to a tradition Marx called "utopian socialism." His two admitted masters were the French socialist Pierre Joseph Proudhon and the Russian anarchist Prince Pëtr Kropotkin, though in a letter of 2 January 1910, Landauer wrote that he had discovered Proudhon only after his own formulations had been completed. Nevertheless, there can be no doubt that these three men all proclaimed the same idea—the desirability of a society composed of small, independent communities—and that Landauer was much indebted to the other two. It was Proudhon who had recognized that socialism is inherent in political economy and that it can assert itself only in a society of independent groups in which membership is voluntary. He stressed the value of tradition in human relationships and saw technology as the new tradition of the Western world. Technological advance, he asserted, could be an incentive toward social decentralization. Landauer agreed, pointing out that distribution of electricity made unnecessary the centralization steam power had demanded. Landauer predicted a new flourishing of small, electrically powered factories that would combine the social benefits of medieval village industry with the technological capacities of the industrial revolution.[15]

The extent to which Landauer wanted to build his new society upon traditional concepts of human social organization becomes increasingly plain as one reads through Kropotkin's *Mutual Aid* (1902), a book Landauer translated from English to German in 1904 (first appearing in German under the title *Gegenseitige Hilfe in der Entwicklung*). Kropotkin seems to have been to Landauer what Darwin had been to Marx. Kropotkin's thesis in this work was that mutual help among members of the same species is as important for the survival and development of the species as is the constant struggle of individual with individual, which according to Darwinism is the fundamental aspect of existence. Kropotkin provided numerous examples from the animal world, showing that individuals often are able to survive only because of common action by the group or groups to which they belong. In Kropotkin's discussion of human social structures, one after another of the elements Landauer advocated for the society he wished to build are seen as concepts that not only had existed but had flourished in earlier periods. The small, independent community, the equal distribution and periodic redistribution of land, cooperative ventures, and the formation of temporary groups for specific purposes —all these had proved viable in the past and in some cases still existed. They all represent attempts by human beings to assist each other in the satisfaction of their various needs. And Kropotkin refused to believe that the tendency toward mutual aid had died out:

It is still flowing and going its way, seeking a new form that should not be the state or the medieval city or the village pasture of the barbarians or the clan of the uncivilized, but something arising from all of these, superior to them in its all-encompassing and deep human import.[16]

It is not enough to say that Landauer might have written this statement. He did write it, frequently, using many different wordings.

In *Paths in Utopia*, Martin Buber compared the work of Proudhon, Kropotkin, and Landauer and showed each one's refinements

of their common idea. Proudhon had demanded that society be established on the basis of economics rather than politics and had insisted that such a basis would be possible only in a society of independent, federated communities. Kropotkin attempted to describe
the structure of this society more carefully than Proudhon and to
show that the state was necessarily the opposite of the desirable
social organization. Like Proudhon, Kropotkin maintained that
the first step toward the new society must be revolution. Landauer
applied Étienne de la Boëtie's concept of servitude to the idea of
the state outlined by Kropotkin and arrived at a new, firmer conviction of how the revolution should be carried out and what its
aims must be. If Landauer was the least original in his social philosophy, it was also he who was most committed to taking practical
steps toward the better life they all envisioned. Following the path
Mauthner had suggested, Landauer sought to penetrate reality by
activity.

The signposts Landauer saw along this path had been placed
by Mauthner's epistemological inquiries, but it was Landauer who
read them. When Mauthner forced him to deny the truth of sense
data and the reality of abstractions, Landauer took refuge in the
one bit of knowledge he could not deny—his own existence—and
used this as the starting point for his new vision of the world. This
was his unique contribution: a synthesis of the metaphysical impasse Mauthner's language theory had created and the social theory
Proudhon, Kropotkin, and others had worked out before him. Un-
willing to abandon humanity to the insecurity his older friend's
insights had wrought, Landauer proposed the possibility of over-
coming it by replacing the values Mauthner had destroyed with
new, willfully created ones, the ones necessary for a life worthy of
man. The sum of these values was *Geist*, which could exert its
influence upon human life, he felt, only if there was a society susceptible to it, the socialist society in which the eternal traditions of
mankind would live and flourish. By this proposal he offered a
metaphysical basis, rooted in the nature of man, for both ethics
and social philosophy; the boundaries between metaphysics, ethics,
and social philosophy shattered under the impact of his personality.

Not everyone was able to recognize how Landauer's efforts were
constantly directed toward the achievement of a new philosophical

unity. Bab pointed out in his eulogy of Landauer that the casual observer often found Landauer exceptionally changeable.[17] In the essay "Die Spitze," * Landauer himself catalogued complaints of former colleagues whose own thoughts had developed along one line or another, while Landauer, as the first remonstrant in the essay suggested, seemed to be six people in one, more than anyone else was able to keep up with.[18] Nor would Landauer help those who were slow or reluctant to follow him. He always put his goals ahead of personal relationships and was sympathetic with others only when they demonstrated that they shared those goals. Even his long friendship with Mauthner suffered during the last year of Landauer's life. He demanded of others what he demanded of himself: unwavering dedication to the cause of a better life for mankind.

In his essay "Zu Tolstois Tagebuch" ("Comments on Tolstoi's Diary," 1918), Landauer issued an ultimatum:

Even if it be called fanatic or terrorist, I demand, for the purification that from now on is our task, without mercy, which I henceforth will not recognize, *one* belief, only one, that one we all of us have, although most people bury it or hide it or deny it or falsify it within themselves. . . .[19]

The conviction that purity is possible in mankind was basic to all his actions and hopes. And the conviction was a part of his nature, as some lines from a letter to Berndl, 16 August 1915—lines reminiscent of *Skepsis und Mystik*—show:

If I feel purity within myself, if I feel that the conditions of men in relation to each other would be different if they were like me—good, then I have the consoling certainty that what is alive in me is not lacking in others as far as tendency, disposition, and potentiality are concerned (all men are equal).

This statement gives a special flavor to the question Landauer asked in his discussion of *Othello:* "For who does not judge mankind according to himself?" [20] But Landauer was wrong to judge humanity by the standards he set for himself, because his purposes were beyond the comprehension of the masses.

He was a revolutionary, but in the sense defined by the nine-

* The word *Spitze* here implies, at one and the same time, "extreme," "the summit," and "jagged edges." Obviously no one English translation will do.

teenth-century socialist philosopher Constantin Frantz, who wrote
that the true revolutionary is really a conservative because he works
to preserve human values that time has distorted or obliterated.[21]
Landauer's new society was to be based firmly on the traditions
handed down through the ages by artists and thinkers. Mauthner's
philosophy had cleared the way by destroying invalid concepts;
Landauer tried to establish valid ones, the ones represented by
Geist. Buber asserted in *Paths in Utopia* that Landauer only once
used the word *religion* in a positive sense; Landauer "always es-
chewed all religious symbolism and all open avowals of religion." [22]
But Buber's desire to stress this point led him to say more than he
meant, for it was precisely a renaissance of religion, a religion one
could truly live, that Landauer envisioned. In *Der Todesprediger*
the heroine says that it is religion she is waiting for; and Landauer
himself, rejoicing in the beginning of the Bavarian Revolution,
expressed the same hope in a letter to Mauthner. In *Skepsis und
Mystik*, the *Aufruf*, and many of the essays, Landauer equated the
socialist society of the future with the return of a valid religion for
mankind. There were people who called him a prophet; they seem
properly to have felt this. But they were few in number. Landauer's
message was for a humanity that was not there to receive it.

When Bab wrote Landauer's eulogy in 1919, he found a telling parallel between Landauer and Shakespeare's Brutus: "Brutus
did not fall as a victor—he fell for a cause that could not prevail,
because it was not even good or wise to desire for the people a
freedom of which they were not in the slightest capable." [23] But
Brutus did not go unrevered, and the words of Mark Antony's last
speech, his praise of Brutus, were the best Bab could find to honor
the memory of his murdered friend: "This was a man." They sum-
marized in one simple sentence a life that had been active in many
fields, but always directed toward a single goal. It was not until a
year later that Bab became acquainted with Landauer's *Shakespeare* and was struck, as any reader of this book who is familiar
with Landauer's life must be, by the discussion of Brutus that
Landauer presented there; for much of what Landauer wrote of
Brutus was prophetic of Landauer's own fate. Landauer's last
words, uttered as he was being beaten to death by a pack of sav-
agely enraged soldiers, were reported to have been, "Erschlagt mich

doch! Das Ihr Menschen seid!" ("Yes, beat me to death! To think that you are human beings!").[24] That same Landauer had written about Brutus: "Precisely because he lived in an illusion about his surroundings, he maintained the original nobility of spirit, which considers it improper to learn from experience." [25] Bab demonstrated this haunting affinity between author and subject by quoting from Landauer's explanation of Brutus' failure:

Thus he trusts mankind and believes in the goodness in human nature that would have to arise again when the commonwealth was reestablished. . . . The absolute is always right—when it remains pure within itself and does not become involved with relativities. If it does, however, its oppressive injustice, its error, begins [to show itself], and it becomes doctrinairism.[26]

The foreword to the second edition of the eulogy ends with Bab's explanation of Landauer's failure, an explanation tinged with wonder:

. . . the future biographer of Landauer will be able to provide a remarkably moving example of how, particularly in exceptional men, there can reside in close association with the most perfect understanding of truth the most basic errors in respect to action.[27]

Bab's eulogy was first delivered at the Freie Volksbühne on 25 May 1919. It was by no means the only recognition Landauer's death—and his life—received. In the weeks after news of the murder came, friends, especially Mauthner and Louise Dumont, looked after the three daughters, who had remained in Krumbach during the revolution. Gustav Lindemann—who, with his wife, had resigned from the Düsseldorfer Schauspielhaus in the face of a staff rebellion (February 1919) but had retained control of *Masken*— dedicated an entire double issue to Landauer's memory.[28] A number of people who had known Landauer contributed to it. Newspapers as far away as the United States (*The New York Times*, 5 May 1919) carried the report of the death. The statement in the *Frankfurter Zeitung* is one of a series connected with that paper that provide an ironic summary of public attitudes toward Landauer. Over the years he had had a number of essays, including the first publication of *Ein Weg deutschen Geistes*, appear in that journal. In 1918 the paper had written him: "We are asking at this time for short but strong articles from our best intellects, who can give our people energy and warmth. We ask you to join in this and would be greatly pleased if you . . . would speak to our readers." [29] A few months later, like all the other papers in Germany, the *Frankfurter Zeitung* was attacking Landauer in the strongest terms for his part in the revolution. As hysteria over the situation in Munich subsided, however, and as the true details of events there became known, the paper remembered what Landauer had always stood for and the respect he had earned from so many prominent individuals of the time. In its obituary (3 May 1919) it took pains to stress that Landauer had in no way been responsible for the bloodshed with which the revolution ended and called his death "a tragic fate." Further homage came from a quite different source in the form of a grave monument, paid for largely by contributions from workers in Munich.

It is possible that there is hidden in the works of Georg Kaiser another kind of tribute. Kaiser's critics do not mention the possibility of Landauer's having influenced the dramatist, but Landauer felt he had. On 26 December 1918 he wrote to Auguste Hauschner of Kaiser's *Gas,* "which is concerned with social colonies and probably . . . , somehow, comes from me." There are certainly parallels between this drama, as well as *Die Bürger von Calais,* and Landauer's *Weltanschauung;* whether there are also points of tangency remains a moot question. Circumstantial evidence, however, suggests the existence of such points. When the call went out for funds for Landauer's tombstone, Kaiser contributed nearly all the money he had.[30]

Unquestionably the greatest tribute the man and his work received came from Martin Buber; it lay in his faithfulness to the task of keeping Landauer's name and thought alive. For ten years he collected and published Landauer's writings and his letters. Landauer left his papers to Buber for this purpose, and Buber responded to the obligation in a manner fully in keeping with their twenty years of close friendship. The *Shakespeare* was first published in 1920 under his editorship. In 1921 appeared the collection *Der werdende Mensch,* essays on life and literature. About this book Hermann Hesse wrote:

One reads and is moved again and again: how this fine, this clear, beautiful soul lived and suffered this time with us, how quietly and modestly, known to few, he did his powerful, bold and loving work! And how his end, the result of his last efforts, exhorts us to contemplation and self-examination.[31]

Beginnen, a collection of essays on socialism, was published in 1924. The plan, announced in the introduction to *Beginnen,* to publish yet another volume of essays, concerned specifically with politics, was not carried out; but *Beginnen* was not the end of Buber's monument to Landauer. The most significant part of it, the two volumes of edited letters, appeared in 1929 as *Gustav Landauer: sein Lebensgang in Briefen.*

Despite these efforts on the part of a man whose reputation as a philosopher has since become world-wide, Landauer's memory has sunk into an undeserved oblivion. The fact that he had something to do with the Bavarian Revolution sticks in many people's minds, but that is scarcely an accurate description of the role he played in the intellectual life of Germany at the beginning of the twentieth century. In fact, close study of the revolution shows that he was at best an important secondary figure in it. He worked hard for the revolution, but it was more important to him than he was to it. Because he remained all his life an isolated thinker removed from the major political and social currents—and because the Socialist Bund, even if it can be said to have had realizable goals, did not have time enough to effect them—Landauer left no group behind him to perpetuate his memory. And then came the Nazis; they remembered Landauer.

The monument erected over Landauer's grave in the Munich Waldfriedhof was dedicated on 2 May 1925, though the authorities prohibited a planned ceremony. Buber described the grave:

The simple but powerful obelisk stands among the fir trees and bears the inscription

1870 Gustav Landauer 1919

and above that the words from his *Aufruf zum Sozialismus:* "It is now necessary to make sacrifices of another kind, not heroic, but quiet, unobtrusive sacrifices, in order to provide an example of genuine life." [32]

The monument is no longer to be found. A man named Dr. Morsbach now lies in the grave. "The urn taken on 22 VI 33 from the concrete base after complete removal of the monument. It was then taken to the mortuary and on 28 VI 33 sent to the Ostfriedhof." [33] Eventually it was interred in the Jewish Cemetery on Ungererstrasse in Munich; according to the caretaker there, this was in 1942.

Also according to the caretaker, almost no one visits the grave. Though a few individuals who survived the Nazi period, among them the writers Arnold Zweig and Theodor Plievier, found their way to Landauer's works, the Nazis' attempt to wipe out his memory has, until recently, been successful. In 1961 the Hamburg publishing house of Rütten and Loening republished the collection of letters from the French Revolution (new title: *Die französische Revolution in Briefen*), and in 1962 it published a slightly abridged version of *Shakespeare*. In 1967 a discussion of Landauer's social writings, with almost no notice of the philosophical and literary works, appeared in Germany.[34] A year later his name was once again brought before the German public, this time in a play about the Bavarian Revolution.[35] The Landauer of this drama, occasionally reciting lines taken directly from the *Aufruf zum Sozialismus*, is little more than a pitiable, intellectual clown.

But the real man behind the name is still unknown. The kind of ironic fate Landauer tried to describe in his story "Lebendig tot" seems better illustrated by the way his own reputation is preserved. He dedicated his life to a revolution that would fundamentally renew all aspects of humanity; what primarily keeps the memory of that life alive is its connection with a short, half-hearted, provincial revolution that made scarcely a ripple in the history of traditional politics. Though the contact between them was slight and does not begin to show the depth and breadth of the work that absorbed Landauer for thirty years, his name is still linked with and overshadowed by that of the man whom he followed into the Bavarian Revolution and into death. It is almost as if fate willed it so, for the remains of Gustav Landauer, who strove all his life for true community among men, now lie in a double grave that serves also as the resting place of Kurt Eisner.

Notes

PREFACE

[1] Julius Bab, *Gustav Landauer*, 2d ed. (Nuremberg and Würzburg, 1924), p. 16.

CHAPTER 1

[1] *Die Nation*, vol. 14, no. 28 (April 1900): 395–97.

CHAPTER 2

[1] Julius Bab, *Das Theater der Gegenwart* (Leipzig, 1928), p. 54.
[2] *Der Sozialist* (Berlin), 29 August 1896, p. 208.
[3] Albert Weidner, "Gustav Landauers Kampf mit der Polizei, Justiz und Partei," *Die Weltbühne,* 8 April 1930, p. 534.
[4] J. Langhard, *Die anarchistische Bewegung in der Schweiz*, 2d ed. (Bern, 1909), pp. 324–25.
[5] Weidner, "Gustav Landauers Kampf," p. 535.
[6] Gustav Landauer, "Der Anarchismus in Deutschland," *Zukunft*, 5 January 1895, pp. 29–34.
[7] *Der Sozialist*, 1 August 1896, p. 186.
[8] Landauer, *Von Zürich bis London* (Pankow [Berlin], n. d. [1896]), p. 3.
[9] Ibid., p. 12.
[10] Julius Bab, *Gustav Landauer*, p. 19.
[11] Bab, *Die Berliner Boheme*, 6th ed. (Berlin and Leipzig, 1904), p. 49.
[12] Landauer, *Gustav Landauer: sein Lebensgang in Briefen*, ed. Martin

Buber, 2 vols. (Frankfort on the Main, 1929), I, vi. Hereafter cited as *Briefe*.
[13] Bab, *Richard Dehmel* (Leipzig, 1926), p. 103.
[14] Ibid., p. 105.
[15] Richard Dehmel, *Ausgewählte Briefe*, ed. I. D. [Ida Dehmel], 2 vols. (Berlin, 1923), I, 107.
[16] Hans Blüher, *Werke und Tage*, 2d ed. (Munich, 1953), p. 390.

CHAPTER 3

[1] Gustav Landauer, ed., *Briefe aus der französischen Revolution,* 2 vols. (Frankfort on the Main, 1919), II, 77.
[2] Landauer, "Der deutsche Multatuli," *Die Gesellschaft*, vol. 3, no. 4 (1899): 230–36.
[3] Landauer, "Die deutsche Multatuli-Ausgabe," *Die Gesellschaft*, vol. 3, no. 3 (1900): 174–79.
[4] Landauer, "Zukunft-Menschen," *Zukunft*, 23 June 1900, pp. 529–34.
[5] Landauer, "Der neue Gott," *Die Gesellschaft*, vol. 4, no. 2 (1899): 119–22.
[6] *Zukunft*, 26 October 1901, pp. 134–40.
[7] Landauer, *Briefe*, I, 115, n.
[8] Landauer, *Macht und Mächte*, 2d ed. (Cologne, 1923), p. 77.
[9] *The Mabinogion*, trans. T. P. Ellis and John Lloyd (Oxford, 1929), I, 2–3.
[10] *Briefe*, I, 164.
[11] Fritz Mauthner, *Beiträge zu einer Kritik der Sprache*, 3 vols.; 1st ed., I and II (Stuttgart, 1901), III (Stuttgart and Berlin, 1902); 3d ed. (Leipzig, 1923). References in my text are to the third edition. All quotations have been compared with the first edition and found to be substantially the same.
[12] Mauthner, *Der Atheismus und seine Geschichte im Abendlande* (Stuttgart and Berlin, 1923), IV, 210.
[13] Landauer, "Mauthners *Sprachkritik*," *Zukunft*, 11 May 1901, pp. 220–24.
[14] "Fritz Mauthner," in Dr. Raymund Schmidt, ed., *Die Philosophie der Gegenwart in Selbstdarstellungen* (Leipzig, 1922), p. 136.
[15] Franz Kobler, ed., *Juden und Judentum in deutschen Briefen aus drei Jahrhunderten* (Vienna, 1935), pp. 381–82.
[16] Landauer, *Skepsis und Mystik: Versuche im Anschluss an Mauthners Sprachkritik*, 2d ed. (Cologne, 1923). All references in my text are to this edition.
[17] Friedrich Nietzsche, *Gesammelte Werke*, Musarion edition (Munich, 1922–28), XIV, 22; quoted in the *Sprachkritik*, I, 366.
[18] Landauer, "Das Liebesleben in der Natur," *Die Gesellschaft*, vol. 4, no. 24 (1898): 400–403.

Notes

[19] *Sprachkritik*, II, 80.
[20] *Briefe*, I, 80.
[21] Landauer, "Richard Dehmel," *Das Blaubuch*, vol. 1, no. 43 (1906): 1690.
[22] Dehmel, *Ausgewählte Briefe*, II, 119.

CHAPTER 4

[1] Auguste Hauschner, "Gustav Landauer," *Zukunft*, 25 January 1904, pp. 163–65.
[2] Quoted in Hermann Friedmann and Otto Mann, eds., *Deutsche Literatur im 20. Jahrhundert*, 4th ed. (Heidelberg, 1961), I, 258.
[3] Gustav Landauer, *Aufruf zum Sozialismus*, 2d ed. (Berlin, 1919), p. 1. All references in my text are to this edition. Hereafter cited as *Aufruf*.
[4] *Briefe*, I, 425.
[5] Landauer, *Der werdende Mensch: Aufsätze über Leben und Schrifttum*, ed. Martin Buber (Potsdam, 1921), p. 110. Hereafter cited as *Der werdende Mensch*.
[6] Landauer, *Rechenschaft*, 2d ed. (Cologne, 1924), p. 80.
[7] *Briefe*, I, 430.
[8] Ibid., II, 36.
[9] Ibid., I, 261.
[10] Ibid., I, 499, n. 2.
[11] Ibid., I, 449.
[12] Ibid., I, 446.
[13] Hans Kohn, ed., *Vom Judentum: Ein Sammelbuch herausgegeben vom verein Jüdischer Hochschüler Bar Kochba in Prag* (Prague, 1913), p. v.
[14] Landauer, "Sind das Ketzergedanken?" in ibid., p. 252.
[15] Ibid., p. 254.
[16] Landauer, *Der werdende Mensch*, p. 133.
[17] Landauer, "Sind das Ketzergedanken?" p. 253.
[18] Landauer, *Beginnen: Aufsätze über Sozialismus*, ed. Martin Buber (Cologne, 1924), p. 7. Hereafter cited as *Beginnen*.
[19] Ibid., p. 8.
[20] Ibid., p. 11.
[21] Landauer, *Aufruf*, pp. 6–7.
[22] Landauer, *Die Revolution*, vol. 13, *Die Gesellschaft*, ed. Martin Buber (Frankfort on the Main, 1907).
[23] Landauer, *Beginnen*, p. 16.
[24] Ibid., pp. 17–18.
[25] *Aufruf*, pp. 19–20.
[26] *Beginnen*, ed. Martin Buber, iii.
[27] Walt Whitman, *Gesänge und Inschriften*, trans. Gustav Landauer (Munich, 1921), p. 13.
[28] Ibid., p. 6.

[29] Landauer, "Richard Dehmel," p. 1690.
[30] Whitman, *Gesänge*, p. 8.
[31] Landauer, "Richard Dehmel," p. 1690.
[32] *Der werdende Mensch*, p. 342.
[33] Ibid.

CHAPTER 5

[1] Landauer, *Aufruf*, p. 129.
[2] Landauer, *Der werdende Mensch*, pp. 58–59.
[3] Ibid., p. 249.
[4] *Briefe*, II, 133–34.
[5] Ibid., II, 45.
[6] Landauer, *Ein Weg deutschen Geistes* (Munich, 1916), p. 17.
[7] *Briefe*, I, 52.
[8] Martin Buber, *Paths in Utopia*, trans. R. F. C. Hull (New York, 1950), p. 46.
[9] Landauer, *Die Revolution*, p. 108.
[10] Ibid.
[11] Werner Sombart, *Der proletarische Sozialismus*, 10th ed. of *Sozialismus und soziale Bewegung*, 2 vols. (Jena, 1924), I, 326–28.
[12] Landauer, *Beginnen*, p. 107.
[13] Ibid.
[14] Ibid., p. 56.
[15] Ibid., p. 107.
[16] Karl Mannheim, *Ideology and Utopia*, trans. Louis Wirth and Edward Shils (New York, 1936), pp. 197–98.
[17] *Beginnen*, p. 16.
[18] Buber, *Paths in Utopia*, p. 50.
[19] Ibid., pp. 48–49.
[20] *Briefe*, I, 359, 365.
[21] Landauer, *Rechenschaft*, p. 49.
[22] Ibid., p. 54.
[23] *Briefe*, I, 459.

CHAPTER 6

[1] Landauer, *Rechenschaft*, p. 180.
[2] Hans Blüher, *Werke und Tage*, p. 361.
[3] Ibid., p. 375.
[4] *Briefe*, II, 125, n. 3.
[5] Reprinted in *Rechenschaft*, pp. 189–95.
[6] Landauer, *Die Revolution*, p. 49. ff.
[7] Buber, *Paths in Utopia,* p. 50.
[8] Landauer, *Ein Weg deutschen Geistes*, p. 15.

Notes

9 Landauer, *Der werdende Mensch*, p. 242.
10 Landauer, *Shakespeare: dargestellt in Vorträgen*, 2 vols., ed. Martin Buber (Frankfort on the Main, 1920), II, 390.
11 *Der werdende Mensch*, p. 256.
12 Julius Bab, *Gustav Landauer*, pp. 13–14.
13 *Briefe*, I, 110.
14 *Ein Weg deutschen Geistes*, p. 14.
15 Ibid., p. 11.
16 Reprinted in *Hölderlin. Beiträge zu seinem Verständnis in unserm Jahrhundert*, vol. 3, *Schriften der Hölderlin-Gesellschaft*, ed. Alfred Kelletat (Tübingen, 1961), 53–78. Also in *Der werdende Mensch*, pp. 155–88.
17 Landauer, *Shakespeare*, II, 290.
18 Hans Franck, "Ein Mensch geht vorüber," in Freihochschulband Düsseldorf, ed., *Das Schauspielhaus Düsseldorf* (Düsseldorf, 1930), p. 107.
19 *Ein Weg deutschen Geistes*, p. 32.
20 Franck, "Ein Mensch geht vorüber," p. 105.
21 Louise Dumont, *Vermächtnis: Reden und Schriften*, ed. Gustav Lindemann and Kurt Loup, 2d ed. (Cologne and Berlin, 1957), p. 42.
22 Ibid., p. 26.
23 *Beginnen*, p. 9.
24 Bab, *Gustav Landauer*, p. 34.
25 Levin L. Schücking, "Neuere Shakespeareliteratur," *Deutsche Vierteljahrschrift für Literaturwissenschaft und Geistesgeschichte*, vol. 6, no. 1 (1928): 183.
26 Ibid., p. 185.
27 *Briefe*, II, 40.
28 *Zeitschrift für Deutschkunde*, vol. 35, no. 3 (1921): 209–210.
29 Ibid., p. 210.
30 *Briefe*, II, 265.
31 Bab, *Gustav Landauer*, p. 26.
32 *Ein Weg deutschen Geistes*, p. 4.
33 Reprinted in *Rechenschaft*, pp. 171–79.

CHAPTER 7

1 Landauer, *Der Todesprediger*, 3d ed. (Cologne, 1923), p. 126.
2 *Briefe*, II, 323.
3 Allan Mitchell, *Revolution in Bavaria, 1918–1919* (Princeton, 1965), pp. 89–90.
4 Erich Mühsam, *Von Eisner bis Leviné* (Berlin-Britz, 1929), pp. 21–22.
5 Hans von Pranckh, ed., *Der Prozess gegen Graf Arco-Valley* (Munich, 1920), p. 46.
6 Mühsam, *Von Eisner bis Leviné*, pp. 40–41.
7 Ibid., p. 42.
8 Ibid., pp. 43–44.

CHAPTER 8

[1] Paul Werner, *Die Bayrische Räte-Republik*, 2d ed. (Leipzig, 1920), p. 19.
[2] *Briefe*, II, 299.
[3] Rudolf Rocker in Mühsam, *et al.*, *Gustav Landauer: Worte der Würdigung* (Darmstadt/Land, n. d. [1951]), p. 39.
[4] *Frankfurter Zeitung*, 18 December 1918, p. 3.
[5] *Rechenschaft*, p. 42.
[6] Bab, *Gustav Landauer*, p. 32.
[7] *Die Revolution*, p. 95.
[8] *Ein Weg deutschen Geistes*, p. 15.
[9] Helmut Rüdiger in *Worte der Würdigung*, p. 15.
[10] *Aufruf*, p. xvii.
[11] Bab, *Gustav Landauer*, p. 33.
[12] Blüher, *Werke und Tage*, 2d ed., p. 378 f.
[13] Mauthner, *Erinnerungen von Fritz Mauthner* (Munich, 1918), p. 349.
[14] Mauthner, *Sprachkritik*, I, 422.
[15] *Aufruf*, p. 49.
[16] Pëtr Kropotkin, *Gegenseitige Hilfe in der Tier- und Menschenwelt*, trans. Gustav Landauer (Leipzig, 1908), p. 204. The 1904 edition bears the title *Gegenseitige Hilfe in der Entwicklung*.
[17] Bab, *Gustav Landauer*, pp. 22–23.
[18] *Beginnen*, pp. 180–84.
[19] *Der werdende Mensch*, p. 211.
[20] *Shakespeare*, I, 326.
[21] Cited by Helmut Rüdiger in *Worte der Würdigung*, p. 22.
[22] Buber, *Paths in Utopia*, p. 55.
[23] Bab, *Gustav Landauer*, pp. 34–35.
[24] *Briefe*, II, 423.
[25] *Shakespeare*, I, 165.
[26] Ibid., I, 160.
[27] Bab, *Gustav Landauer*, p. 7.
[28] *Masken: Halbmonatschrift des Düsseldorfer Schauspielhaus*, 14 (1919): 282–314.
[29] *Briefe*, II, 398.
[30] Brian J. Kenworthy, *Georg Kaiser* (Oxford, 1957), p. xviii.
[31] Hermann Hesse, *Vivos Voco*, 2 (1921): 275.
[32] *Briefe*, II, 424.
[33] Grabbuch, Gräberfeld 95 of the Münchner Waldfriedhof.
[34] Wolf Kalz, *Gustav Landauer: Kultursozialist und Anarchist* (Meisenheim on the Glan, 1967).
[35] Tankred Dorst, *Toller* (Frankfort on the Main, 1968).

A
Selected
Bibliography

This bibliography includes only the major titles used in the preparation of the present work. For a more detailed catalog of Gustav Landauer's writings, the reader is referred to the book by Wolf Kalz, a complete reference for which is given below. Despite a few minor inaccuracies and omissions, Mr. Kalz's list may be regarded as complete. For Landauer's major articles and essays, check the contents notes for *Beginnen*, *Rechenschaft*, and *Der werdende Mensch*.

WORKS BY GUSTAV LANDAUER

Philosophy

Die Revolution. Die Gesellschaft, edited by Martin Buber, vol. 13 (Frankfort on the Main, 1907).

"Sind das Ketzergedanken?" In *Vom Judentum: Ein Sammelbuch herausgegeben vom Verein Jüdischer Hochschüler Bar Kochba in Prag*, edited by Hans Kohn (Prague, 1913).

Skepsis und Mystik: Versuche im Anschluss an Mauthners Sprachkritik. 2d ed. (Cologne, 1923).

Politics and Socialism

Aufruf zum Sozialismus. 2d ed. (Berlin, 1919).

Beginnen: Aufsätze über Sozialismus. Edited by Martin Buber (Cologne, 1924).

Call to Revolution
The Mystical Anarchism of Gustav Landauer

Contents: "Volk und Land: Dreissig sozialistische Thesen." "Vom Sozialismus und der Siedlung." "Einkehr." "Vom Weg des Sozialismus." "Schwache Staatsmänner, schwächeres Volk!" "Der Arbeitstag." "Wohin?" "Die Siedlung." "Vom geistigen Privileg." "Stelle dich, Sozialist!" "Das erste Flugblatt: Was will der sozialistische Bund?" "Das zweite Flugblatt: Was ist zunächst zu tun?" "Das dritte Flugblatt: Die Siedlung." "Die zwölf Artikel des sozialistischen Bundes." "Sätze vom sozialistischen Bund." "Der Schlendrian." "Die zwei Seiten." "Sozialistisches Beginnen." "Ein Brief über die anarchistischen Kommunisten." "Zum Thema: Sozialismus und Wissenschaft." "Antwort auf einen kritischen Brief." "Die Spitze."

Rechenschaft. 2d ed. (Cologne, 1924).

Contents: "Vom Schnee und vom König von England usw." "Der Krieg." "Bairam und Schlichting." "Marokko." "An die deutschen Arbeiter." "Die Abschaffung des Kriegs durch die Selbstbestimmung des Volks. Fragen an die deutschen Arbeiter." "Vom freien Arbeitertag." "Rede von der Reichstagsgalerie." "Revolution, Nation und Krieg." "Das glückhafte Schiff." "Vom Krieg." "Die Sozialdemokratie und der Krieg." "Deutschland, Frankreich und der Krieg." "Kriegsanstifter." "Vor fünfundzwanzig Jahren." "Der Kanzler des deutschen Volkes." "Die Erschiessung des österreichischen Thronfolgers." "Italien." "Ein Protest in Volksliedern." "Veitstag." "Der europäische Krieg." "Zum Gedächtnis." "Aus unstillbarem Verlangen." "Anhang: Brief an Wilson."

Von Zürich bis London (Pankow [Berlin], n.d. [1896]). [An English translation appeared during the same year under the title *Social Democracy in Germany.*]

Fiction

Macht und Mächte. 2d ed. (Cologne, 1923).
Der Todesprediger. 3d ed. (Cologne, 1923).

Criticism

"Richard Dehmel," *Das Blaubuch,* vol. 1, no. 43 (1906): 1685–92.
Shakespeare: dargestellt in Vorträgen. Edited by Martin Buber. 2 vols. (Frankfort on the Main, 1920). [A new edition appeared at Hamburg, 1962.]
Ein Weg deutschen Geistes (Munich, 1916).
Der werdende Mensch: Aufsätze über Leben und Schrifttum. Edited by Martin Buber (Potsdam, 1921).

A Selected Bibliography

Contents: "Musik der Welt." "Gott als Band." "Gott und der Sozialismus." "Von der tierischen Grundlage." "Tarnowska." "Von der Ehe." "Selbstmord der Jugend." "Polizisten und Mörder." "Vom Dilettantismus." "Arbeitselig." "Puppen." "Die Botschaft der 'Titanic'." "Zum Problem der Nation." "Sind das Ketzergedanken?" "Zum Beilis-Prozess." Dem grössten Schweizer" (Rousseau). "Goethes Politik." "Friedrich Hölderlin in seinen Gedichten." "Walt Whitman." "Lew Nikolajewitsch Tolstoi." "Zu Tolstois Tagebuch." "Peter Kropotkin." "Die Lehre von den Geistigen und vom Volke." "Martin Buber." "Strindberg." "Strindbergs Historische Miniaturen." "Strindbergs Traumspiel." "Strindbergs Gespenstersonate." "Walter Calé." "Fragment über Georg Kaiser." "Eine Ansprache an die Dichter."

Translations

Briefe aus der französischen Revolution. 2 vols. (Frankfort on the Main, 1919). [A new edition, Hamburg, 1961, has the title *Die französische Revolution in Briefen.*]

Kropotkin, Pëtr. *Gegenseitige Hilfe in der Tier- und Menschenwelt* (Leipzig, 1908). [Title of 1904 edition: *Gegenseitige Hilfe in der Enwicklung.*]

Meister Eckharts mystische Schriften (Berlin, 1903).

Whitman, Walt. *Gesänge und Inschriften* (Munich, 1921).

BIOGRAPHICAL AND CRITICAL SOURCES

Bab, Julius. *Die Berliner Boheme.* 6th ed. (Berlin and Leipzig, 1904).

————. *Gustav Landauer.* 1st ed. (Berlin, 1919); 2d ed. (Nuremberg and Würzburg, 1924). (The two editions are essentially the same.)

————. *Richard Dehmel* (Leipzig, 1926).

————. *Über den Tag hinaus.* Edited by Harry Bergholz (Heidelberg and Darmstadt, 1960).

————, ed. *Wesen und Weg der Berliner Volksbühnebewegung* (Berlin, 1919).

————. *Wien und Berlin* (Berlin, 1918).

Blüher, Hans. *Gesammelte Aufsätze* (Jena, 1919).

————. *Werke und Tage.* 1st ed. (Jena, 1920). 2d ed. (Munich, 1953).

Briefe an Auguste Hauschner. Edited by Martin Beradt and Lotte Bloch-Zavrel (Berlin, 1929).

Buber, Martin, ed. *Gustav Landauer: sein Lebensgang in Briefen.* 2 vols. (Frankfort on the Main, 1929).

————. *Paths in Utopia.* Translated by R. F. C. Hull (New York, 1950).

Dehmel, Richard. *Ausgewählte Briefe.* Edited by I. D. [Ida Dehmel]. 2 vols. (Berlin, 1923).

Esper, Thomas. "The Anarchism of Gustav Landauer." Master's thesis, Department of History, University of Chicago, 1961.
Franck, Hans. "Ein Mensch geht vorüber." In Freihochschulband Düsseldorf, ed., *Das Schauspielhaus Düsseldorf* (Düsseldorf, 1930).
Kalz, Wolf. *Gustav Landauer: Kultursozialist und Anarchist* (Meisenheim on the Glan, 1967).
Kobler, Franz, ed. *Juden und Judentum in deutschen Briefen aus drei Jahrhunderten* (Vienna, 1935).
Langhard, J. *Die anarchistische Bewegung in der Schweiz.* 2d ed. (Bern, 1909).
Mannheim, Karl. *Ideology and Utopia.* Translated by Louis Wirth and Edward Shils (New York, 1936).
Masken: Halbmonatschrift des Düsseldorfer Schauspielhaus, 14 (1918–19).
Michel, Wilhelm. "Gustav Landauer." *Die Silbergäule*, 33 (1920): 4–5.
Mühsam, Erich. *Namen und Menschen* (Leipzig, 1949).
Mühsam, Erich, Rudolf Rocker, Helmut Rüdiger, and Diego Abad de Santillan. *Gustav Landauer: Worte der Würdigung* (Darmstadt/Land, n. d. [1951]).
Oschilewski, Walter. *Freie Volksbühne Berlin* (Berlin, 1965).
Pranckh, Hans von, ed. *Der Prozess gegen Graf Arco-Valley* (Munich, 1920).
Slochower, Harry. *Richard Dehmel* (Dresden, 1928).
Sombart, Werner. *Der proletarische Sozialismus.* 10th edition of *Sozialismus und soziale Bewegung.* 2 vols. (Jena, 1924).
———. *Sozialismus und soziale Bewegung.* 6th ed. (Jena, 1908).
Spohr, Wilhelm. *O ihr Tage von Friedrichshagen!* (Berlin, 1949).
Weidner, Albert. "Gustav Landauers Kampf mit Polizei, Justiz und Partei." *Die Weltbühne*, vol. 26, no. 15 (8 April 1930).
Werner, Paul. *Die Bayrische Räte-Republik.* 2d ed. (Leipzig, 1920).

OTHER SOURCES

Bab, Julius. *Das Theater der Gegenwart* (Leipzig, 1928).
———. *Das Theater im Lichte der Soziologie* (Leipzig, 1931).
Bayerische Staatszeitung (Munich). [Various news articles from January to May 1919.]
Dubnow, S. M. *History of the Jews in Russia and Poland.* Translated by I. Friedlaender. 3 vols. (Philadelphia, 1920).
Dumont, Louise. *Vermächtnis: Reden und Schriften.* Edited by Gustav Lindemann and Kurt Loup. 2d ed. (Cologne and Berlin, 1957).
Eisner, Kurt. *Gesammelte Schriften.* 2 vols. (Berlin, 1919).
Fischer, Ruth. *Stalin and German Communism* (Cambridge, Mass., 1948).
Frankfurter Zeitung (Frankfort on the Main). [Various news articles from December 1918 to May 1919.]
Kenworthy, Brian J. *Georg Kaiser* (Oxford, 1957).

A Selected Bibliography

Loup, Kurt, ed. *Das festliche Haus: Das Düsseldorfer Schauspielhaus Dumont-Lindemann* (Cologne and Berlin, 1955).

The Mabinogion. Translated by T. P. Ellis and John Lloyd. 2 vols. (Oxford, 1929).

Mauthner, Fritz. *Der Atheismus und seine Geschichte im Abendlande.* 4 vols. (Stuttgart and Berlin, 1920–23).

———. *Beiträge zu einer Kritik der Sprache.* 3 vols. 1st ed. (Stuttgart and Berlin, 1901–02); 3d ed. (Leipzig, 1923).

———. *Erinnerungen von Fritz Mauthner* (Munich, 1918).

———. "Fritz Mauthner." In Dr. Raymund Schmidt, ed., *Die Philosophie der Gegenwart in Selbstdarstellungen* (Leipzig, 1922), pp. 121–44.

———. *Die Sprache* (Frankfort on the Main, 1906).

Mitchell, Allan. *Revolution in Bavaria, 1918–1919* (Princeton, 1965).

Mühsam, Erich. *Von Eisner bis Leviné* (Berlin-Britz, 1929).

Der Sozialist (Berlin). 1891–99.

Der Sozialist (Berlin). 1909–15.

Tormin, Walter. *Zwischen Rätediktatur und sozialer Demokratie* (Düsseldorf, 1954).

Index

Charles B. Maurer is Director of the W. H. Doane Library at Denison University, Granville, Ohio. He received a Ph.D. in German Language and Literature from Northwestern University in 1965. He has held an assistant professorship of German at The University of Michigan and has been Coordinator of the Foreign Language Program at The University of Michigan's Residential College.

The manuscript was edited by Aletta Biersack. The book was designed by Gary Gore. The type face for the text is Linotype Electra designed by W. A. Dwiggins about 1935. The display face is Weiss designed by E. R. Weiss.

The text is printed on S. D. Warren's Olde Style Antique paper; and the book is bound in Interlaken's cloth over binders' boards. Manufactured in the United States of America.